SELF-REGULATION IN THE EARLY YEARS

SUE ROBSON
ANTONIA ZACHARIOU

SELF-REGULATION IN THE EARLY YEARS

Learning Matters
A SAGE Publishing Company
1 Oliver's Yard
55 City Road
London EC1Y 1SP

SAGE Publications Inc.
2455 Teller Road
Thousand Oaks, California 91320

SAGE Publications India Pvt Ltd
B 1/I 1 Mohan Cooperative Industrial Area
Mathura Road
New Delhi 110 044

SAGE Publications Asia-Pacific Pte Ltd
3 Church Street
#10-04 Samsung Hub
Singapore 049483

Library of Congress Control Number: 2022930442

British Library Cataloguing in Publication Data

A catalogue record for this book is available from the British Library

Editor: Amy Thornton
Senior project editor: Chris Marke
Project management: TNQ Technologies
Marketing manager: Lorna Patkai
Cover design: Wendy Scott
Typeset by: TNQ Technologies
Printed in the UK

ISBN: 978-1-5297-7100-8
ISBN: 978-1-5297-7099-5 (pbk)

For David Whitebread, whose inspirational work in the field of self-regulation has been, and continues to be, hugely influential on both authors, and for the early childhood world in general.
We are both personally indebted to David, for making our learning about self-regulation so enjoyable and meaningful, and for his insistence, in the most positive way, on the importance of putting children and playfulness at the centre of what we do.

Thank you, David

Contents

vii

Contents

About the authors

Dr Sue Robson is Honorary Research Fellow at the University of Roehampton. She has worked in higher education for over 30 years, most recently as Principal Lecturer and Subject Leader for Early Childhood Studies at Roehampton. Sue has worked as a teacher in nurseries and primary schools, including as Deputy Head teacher of a Nursery and Infant School and co-leading a large nursery. Sue is a former Trustee of the Froebel Trust, and currently sits on the Education and Research Committee and the Research Sub-committee. She is also a National Teaching Fellow and a Fellow of the Higher Education Academy. Her research interests are particularly in the field of young children's thinking, especially self-regulation and metacognition, and creative thinking, as well as young children's play, well-being and autonomy. Her PhD research looked at the relationship between responsibility for children's choice of activity and evidence of self-regulation and metacognition. Sue is also interested in practice development, and support for practitioners, and has had long involvement with practitioner support and development in local authorities in England. She contributed as a Member of a Working Group to *Birth to Five Matters*, and has worked as part of a team looking at the value of Work Discussion groups for early childhood practitioners. Sue has collaborated on a range of international projects, including in Denmark, Ireland, Lithuania, Norway, Scotland, Sweden, the United States and Wales, and on international publications. She is currently working on a funded international project looking at children's perspectives about their play experiences in settings, alongside supporting practitioner development in implementing guided play. Sue has written and published widely, including *Developing Thinking and Understanding* and *The International Handbook of Young Children's Thinking and Understanding*, both for Routledge, and *Young Children's Creative Thinking* for Sage.

Dr Antonia Zachariou is Senior Lecturer at the University of Roehampton, London. Her teaching and research interests lie in the areas of educational psychology, developmental psychology and education. She is a Fellow of the Higher Education Academy. She is also a Visiting Senior Lecturer at New York University London where she lectures in the areas of Developmental Psychology and Human Development, and at the Royal College of Music where she teaches on prenatal and infant development. Antonia has collaborated with various universities around the world, including the University of Cyprus where she was a specialist scientist and the University of Florence in Italy where she was an Erasmus+ Academic. She studied for her PhD in Psychology and Education under the guidance of Dr David Whitebread, at the University of Cambridge. She also holds an MPhil in Psychology and Education from the University of Cambridge, and a BA (Honours) in Education from the University of Cyprus. Before starting her tenured career, Antonia worked as a researcher on various projects at the Faculty of Education of the University of Cambridge, where she also taught for three years at undergraduate and post-graduate levels. She has published widely in the areas of self-regulation, meta-cognition, the role of the context, play, and musical play in young children's self-regulation and broader development. Recent externally funded projects include the study of links between autonomy support from teachers and self-regulation from pupils during learning, and the investigation of musical play's potential as an intervention for promoting children's self-regulation. Antonia holds Qualified Teacher Status and has worked as a primary school teacher at schools abroad. She is passionate about making a change in the lives of children, practitioners and families and has contributed as a Member of a Working Group to *Birth to Five Matters*, guidance for the Early Years Foundation Stage in the UK. She is also the co-founder of the Play, Learning and Development Special Interest Group at the European Association for Research on Learning and Instruction (EARLI).

Acknowledgements

We would like to extend our heartfelt thanks and gratitude to all of the people who have helped us to get to this point with the book. In particular, we wish to thank all of the children and practitioners we have been privileged to work with over many years, and especially those whose thinking and ideas are included here. We are indebted to them for their openness and welcome, and their generosity in allowing us to represent them here. We also wish to thank colleagues and students past and present, for the opportunities to discuss self-regulation (among many other things!), all of which has, we hope, made this a better book. Last, but not least, our thanks go to family and friends, for their support and encouragement, in particular love and thanks to Irene, Stavros and Harry from Antonia and to Charlotte and Isabella from Sue.

Introduction

Self-regulation is an area of huge interest in early childhood, for practitioners, researchers and policymakers. For both of us personally it has been a vital focus of our work for, between us, over 35 years! Unsurprisingly perhaps, we believe it is one of the most important areas for all of those working with or for young children to know about. It is also endlessly fascinating, and we hope that one of the things we have been able to do here is to highlight and illustrate this fascination, and the joy of engaging with children and watching its development as they play and work, at home, in communities and in education and care settings. At the same time, self-regulation remains an area in which clarity can be much needed, with diverse theoretical positions, curricula and policies often emphasising different aspects. What we have tried to do throughout this book is to present a clear picture of what we think self-regulation is – and also what it is not. In Chapter 1, we set out our perspective, which we paraphrase here:

Self-regulation is a holistic process, with emotion regulation and cognitive regulation supporting the regulation of behaviour. It is not just a matter of regulating behaviour, nor is it only concerned with cognition. It affects (and is affected by) all aspects of children's development.

The cover of this book exemplifies this. Learning to ride a bicycle is an inherently social process, as the adult supports and co-regulates the child's efforts, gradually withdrawing this support as the child becomes more skilled, and able to self-regulate. The adult also offers encouragement, supporting and co-regulating the child's emotional state. In turn, the child needs to be emotionally engaged and motivated to persist, as they gradually learn to regulate their emotions when things are tricky or challenging.

Self-regulation also seems to be crucially significant in all aspects of development, making it important to look at it from the perspective of practice, informed by what we know from theory and research. Throughout the book we draw on our own research, which has been conducted in early childhood settings with practitioners and children. The examples we give are of children in everyday contexts, and we hope they demonstrate just how competent and skilful we think young children are.

The focus of the book is on self-regulation in young children up to the age of eight, generally considered globally as the period of early childhood. Our approach throughout is to present a mix of theory, practice, reviews of the literature, and accounts of research projects. We want to emphasise the importance of translating theory and research to practice, to support students and practitioners working with young children. In putting this book together, we have tried to organise chapters so that they can be read independently but also so that readers, as they move from one chapter to the next, can build on the understandings established in previous chapters. As could be expected when looking at such a holistic concept, some topics appear time and again in different chapters. We have tried to ensure that there are signposts to other chapters when this occurs, both to ensure that the reader can move effortlessly between chapters, and to highlight the connections across ideas.

Learning features

Throughout, we have included opportunities for you to stop, reflect on what you have been reading, and implement ideas, or read in further depth. 'Think about/ Activities' ideas encourage you to put your learning into practice, whilst we also identify opportunities for you to further 'Develop your understanding', by reading more challenging texts or developing your thinking about important concepts. In the 'Observation' examples, we share with you observations that elucidate key concepts. The sections on 'What does research tell us?' focus on specific projects which have been influential in establishing current understandings about self-regulation, and 'What does policy tell us?' sections highlight current policy frameworks. We have also tried throughout to highlight the implications for practice, both in working with children, and in working with parents and carers (please note, that throughout the book when we refer to 'parents' we include carers and guardians in this term).

Book structure

The book is structured in eight chapters:

In *Chapter 1*, 'What is self-regulation, and why does it matter?', we address the core challenge of defining self-regulation, both for what it is, and what we think it is not. We also look at it alongside a range of other, closely related areas, including meta-cognition, executive function, effortful control, co-regulation and socially shared regulation. Self-regulation is a field in which many of these terms crop up time and again, and it is valuable to know what they mean, and how they relate to our subject. We look at key theorists' perspectives on self-regulation, and the evidence for self-regulation's importance for children's emotional, social, cognitive and behavioural development, both in early childhood and for their lifelong development.

This development is set out in *Chapter 2*, 'How does self-regulation develop in early childhood?' which looks at self-regulation through a developmental lens. We describe how self-regulation develops with age, and look at why young children were traditionally thought to be unable to self-regulate. Building on ideas intro-duced in Chapter 1, we look at the development of a range of higher mental processes related to self-regulation, alongside emerging understandings about processes such as co-regulation and socially shared regulation.

In recent years, self-regulation has become more noticeable in curriculum frameworks for young children, and it is increasingly evident in local and national policies, and in international initiatives such as the OECD *International Early Learning and Child Well-Being Study*.

In *Chapter 3*, 'Where can we find self-regulation in policy and curriculum frameworks?', we look at some of these frameworks and policies from around the globe, both for themselves and for how they can help us to make sense of policies in our own countries. We ask, do these policy and curriculum frameworks do justice in presenting the significance of self-regulation?, as well as highlighting the lack of consensus about a definition of self-regulation amongst them.

In *Chapter 4*, 'Relationships and self-regulation', the emphasis is on how relationships with parents and peers can affect children's self-regulation. We look at how parental scaffolding and support can be beneficial for young children's self-regulation, and at the importance of peer interactions and friendship. This relationship seems to be bi-directional, so we also explore the ways in which self-regulation can also affect children's relationships with their peers.

Chapter 5, 'Observing and assessing self-regulation in young children' explores different approaches to observing, assessing and documenting self-regulation in young children. We look at frameworks which enable practitioners and researchers to assess children in everyday contexts, observing them as they play and work, and listening to what they say. In so doing, we highlight the importance of valuing and prioritising children's perspectives and input.

In *Chapter 6*, 'Communication and language for self-regulation', we look at how communication with others and communication with the self, so-called 'private speech', can support young children's self-regulation. Importantly, we do not focus only on oral language, but include gesture and embodied cognition as ways of communicating. Here we also begin to look in detail at social contexts for talk, and the important parts played by narrative and pretend play in young children's self-regulation. The following chapter, 'Contexts for self-regulation', takes this discussion further, focusing on play, particularly pretence and musical play, and problem-solving, as contexts fostering self-regulation. We also broaden this discussion, looking at self-regulation across the early childhood curriculum.

Chapter 8, 'Planning – and not planning – for self-regulation', acts to look both at how we can plan for young children's self-regulation, and as a way of bringing together insights from across the book as a whole. Here we look particularly at what it means for children's self-regulation in contexts ranging from child-initiated to adult-directed and at the possible effects of adult involvement or absence as children play and work. We explore some of the ways in which the physical environment, including materials and resources, can act to support self-regulation development.

1 What is self-regulation, and why does it matter?

In this chapter, we look at:

- What self-regulation is – and what it is not;
- How ideas about self-regulation have developed;
- Key theorists and their perspectives on self-regulation;
- Other regulation, self-regulation, co-regulation and socially shared regulation;
- Relationships between self-regulation, metacognition, executive function, effortful control and theory of mind;
- Why self-regulation is so important for young children's development: emotionally, socially, cognitively and behaviourally.

Keywords: self-regulation, co-regulation, executive function, metacognition, self-regulated learning, socially-shared regulation.

Introduction

In this opening chapter, we introduce some of the key ideas that run throughout the book. Starting with self-regulation (SR) itself, we also look at the related term self-regulated learning (SRL), as well as exploring the relationships between self-regulation, other regulation, co-regulation (CR) and socially shared regulation (SSR). We also look at the ways in which self-regulation has been linked to a variety of other mental processes, notably metacognition, executive function (EF), effortful control (EC) and theory of mind (ToM).

The fact that self-regulation has been of interest to a wide range of disciplines – cognitive and developmental psychology, education and health, for example – has contributed to the range of ways in which it has been conceptualised, described and defined. What unites these different perspectives is a recognition that self-regulation plays a 'central role in influencing learning and achievement in school and beyond' (Boekaerts & Cascallar, 2006: 199), from the early years onwards. In England, self-regulation is included for the first time in the 2021 version of the Early Years Foundation Stage, as shown in the box below.

Statutory framework for the early years foundation stage in England

Since 2021, self-regulation has been included in the English Early Years Foundation Stage (EYFS). In the EYFS, it appears in the Early Learning Goals for Personal, Social and Emotional Development. As we shall see, this represents only a part – albeit important! – of self-regulation.

ELG: Self-Regulation

Children at the expected level of development will:

- Show an understanding of their own feelings and those of others, and begin to regulate their behaviour accordingly;
- Set and work towards simple goals, being able to wait for what they want and control their immediate impulses when appropriate;
- Give focused attention to what the teacher says, responding appropriately even when engaged in activity, and show an ability to follow instructions involving several ideas or actions.

(Department for Education, 2021: 12)

What is self-regulation – and what is it not?

In education, self-regulation features in the theories of major figures such as Piaget and Vygotsky, as well as Behaviourist and psychoanalytic ideas. This breadth of interest has contributed to the range of definitions, and even to ways of describing self-regulation. These include ideas of self-regulation as 'impulse control, self-control, self-management, self-direction, independence' (Bronson, 2000: 3), and 'problem-solving, behavioral control, mood control, self-regulated learning' (Zeidner et al., 2000: 750).

In all of these varied perspectives, self-regulation is seen as having implications for children's affective (emotional and social), cognitive and behavioural development. Zimmerman's 'widely accepted' (Whitebread, 2016: 3) definition of self-regulation highlights the interrelationships between them:

> The processes whereby learners personally activate and sustain cognitions, affects and behaviors that are systematically oriented towards the attainment of personal goals.

(Zimmerman, 2011: 1)

5

Zimmerman's description of a self-regulated learner emphasises the close relationship between motivation and self-regulation, which Bronson (2000) believes are inseparable in most situations, particularly for young children. Zimmerman suggests that children:

> *can be described as self-regulated to the degree that they are metacognitively, motivationally and behaviourally active participants in their own learning process.*

> (Zimmerman, 1989: 329)

The ideas looked at so far suggest that self-regulating learners are motivated and active participants in their own learning, with skills in managing their emotions, thoughts and behaviour. **Self-regulation is not just a matter of regulating behaviour, nor is it only concerned with cognition. Above all, it is a holistic process, with emotion regulation and cognitive regulation supporting the regulation of behaviour. It affects (and is affected by) all aspects of children's development.**

GUIDANCE FROM THE EARLY YEARS SECTOR: BIRTH TO 5 MATTERS *(2021)*

Birth to 5 Matters has been developed by the Early Years Coalition to support practitioners in implementing the EYFS. They are clear on what self-regulation is *not*:

> *Self-regulation is not the same thing as compliance, such as sitting still and listening when expected to. A child who is stressed and struggling to resist the impulse to move or speak is very different from a child who is calm and alert, in a balanced state of feeling, thinking, and behaviour.*

> (Early Years Coalition, 2021: 21)

Developing behavioural self-regulation involves much more than learning to do what you are told, or what is expected of you – both at home and in school. As the Early Years Coalition suggest, expecting children to do so without understanding *why* it can be very important to sit still and listen, for example, may lead to children being both stressed and/or unable to resist the desire to wriggle and talk. It serves as a good example of being regulated by others, rather than self-regulation.

The development of theories about self-regulation

How, though, did we get to this point? Interest in self-regulation (although it was not referred to as that) probably begins with Freudian psychoanalytic ideas and

Behaviourist approaches to learning in the late nineteenth and early twentieth centuries (Bronson, 2000). From a psychoanalytic perspective, the development of self-regulation is an outcome of emotional needs and drives. Behavioural perspectives on self-regulation see it as learnt self-control, and largely attributable to factors outside the child, such as reward and punishment (Bronson, 2000).

By the mid-twentieth century, the work of Jean Piaget had become influential on ideas about self-regulation. In Piaget's model, two complementary processes, assimilation and accommodation, are responsible for cognitive development through their impact on a child's existing mental structures or 'schemas' (Piaget, 1953). Assimilation is about the way in which we fit incoming information into our existing way of thinking about a schema, for example, a family might have a pet dog, so a baby might call all small animals 'dog'. Accommodation is what happens when we adjust a schema, and adapt our thinking, in light of new information – to continue the example, a child's realisation that a small animal might be a dog, or it could be a cat. These processes are, in Piaget's view, automatically self-regulating, in that the child's current level of development governs what information is incorporated into an existing schema, via the innate self-regulatory processes of equilibration (balance), which arises as a result of these changes in our thinking.

Lev Vygotsky and self-regulation

It is, though, from the ideas and writings of Lev Vygotsky that many of the most influential ideas about self-regulation have been drawn. For Vygotsky, self-regulation is a prime example of a 'higher mental process' (Vygotsky, 1978: 57), a term which refers to any consciously directed thought process, in contrast to elementary mental processes such as reactive attention. Self-regulation includes the coordinated exercise of other higher mental functions such as memory, analysis, evaluation, synthesis and planning. For Vygotsky all learning is social in origin, and the development of self-regulation is a co-constructive process, in which the child learns with the assistance of others. The role of these more experienced others is to guide a child to a more sophisticated solution to a task in order to support the move from regulation by others to self-regulation.

There are two critical ideas that Vygotsky uses to explain the ways in which children develop self-regulation. One is the zone of proximal development (ZPD), the other is speech and interaction. We shall return to these ideas throughout the book, but here it is useful to introduce the key idea of the ZPD. For Vygotsky, the most powerful and effective learning takes place within the ZPD, defined by Vygotsky as set out below and as shown in Figure 1.1:

> *the distance between the actual developmental level as determined by independent problem solving and the level of potential development as determined through problem solving under adult guidance or in collaboration with more capable peers.*

> (Vygotsky, 1978: 86)

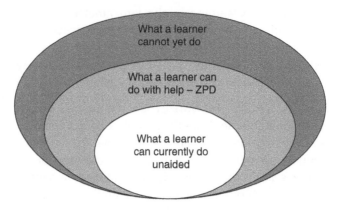

Figure 1.1   The zone of proximal development

Learning, then, is a process of internalisation, in which adults or more experienced others are initially responsible for providing the means for successful problem-solving and regulating learning. We are familiar with this as an idea, often referred to as scaffolding, although this term was actually coined by Wood et al. (1976). Gradually, children start internalising these means for successful problem-solving and regulating learning, and become able to take on more of the responsibility for learning themselves, becoming self-regulating. Central in this process, particularly for young children, are play and language. In play, the 'rules' of the game require children to act against their immediate impulses, so that the game can continue, which supports the development of self-regulation (Vygotsky, 1978). Language, for Vygotsky, is the primary vehicle for both transmitting the ideas of a culture, and thought and self-regulation. His ideas about play and language are looked at in detail in Chapters 6 and 7, but perhaps the most important point for practice to draw out here is that, if the move from other regulation to self-regulation happens as a result of children's social interactions with others (including parents and practitioners), then there is the potential for self-regulatory skills to be taught and learnt.

The move from other regulation to self-regulation: looking at co-regulation and socially shared regulation

In Chapter 2, we look in more detail at the ways in which self-regulation develops during childhood, but it is useful here to introduce the ideas of co-regulation (CR), and socially shared regulation (SSR).

Co-regulation is a transitional process, between being regulated by others, and self-regulation. Think, for example, of the ways in which adults use soothing and distraction to calm a distressed or frustrated young baby, holding, rocking and singing to them, for example. In so doing, they are supporting the baby, and helping them to reduce their distress, by co-regulating their emotion. The Early Years Coalition (2021) emphasise the importance of co-regulation in their guidance on implementing the EYFS.

GUIDANCE FROM THE EARLY YEARS SECTOR: BIRTH TO 5 MATTERS (2021) AND CO-REGULATION

Birth to 5 Matters emphasises the importance of co-regulation:

- A pedagogy which includes co-regulation strategies will help children develop self-regulatory skills.

- Researchers have identified three basic strategies for co-regulation:

  - **Positive Relationships** – Provide a warm, responsive relationship where children feel respected, comforted and supported in times of stress, and confident that they are cared for at all times.

  - **Enabling Environments** – Create an environment that makes self-regulation manageable, structured in a predictable way that is physically and emotionally safe for children to explore and take risks without unnecessary stressors.

  - **Learning and Development** – Teach self-regulation skills through modelling, suggesting strategies, providing frequent opportunities to practice, and scaffolding to support children to use self-regulation skills.

  (Early Years Coalition, 2021: 21)

Co-regulation does not necessarily mean that it is an adult who is doing the regulating. Another child can also do this. Co-regulation occurs in situations when one partner (adult or child) masters a key element of the task but the other does not (Hadwin et al., 2011). This could be, for example, in the form of peer-tutoring or the asymmetric development of ideas among children (Grau & Whitebread, 2012). The goal of co-regulation is either a transition towards self-regulation or coordination of independent self-regulation among group members. For example, one of us studied children's self-, co- and socially shared regulation in musical play. We have examples of children engaging in instrumental play in groups, in which one girl closely monitors a peer to check that they are playing correctly, and nods her head in approval (Zachariou & Whitebread, 2017).

Socially shared regulation is fundamentally a collective process. While both self-regulated learning and co-regulated learning can be either individual or collaborative, by contrast, socially shared regulation of learning is located in collective, collaborative activity. As Hadwin and Oshige (2011: 258) define it, SSR comprises: 'Processes by which multiple others regulate their collective activity. From this perspective, goals and standards are co-constructed, and the desired product is socially shared cognition.' Continuing from the previous example, in musical play, socially shared regulation was observed when the children in a circle game carefully monitored each other and the team, so that they could manage to pass the tambourine around the circle without making any noise (Zachariou & Whitebread, 2017). As with SR and CR, socially shared regulation

Look at the three basic strategies for co-regulation identified by the Early Years Coalition:

POSITIVE RELATIONSHIPS	ENABLING ENVIRONMENTS	LEARNING AND DEVELOPMENT

1. Reflect back to an occasion when you felt that you were able to successfully co-regulate a child's thinking and learning. What helped to make it successful? Can you relate this to the three basic strategies here?

2. Try to think back to an occasion when you felt you were not successful – what do you think made it less successful? Can you relate this to the three basic strategies here? What might you do now to make it more successful?

gives motivation an important role, except that here it is socially constructed and enacted, as part of a process of engagement and involvement in a collaborative social activity.

Co-regulation and socially shared regulation, then, are rooted in Vygotsky's ideas about the ways in which higher mental processes like self-regulation are socially embedded, and in which scaffolding and intersubjectivity (mutual understanding between people of each other's thoughts and feelings) are central.

How is self-regulation related to other higher mental processes?

There has been much debate about the relationship between self-regulation and other higher mental processes, particularly metacognition, executive function, effortful control and theory of mind. As we shall see in Chapter 3, the International Early Learning and Child Well-Being Study developed by the Organisation for Economic Co-operation and Development often uses 'self-regulation' and 'executive function' interchangeably. There is, though, growing consensus, reflected throughout this book, that self-regulation is the overarching construct. Within this, metacognition is a 'key subprocess of and vital to effective self-regulation' (Tarricone, 2011: 168), but not, by itself, sufficient to enable successful self-regulation. Similarly, EF can be seen as a subcomponent of self-regulation (Monette et al., 2011) and a facilitator of metacognitive processes (Brown, 1987). Blair and Ursache (2011) suggest that the relationship is bidirectional, with executive functions

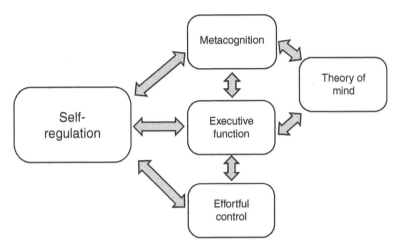

Figure 1.2   How is self-regulation related to other higher mental processes?

serving as important contributors to self-regulation while also being dependent upon self-regulatory processes such as emotion regulation, attention and stress arousal.

It is helpful to look at all of these processes together. The emergence of the term self-regulated learning (SRL) in the 1980s reflects this, as most models of SRL integrate aspects of metacognition and self-regulation. Goswami (2008) suggests that one further reason for this growing unification is the emergence of cognitive neuroscience, and our developing knowledge of the co-location of features such as inhibitory control, strategic control and working memory in the frontal cortex of the brain. The two-way relationships between these processes are shown in Figure 1.2.

It is worth taking some time now to look briefly at these different processes.

What is metacognition?

We look first at metacognition because it has such strong links to self-regulation. At times, the two terms have been used together. For example, Sperling et al. (2000) refer to 'metacognitive self-regulation'. We can date use of the term itself to John Flavell in 1976, even if ideas about metacognition have been around for much longer. He describes it:

> *'Metacognition' refers to one's knowledge concerning one's own cognitive processes and products or anything related to them, e.g. the learning-relevant properties of information or data.*

> (Flavell, 1976: 232)

Metacognition, then, is about how we think about, and what we know about, our thinking. But, as Flavell himself emphasises, metacognition is not just about cognition; it is also about social and emotional processes and experiences. Feelings play an important part in metacognition, as they do in self-regulation. Feeling confident, interested and motivated, or alternatively, insecure, bored or discouraged, will affect how we approach something, and our likelihood of success.

The components of metacognition

We can think about metacognition as having two components, which affect and influence one another. These are metacognitive knowledge and metacognitive regulation. Both are also affected by our metacognitive experiences as we engage in an activity. These experiences can lead us to revise our goals, and establish new ones or abandon old ones. They can also add to or revise our metacognitive knowledge, and help to activate strategies (metacognitive regulation) that may be useful to us in attaining a goal. Think of yourself reading this book – as you do so, you may slow down when your experience tells you that you have not fully understood something, or you may use another strategy, such as re-reading a paragraph. You may also skim-read in places where you feel confident about your understanding, using a strategy such as looking for a particular term or word. As a result, you may decide that your goal this time is to finish reading a particular chapter, or to look through the book as a whole to find out about a particular topic. Whether or not these processes are deliberate and consciously activated, or automatic, is a question that is much debated, as we shall see in Chapter 2. Figure 1.3 sets these components out.

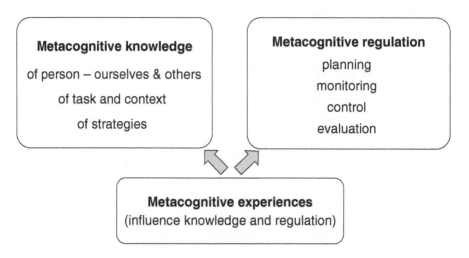

Figure 1.3   Components of metacognition

We can see evidence of children's metacognition as they play, work and talk. Children's metacognitive knowledge, in particular, is often most evident when we listen to what they are saying. The following examples show both metacognitive knowledge and regulation.

Metacognitive knowledge:

ORRIN (5.1): 'I know how to build a ship, by myself': *knowledge of person (himself)*

JOSHUA (4.10): 'We need to dig over here' (in the sand with friends): *knowledge of task*

ARIA (4.9): 'You need loads of glue, Jayvon, loads of glue': *knowledge of strategies*

Metacognitive regulation:

SUBIRA (5.3): (picking up a piece of paper) 'I'm doing a beautiful picture. I'm going to make a sun now' (picks up yellow felt tip pen). 'I'm going to make a sun': *planning*

SAM (5.2): 'You know what, they're not enough' (to self, as he collected resources): *monitoring*

Safi (5.2) holds out his model to Reuben, and gestures in a silent request for Reuben to wind sellotape around the joint between a box and a tube in his model: *control*

JOSHUA (4.9): (making a hat, commenting on his success in gluing) It works, it will stay there for ever: *evaluation*

As we noted earlier, there is growing emphasis now on looking at self-regulation and metacognition together. The development of the term self-regulated learning (SRL) in the 1980s has probably contributed to this, as most models of SRL combine the two. A good example of this in early childhood is the Cambridge Independent Learning (C.Ind.Le) project, which includes an observational tool which comprises three areas of metacognitive knowledge, metacognitive regulation, and emotional and motivational regulation (Whitebread et al., 2009b). We shall look at this in more detail in Chapter 5.

What is executive function?

As with self-regulation and metacognition, there are differing definitions of executive function, but Drayton et al.'s (2011: 534) view of EF as a 'cognitive system that controls and manages other cognitive processes, including flexibility of thought, planning, inhibition, and coordination and integration of information' is a helpful summary. Executive function comprises three interrelated sets of cognitive abilities:

- cognitive flexibility and the ability to 'set shift' (for example, sorting a set of plastic toys according to colour, then switching to sorting by shape);
- inhibitory control (resisting distraction and delaying gratification);
- working memory (in particular the ability to update and monitor working memory representations).

Neuroimaging studies support the idea that these cognitive abilities are interrelated (Monette et al., 2011). Working together, they 'support children's ability to monitor and control thought and action' (Razza & Raymond, 2015: 133).

WHAT DOES POLICY TELL US?

Development Matters: Self-regulation and executive function

Development Matters is the non-statutory guidance for the EYFS, published by the Department for Education in England. Self-regulation appears here as one of seven key features of effective practice, and is particularly related to executive function in the document:

Self-regulation and executive function

- Executive function includes the child's ability to:
  - hold information in mind
  - focus their attention
  - regulate their behaviour
  - plan what to do next.

- These abilities contribute to the child's growing ability to self-regulate:
  - focus their thinking
  - monitor what they are doing and adapt
  - regulate strong feelings
  - be patient for what they want
  - bounce back when things get difficult.

(Department for Education, 2020b: 11)

WHAT DOES RESEARCH TELL US?

Digital technologies and self-regulation: The effects of screen media content on young children's executive functioning

Children's exposure to screen-based media is a topic of much concern for parents and practitioners alike, given that the majority of even very young babies see and use screens on a daily basis (https://blogs.lse.ac.uk/parenting4digitalfuture/2016/12/28/what-are-the-effects-of-touchscreens-on-toddler-development/). But not all 'screens' are the same, and there is a growing body of research which looks at the potential advantages and disadvantages of different types of screen use. Are touchscreens the same in their effects as television watching, for example?

Huber and colleagues' (2018) study looked in particular at the effect of touchscreens on young children's executive functioning. In this study, 96 two- and three-year-old children completed executive functioning measures of working memory and response inhibition and task switching before and after watching an educational television show, playing an educational app, or watching a cartoon. Results show that the type of screen intervention had a significant effect on executive functioning performance. Children were more likely to delay gratification after playing an educational app than after viewing a cartoon. In particular instances, children's working memory improved after playing the educational app.

As the authors emphasise, their findings suggest that factors such as interactivity and content may be more important to consider than just 'screen time'. In other research, Fletcher-Flinn and Suddendorf (1996) found that digital technologies can benefit metacognitive development, and Fleer (2017) suggests that the creation of narratives on a tablet led to perspective taking on the part of the children, which is linked with the development of theory of mind.

This is an area about which parents often ask for guidance from practitioners. A useful starting point is the blog 'Toddlers and touchscreens: a parent's guide': https://blogs.lse.ac.uk/parenting4digitalfuture/2018/07/04/toddlers-and-touchscreens/

Why is executive function important and how does it contribute to young children's development?

EF is a key aspect of self-regulation, and may be a predictor of both academic achievement and socioemotional competence across childhood (Razza & Raymond, 2015). The cognitive processes of EF may directly support children's acquisition of knowledge by helping them to monitor their thinking, focus their attention and flexibly apply problem-solving strategies (Razza & Raymond, 2015). Strong executive functions have been associated with positive approaches to learning (Vitiello et al., 2011), and there is evidence of its importance for children's achievement in mathematics and language development (Razza & Raymond, 2015), science (Roebers, 2017) and creative thinking (Krumm et al., 2018). EF may also be associated with socioemotional competence, including emotion regulation and peer relationships (Qu, 2011; Razza & Raymond, 2015). A deficit in executive function has been linked to autism spectrum disorder (ASD) (Monette et al., 2011) and attention-deficit/hyperactivity disorder (ADHD) (Roebers, 2017). Some studies have observed less mature development of the region of the brain with primary responsibility for inhibition, planning and conceptualisation of complex tasks in children with ADHD (Bergen et al., 2018). Panksepp (1998) suggests that a longer period of opportunities for play, particularly physical rough and tumble play, may be valuable for children with ADHD, helping to develop the frontal lobes of their brains. At a time when many children's opportunities for play in school may be less than in times past, this may be important to think about.

WHAT DOES RESEARCH TELL US?

The Marshmallow Test: Inhibitory control and delaying gratification

Inhibitory control is one of the three aspects of executive function, and an important aspect of this is the ability to delay gratification – for example, waiting until the girl next to you has finished using the crayon rather than trying to snatch it from her hand. In the 1960s the 'marshmallow test' was developed to look at this aspect of EF. In this test, children aged 3–5 years are given a marshmallow which they can eat immediately, but they are also told that, if they wait for 10 minutes (that is, delay gratification and control the impulse to eat) they will be rewarded with two. Results of this test suggest that the willpower to wait may be associated with better social and emotional coping in adolescence and higher test scores, with such advantages persisting into adulthood (Mischel et al., 2011).

A recent replication of the study (Watts et al., 2018), however, found that, while there were still benefits for those children who could delay gratification, these were not as significant as those found by Mischel et al., and that any effect had largely disappeared by the age of fifteen. In addition, there may be cultural variance, dependent upon the kinds of behaviours children experience within their families and communities (Lamm et al., 2018).

What is effortful control?

Effortful control is about temperament, particularly being able to voluntarily manage attention, and inhibit a response, or adapt your behaviour as needed. It is clear to see how this is related to self-regulation generally, particularly from a socioemotional perspective, and also to executive function in particular. Blair and

Razza (2007), for example, found that aspects of executive function were related to effortful control in 3–5-year-olds. It plays a pivotal role in the self-regulation of emotion, social competence and prosocial behaviour (Eisenberg et al., 2010b), positive attitudes to school and positive teacher–child relationships (Silva et al., 2011).

OBSERVING EXECUTIVE FUNCTION AND EFFORTFUL CONTROL: IMRAN

This observation takes place in a Reception class of 4–5-year-old children, in London. Imran (age five) is kneeling on the floor. He has built a tall thin block construction, of cuboids and a cylinder. He stands up, carefully places another cuboid on top and stands back. The construction stays up, and he tells James nearby about it. He kneels down, stands a long cuboid on its end next to the tower, then puts another similar sized piece next to it. This falls back, and he catches it in his arms.

IMRAN: (to himself) Ups, again. Go on, ups again.

He continues building, repeating 'ups again'. He looks briefly at the adult nearby and smiles broadly. He stands up and tries to rest one block on top of another, but this is not stable, and it falls back towards him. In catching these he knocks his other tower, this topples forward and knocks over his original tower. He looks around, collapses on the floor with his blocks and smiles at James.

He continues to build. Amir arrives, and Imran pushes him away gently with his palm on Amir's chest. Amir picks up a long cuboid, and reaches up to put it on. Imran puts his hand over the top of the tower, in a gesture to stop Amir, but Amir carries on, and pushes the tower over as he does so. Amir walks away.

Imran does not react, but starts again, further experimenting with different sizes and shapes of blocks. He picks up a plank and balances it on top of a cylinder. He stands up, picks up another plank from nearby and balances this on top, in a T-formation. He stands back.

IMRAN: (shouting, to nobody) I've done the letter T̲. I've done the letter T!

JAMES: (turns, looks and prods Tahir, who is building nearby) Look!

TAHIR: (turns and looks): Yeah! That's mine.

Tahir walks over, leans forward and knocks the construction over with his chest. Imran smiles, and starts again. He makes another T-shape, then tries to put a small block at the end of one arm of the T. This destabilises it and it all falls down. He begins again, but this falls towards him. He looks around at what Bill, James and Tahir are doing, and joins them. The group continue to work together building the wall. The wall grows to about 70-cm high, then gets knocked over, collapsing. Ben, James and Tahir complain about this, blaming some nearby girls, but Imran continues to kneel down, and starts rebuilding. The other boys go away and Imran is left alone, rebuilding the wall.

(Continued)

OBSERVING EXECUTIVE FUNCTION AND EFFORTFUL CONTROL: IMRAN continued

This observation shows Imran displaying many of the characteristics of both executive function (EF) and effortful control (EC) – with clear overlap between the two in places. Looking at EF, Imran's change of focus from building tall towers to making the letter T shows his cognitive flexibility. The second aspect of EF, inhibitory control, is particularly characteristic of Imran's behaviour, as he focuses his attention and resists being distracted from his task, despite repeated collapses, and the interventions of others (for example, when Tahir knocks over his construction). This is also related to the EC characteristics of voluntarily managing attention (for example, as he says 'Ups, again. Go on, ups again') and inhibiting a response (for example when he looks around and smiles at James when he knocks his tower over). Imran also shows he is able to adapt his behaviour, with his protective gestures towards Amir when he tries to add to the construction. Finally, he shows his ability to self-regulate his emotions, smiling when his constructions fall down. Throughout, he shows prosocial behaviour, proactively engaging with both adults and children.

What about theory of mind?

Theory of mind (ToM) is really about our ability to understand that people have thoughts, beliefs and desires, and that other people's thoughts, beliefs, feelings and desires may differ to our own. As we have seen, metacognition is very much concerned (but not only) with what children know about their own minds. The links between the two are clear, and both are concerned with what we know about cognition, and the vocabulary we develop for talking about it. While research about the two has often been separate and unconnected, there is now more emphasis on thinking about them together, in what Kuhn (2005) calls 'meta-knowing'. Papaleontiou-Louca (2008) suggests that the underlying links between metacognition, theory of mind and executive function means that there is a case for uniting all three under one model of cognitive development.

Theory of mind may be associated with classroom skills (Razza & Blair, 2009) and academic achievement (Lecce et al., 2014). Perhaps most importantly in the context of self-regulation, it is linked to the development of social understanding in young children, including perspective taking and the ability to use persuasive arguments in our interactions with others (Slaughter et al., 2013). As Astington suggests:

> *Social interaction is really an interaction of minds, of mental states, but we have to communicate those states to others. We have to let the other person know we want something, or that we want them to believe something.*

> (Astington, 1994: 43)

OBSERVING THEORY OF MIND: LIVIE

Livie, aged 2 years 6 months, is visiting her grandparents' house with her parents. Her grandmother comes home with four ice-lollies. Livie, her parents and grandmother start having the four ice lollies, while her grandad is having a rest in his bedroom. With her almost-finished ice lolly, Livie walks up to her grandad's room, and looks at him:

LIVIE: I am having a lolly! (she gives him a second look, probably realising that there are no more ice lollies for her grandad) Don't worry grandpa! There must be something else for you to have!

Livie provides a brilliant example of a young child's Theory of Mind. Even though she is only two-and-a-half years old, this example shows that she can put herself into her grandad's 'mental shoes'. Livie saw the situation from her grandfather's perspective, and realised that her grandad would probably also want to have an ice lolly. This indicates that she understands that people have thoughts and desires and feelings, which can be different to the child's own feelings. So, she could understand that, even though she was happy having had her ice lolly, her grandfather would be disappointed. As we will see below, Theory of Mind is linked to the development of perspective taking, and this is evident here.

Children with ASD generally experience more difficulty in developing a theory of mind. They may develop ToM much later than their peers, in a different sequence, or not at all (Jenvey & Newton, 2015). Child-centred communication programmes and behaviour-based interventions have shown success in developing areas such as shared attention and social interaction (Carpendale et al., 2018), both important for ToM.

Why is self-regulation so important for young children's development?

We have seen throughout this chapter that there is some overlap between ideas about self-regulation, and other processes, particularly executive function and metacognition. Here we look at some of the evidence relating to all of these ideas, and why they are so important for the development of young children – and older ones too!

The importance of self-regulation for lifelong learning

There is good evidence to point to the significance of self-regulation for all aspects of development (Rademacher & Koglin, 2019; Whitebread, 2016), and important for lifelong learning and life skills (Shuey & Kankaraš, 2018), influencing classroom behaviour, academic achievement and school success (McClelland & Tominey, 2011). Flavell claims that the importance of metacognition lies in 'teaching children and adults to make wise and thoughtful life decisions as well as to comprehend and learn better in formal educational settings' (Flavell, 1979: 910). Fitzsimons and Finkel (2011) emphasise long-term effects, suggesting that 'good self-regulators' may be physically healthier, have more career success, and experience higher levels of well-being.

Looking back at the range of skills and dispositions that are attributed to successful self-regulation, it is clear that an important reason why self-regulation matters is the influence it may have on children's academic achievement and success in school. This is apparent from the early years onwards (McClelland et al., 2006; Shuey & Kankaraš, 2018), and long term in its effects (McClelland et al., 2006). Blair and Razza (2007), for example, found that features of self-regulation, particularly attention and inhibitory control, predicted progress in mathematical and reading ability a year later in 3–5-year-olds from low-income families in America. Bryce et al. (2015) concluded that metacognitive skills were the most important predictors of educational achievement in the 5- and 7-year-olds in their study. Self-regulation and metacognition may be significant for, among other things, mathematics (Larkin, 2010), science (Georghiades, 2006; Larkin, 2010), music (see Chapter 7), thinking skills (McGuinness, 1999), problem-solving (Bryce & Whitebread, 2012; Robson, 2016a), memory and attention (Flavell, 1979) and motor development (Whitebread, 2012). Some of the strongest evidence is to be found in studies of young children's talk, including the contribution of metacognitive talk to young children's emerging literacy (Annevirta et al., 2007; Degotardi & Torr, 2008). This area is looked at in more detail in Chapter 6.

ACTIVITY: THINKING ABOUT METACOGNITIVE TALK

Caroline, a teacher working with a Reception class of 4–5-year-olds in London, made regular use of metacognitive ideas and terms with the children, particularly in group discussions. She exhorted the children to 'think about your learning' and asked them 'What do we have to remember?' and 'What did you learn today?', highlighting the significance of 'learning' rather than 'doing'. She also praised them using expressions such as 'good remembering', 'good thinking' and even 'good theory'.

We have noted that this kind of metacognitive talk may be especially valuable for the development of metacognition and self-regulation (Annevirta et al., 2007; Degotardi & Torr, 2008).

(Continued)

ACTIVITY: THINKING ABOUT METACOGNITIVE TALK continued

1. Try to make a list of different words and phrases that support metacognition, and metacognitive talk.

2. Think about how you might incorporate more of these metacognitive talk words and phrases into your interactions with children, both individually and in groups.

Self-regulation and children's affective development

A number of studies highlight the significance of self-regulation for affective development (Rademacher & Koglin, 2019), including social cognition and self-control (Flavell, 1979). It is associated with social well-being and social success (Fitzsimons & Finkel, 2011) and positive peer relationships (Denham et al., 2010; Robson, 2016a) with children's ability to regulate their emotions affecting the way they are seen by others (Smith-Donald et al., 2007). These things may, in turn, support children's positive engagement with school life (Denham et al., 2010; Eisenberg et al., 2010b).

This emotion regulation overlaps with and mutually influences behavioural regulation (Smith-Donald et al., 2007), seen as critical to children's success (Wanless et al., 2011). This includes key aspects of behavioural regulation such as the ability to follow classroom rules, take turns and share, all of which are routinely expected of young children in their school lives. The development of such skills may be cumulative, suggesting that young children with poor behavioural regulation skills may be at greater risk of academic difficulty than their peers, with an ever-widening gap over time (Blair & Razza, 2007; McClelland et al., 2006).

What can practitioners do?

Perels et al. (2009) believe that the development of self-regulated strategies should be one of the main aims of education, particularly now, when there is increased emphasis on people's capacity to adapt to changing circumstances and new ways of working. Self-regulation may be a crucial factor in understanding and intervening to support children at risk of academic difficulty (McClelland & Cameron, 2012). Happily, there is strong evidence to suggest that efforts to enhance children's self-regulation (including in early childhood) may be among the most effective interventions (Durlak et al., 2011; Education Endowment Foundation, 2019). Interventions may be particularly valuable for children with low levels of self-regulatory skill at the outset (Tominey & McClelland, 2011), including those at risk because of academic difficulty (McClelland & Cameron, 2012), poverty and income inequality (Raver, 2012).

Looking at what practitioners can do to support the development of self-regulation is one of the main focuses of this book, and ideas are set out throughout. Here, we reflect back on what has been looked at in this chapter, and set an agenda which will be looked at in detail in the following chapters.

Both practitioners and parents and carers can actively help children to develop self-regulation by:

- interacting and talking with children;
- fostering warm, responsive relationships, between adults and children and between children themselves;
- providing an environment that supports the potential for self-regulation;
- scaffolding children's thinking, suggesting strategies and modelling ideas and self-regulatory behaviour;
- ensuring sufficient opportunities for children's play;
- using classroom routines productively as a way to support self-regulation.

WHAT DOES RESEARCH TELL US?

Metacognition and self-regulated learning guidance report

The Education Endowment Foundation concludes that teaching for self-regulation and metacognition has a high impact on children's achievement, for a low cost. Looking at a wide range of research in the area, and talking to teachers, researchers and academics, they put together a set of seven practical recommendations, for individual practitioners and schools:

Recommendation 1 Teachers should acquire the professional understanding and skills to develop their pupils' metacognitive knowledge

Recommendation 2 Explicitly teach pupils metacognitive strategies, including how to plan, monitor and evaluate their learning

Recommendation 3 Model your own thinking to help pupils develop their metacognitive and cognitive skills

Recommendation 4 Set an appropriate level of challenge to develop pupils' self-regulation and metacognition

Recommendation 5 Promote and develop metacognitive talk in the classroom

Recommendation 6 Explicitly teach pupils how to organise, and effectively manage, their learning independently

Recommendation 7 Schools should support teachers to develop their knowledge of these approaches and expect them to be applied appropriately

(Education Endowment Foundation, 2019: 3)

Conclusion

Self-regulation is recognised as crucial to young children's holistic development – emotionally, socially, cognitively and behaviourally. It has been described in a number of ways, but can be summed up here as being concerned with strategically planning, monitoring and regulating emotion, cognition and behaviour. Self-regulating learners are motivated and active participants in their own learning. The ideas of Vygotsky have been particularly important in helping us to think about what self-regulation is. It is also from Vygotsky that we can identify some key processes in supporting and developing self-regulation, particularly the idea of co-regulation, and the key role of more experienced others, often parents and practitioners, in scaffolding children's development, and in support of the move from regulation by others to self-regulation. Vygotsky also draws attention to the crucial roles of play and talk.

We have also seen how self-regulation is related to other higher mental processes, particularly metacognition, executive function, effortful control and theory of mind. At the same time, there is now much agreement that self-regulation is the overarching 'superconstruct', with these other processes being seen as key sub-processes.

Self-regulation seems to be important for lifelong learning and achievement. It is also significant for young children's affective development, contributing to social well-being and positive peer relationships, as well as many of the key skills important for managing behaviour, both in and out of school. Crucially, there is strong evidence that efforts to enhance young children's self-regulation can be highly effective, particularly for children with lower levels of self-regulation. The key ways in which practitioners can support young children's self-regulatory development introduced here set a context for the following chapters.

Key further reading

Bronson, M. (2000). *Self-regulation in early childhood: Nature and nurture*. New York, London: Guilford Press.

Education Endowment Foundation (EEF) (2019). *Metacognition and self-regulated learning*. online: https://educationendowmentfoundation.org.uk/public/files/Publications/Metacognition/EEF_Metacognition_and_self-regulated_learning.pdf.

Razza, R., & Raymond, K. (2015). 'Executive functions and school readiness: Identifying multiple pathways for success', in S. Robson & S. Flannery Quinn (Eds.), *The Routledge International Handbook of young children's thinking and understanding* (pp. 133–149). Abingdon: Routledge.

Roebers, C. M. (2017). Executive function and metacognition: Towards a unifying framework of cognitive self-regulation. *Developmental Review*, 45, 31–51.

Website

TABLET (Toddler Attentional Behaviours and Learning with Touchscreens) project. https://www.cinelabre-search.com/tablet-project.

2   How does self-regulation develop in early childhood?

In this chapter, we look at:

- The development of cognitive self-regulation and metacognition;
- Why it was traditionally thought that young children cannot self-regulate;
- The development of cognitive, affective and behavioural regulation;
- Self-regulation, executive function and effortful control development;
- Development of co-regulation and socially shared regulation;
- How practitioners and parents can support children's self-regulation development.

Keywords: development, cognitive regulation, metacognition, emotional regulation, behavioural regulation, co-regulation, socially-shared regulation.

Introduction

In this chapter, we explore how self-regulation develops. As we saw in Chapter 1, a child's self-regulation is related to their academic achievement (Pintrich, 2000) and how well they may do in life, including aspects such as income, health and even criminality (Moffitt et al., 2011). We also know that self-regulation is malleable and can be learnt from an early age (Dignath et al., 2008). This makes it important to develop an understanding about how self-regulation develops, in order to scaffold and support its development in children.

The chapter begins with an introduction to the development of self-regulation. Traditionally, it was thought that young children below the age of 8 could not self-regulate, so we look at why young children's self-regulatory capabilities may have been underestimated in the past. This provides important lessons for how we can look at self-regulation in young children. We then separately consider the development of cognitive self-regulation and metacognition (reflecting the close links between them that we saw in Chapter 1), emotional regulation and behavioural self-regulation. It is evident throughout that executive function and effortful control play a significant role in children's self-regulatory development, so we also look at their development. Lastly, as we saw in Chapter 1, nowadays research looks not just at self-regulation, but also co-regulation and socially shared regulation. So, we look at some of the research on co-regulation and socially shared regulation development and conclude the chapter with ideas for practitioners on how to support children's self-regulation development when working with children and with their parents.

The development of self-regulation

Historically, theories of self-regulation assumed that young children below the age of 8 were not capable of self-regulatory behaviours (Veenman et al., 2006). However, in the last 20–30 years, the evidence gained from observation of young children in natural circumstances, in homes and settings, suggests that very young children can self-regulate and socially regulate (Perry & VandeKamp, 2000; Rodríguez & Palacios, 2007; Whitebread et al., 2009b).

In fact, early indicators of self-regulation are apparent in the first months of life. Babies between 2 and 4 months old are thought to be able to participate in monitoring and control exchanges with adults (Brinck & Liljenfors, 2013). We can also see rudimentary self-regulation behaviours when infants try to reduce negative emotions by turning their heads away from a negative trigger such as their mother being unresponsive to them, or by attempting to soothe themselves, as early as 5 months of age (Kopp, 1989). From around the age of 3, there is clear evidence of self-regulatory abilities, particularly when we observe children in activities that are child-initiated, playful and meaningful to the children (Robson, 2016a; Whitebread et al., 2012). For example, in playing 'mummies and daddies' young children have to control their behaviour to resemble that of an adult. They also have to negotiate with their peers about roles, resolve arguments, and monitor and control their feelings. Early childhood is full of opportunities for children to develop their self-regulation. This development continues into middle childhood, adolescence and early adulthood.

DEVELOP YOUR UNDERSTANDING: WHY DID RESEARCHERS UNDERESTIMATE CHILDREN'S SELF-REGULATORY ABILITIES?

Researchers traditionally viewed self-regulation as an aptitude (a natural ability), and self-regulation research was dominated by techniques such as self-report measures (where participants report what they did, are doing or will do), or verbally based methodologies (for an overview, see Patrick & Middleton, 2002; Whitebread et al., 2005, 2009b; Winne & Perry, 2000). These methods may have two disadvantages for young children. First, they rely on children's verbal understanding and fluency, which is not necessarily well-developed in young children, and second, they can lead to working memory overload (children have too many

(Continued)

things to remember). As a result, children's abilities were often underestimated (Whitebread et al., 2005, 2009b; Winne & Perry, 2000).

In addition, especially for young learners, talking about self-regulation can be particularly difficult, possibly because their actions do not remain stable, but rather change across settings and situations (Hadwin et al., 2001; Perry & Rahim, 2011). Therefore, research that relies on talk reveals only what learners say they do, but does not reveal what they actually do. Such research also tends to underplay the importance of context/environment (Patrick & Middleton, 2002; Perry, 2002).

Meanwhile, there was a realisation that research needed to reflect individuals acting within contexts in order for it to be relevant for practice (Perry, 2002; Winne, 2010). These developments pioneered a shift to investigating self-regulation as an *event* instead of an aptitude. When examining self-regulation as an event, observations of children, rather than self-report measures, were appropriate. Studies also moved from laboratory settings to more naturalistic contexts such as classrooms (Patrick & Middleton, 2002; Perry, 2013; Whitebread et al., 2007). This made it possible to capture young children's self-regulation and revealed that they were capable of acting in a self-regulatory way.

Cognitive self-regulation and metacognition: how do they develop?

We need to begin here by first explaining that there is a lack of longitudinal studies (conducted over long periods of time) looking at the development of cognitive self-regulation and metacognition in young children (Grau & Preiss, 2019). This means that there are not many studies assessing the same children's self-regulation over time. Studies like this can be valuable in giving us a developmental trajectory. What we can do, though, is to bring together information from different studies which look at children of different ages, in order to build a picture of development over time.

Robson (2019) has collated information from a range of studies which help to evidence how children progress. These show how, from 6 months old, babies show some evidence of cognitive self-regulation. From 3 years onwards we observe intentionality in what young children do, indicating that the children are self-regulated. With age, children's metacognitive and cognitive self-regulatory skills develop. For example, 5-year-olds are much better than younger children at predicting how they will perform at a task and at evaluating their performance. Table 2.1 presents an overview of this. Looking at the studies in the table, you will see that researchers use measures of executive functions (introduced in Chapter 1) as proxies for children's self-regulation. The relevance of executive functions for self-regulation

Age	What does the child do in terms of cognitive self-regulation and metacognition?	Where can we find evidence?
6 months	Make simple plans to achieve a goal	Karmiloff-Smith (1994)
1–3 years old	Planning skills and problem solving strategies develop Abilities to engage in goal directed activities increase	Karmiloff-Smith (1994) Roebers (2017)
3 years old	Monitor their problem-solving	Sperling et al. (2000)
4 years old	Use strategies (metacognitive control) in puzzle tasks	Sperling et al. (2000)
3–5 years old	Evidence of metacognition and metacognitive self-regulation in self-directed activities	Robson (2010, 2016a) Whitebread et al. (2007)
4–5 years old	Improve at predicting their performance and at judging their performance	Sperling et al. (2000)
5–6 years old	Use strategies (e.g. naming, grouping) to help them remember when they are shown group of objects that they will then have to recall Most can talk about their memory and how it works	Larkin (2007)
6–8 years old	Children show all metacognitive regulation skills. 8-year-olds show significantly more metacognitive monitoring and planning compared to 6-year-olds	Zachariou and Whitebread (2019)

Table 2.1   Trajectory of development for cognitive self-regulation and metacognition

Source: Table drawing on Robson (2019).

development is something we look at in Chapter 1 and in the section below on 'Self-regulation, executive function and effortful control development'.

Is there a particular way in which this development over time occurs? There are two ways of thinking about this question. First is the idea of the development of cognitive self-regulation and metacognition from a traditional, age-graded, maturational developmental perspective. So we look at metacognitive monitoring and control for what they can tell us about how self-regulation develops over time. Second, we look at the idea of whether cognitive self-regulation and metacognition are domain-specific or general, that is, if self-regulation is acquired in specific areas first and then generalised, or vice-versa.

First approach: the development of cognitive self-regulation and metacognition (mainly monitoring and control) with age and maturation

Studies show that, as children grow up, their cognitive self-regulatory abilities increase in both how frequently they occur and in their quality. Keep in mind that most studies in this area are with children aged 5 and older (but exploring these can help to give us an understanding of the trajectory of development), and that they focus on two specific elements of cognitive self-regulatory behaviour, namely metacognitive monitoring (ongoing on-task assessment of how one is doing) and metacognitive control (changing the way a task has been conducted as a result of monitoring).

Monitoring skills are thought to be fairly established by 9 years of age. This implies that monitoring skills develop up to that age. Their development appears to be mainly a maturational process, depending upon age and not particularly affected by ability. For example, when children complete text comprehension tasks, skilled and non-skilled readers show similar levels of monitoring (Eme et al., 2006). Ability, then, does not seem to have a role to play in the development of monitoring.

Metacognitive control skills are still developing after age 9 (Roebers et al., 2009). Contrary to monitoring abilities, the development of control depends upon ability. For example, looking at children's control during problem-solving tasks showed that mathematical skills were more important than age for how well children would perform in terms of metacognitive control (Puustinen, 1998). Alexander et al. (1995) reviewed projects on children's self-regulation in academic tasks, and suggested that, while monitoring showed typical developmental improvements in gifted children with higher IQs, their development of control capabilities was accelerated.

More recently, Bryce and Whitebread (2012), looking at younger children, observed 5- to 7-year-olds completing a train-track task. They report that, as with the studies of older children, monitoring processes improved with age, and control also improved with task-specific ability.

The development of metacognitive skills: evidence from observational analysis of young children's behaviour during problem-solving

In this study, Bryce and Whitebread (2012) explored how metacognitive skills develop in young children aged 5 and 7. The researchers observed and video-recorded 66 children engaged in a problem-solving task, in which they had to complete a train track. The children were asked to use as many train-track pieces as required in order to build a track to match a predefined shape from a plan (see image). The videos of children problem-solving were analysed to assess metacognitive skills, among which were monitoring and control.

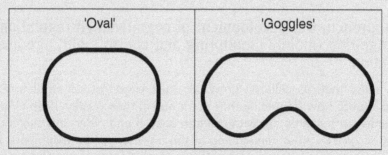

| 'Oval' | 'Goggles' |

Figure 2.1   Example of a predefined plan for a train track

(Continued)

The authors report that, between younger and older children, there was a *quantitative* increase in their metacognitive skills. Older children showed significantly more monitoring (e.g. checking the plan) and control (e.g. clearing space and seeking the correct piece) compared to younger children.

The authors also report *qualitative* changes in younger and older children's metacognitive skills. Older children illustrated different types of monitoring and control compared to younger children. For example, older children showed significantly more behaviours such as clearing their space and seeking, while younger children engaged in more verbally expressed planning. Older children also tended to check their plan more, while younger children would check their actual track.

Bryce and Whitebread were able to show a quantitative increase in metacognitive skills and qualitative changes in the types of monitoring and control between younger and older children. This suggests that it is not just the *amount* of metacognitive skills that changes as children grow older, but also the *type* of metacognitive skills (Bryce & Whitebread, 2012).

Source: Bryce and Whitebread (2012).

Second approach: is the development of cognitive self-regulation and metacognition from domain-specific to general or vice-versa?

In the second approach, we explore the question of whether cognitive self-regulation and metacognition are acquired in a general way, following age-related, maturational changes and are then applied in specific domains (for example, mathematics or problem-solving), or if they initially develop in domain-specific contexts, perhaps related to domain-specific knowledge, and then generalise at a later stage (Pintrich & Zusho, 2002; Van der Stel & Veenman 2010; Zeidner et al., 2000). This has considerable relevance when we think about how to support children's development.

On the one hand, there is evidence for general metacognitive skills (Van der Stel & Veenman, 2014). For example, Veenman et al. (2004) found support for metacognition development being a general, person-related characteristic across age groups (10-, 12- and 14-year-olds). On the other hand, some studies suggest that metacognition is task-specific. For example, Thorpe and Satterly (1990) used memory tasks with children aged 7–11 and suggested that metacognition appears to be task-specific within this age range. If we look closely at the age groups, this might suggest a trend where metacognition is task-specific for younger children and becomes more generalised for older children.

The latest developments in this area suggest that metacognitive skills might be initially acquired within separate tasks and domains and then gradually become generalised. Again, it is important to note that most research has been conducted with older children. Some research suggests that, until the age of 14, the metacognitive skills of children have a substantial domain- or task-specific orientation.

Between the ages 14 and 15 years, however, metacognitive skills generalise across tasks and domains (Van der Stel & Veenman, 2010, 2014; Veenman & Spaans, 2005). Veenman and Spaans' (2005) study of mathematics word problems and a biology task showed that the metacognitive skills of the 13-year-olds seemed to be rather domain-specific, whereas those of the 15-year-olds were general. It is interesting though to also look at a more recent study with younger children, aged 6–8, where regulatory abilities appeared to have a domain-specific element for the younger children, but gradually became fully general for the older children (Zachariou & Whitebread, 2019).

What this means is that it is important to start supporting children's metacognitive development early and certainly before the age of 8. This also suggests that attempts to improve children's metacognition and cognitive self-regulation should target the child's abilities on the specific task that is employed. Additionally, when supporting children's metacognitive development, practitioners should look at a variety of tasks, in order to support the potential for children to generalise these skills.

Emotional self-regulation: how does it develop?

We move on now to exploring how affective self-regulation, particularly emotional self-regulation, develops. Children's emotional self-regulation develops from early on in life. Very young babies usually rely on their caregivers to help them regulate and control their emotional states (Siegler et al., 2017). When an infant is distressed or frustrated, their parent will usually try to soothe or distract them (Gianino & Tronick, 1988). As we saw in Chapter 1, this is termed as 'co-regulation'.

Gradually, in their first year of life, infants show rudimentary signs of starting to self-regulate their emotions (Kopp, 1982). Infants show early indications of this when they engage in self-soothing behaviours. For example, by 5 months old, a baby will engage in repetitive actions such as sucking their fingers or rubbing their hands together, which help regulate their arousal (Planalp & Braungart-Rieker, 2015). They also discover that they are in control, and that looking away from an upsetting stimulus can help them regulate their level of arousal (Ekas et al., 2013). This is called self-distraction. As babies mature, they use these more reflexive, self-comforting behaviours less, and use more sophisticated and effective strategies, such as self-distraction, more (Ekas et al., 2013). In the first years of life, children develop their abilities for self-distraction, by playing on their own when they are distressed (Bridges & Grolnick, 1995).

As we have already noted in Chapter 1 (and look at in more detail in Chapter 6), children's language abilities also have a significant role to play. As children become more proficient language users, when feeling upset they are more likely to talk about their emotions, protest, and argue with their caregivers rather than, for example, burst into tears (Siegler et al., 2017). Additionally, when encountering emotionally difficult situations, older children use cognitive strategies and problem-solving (Zimmer-Gembeck & Skinner, 2011). For example, a child who is being teased by their peers may try to ignore them, rather than react in an aggressive way.

Much of the research focusing on emotional regulation, particularly with very young children, has looked at the home and the roles parents play in its development. Young children now spend increasing amounts of time in settings, making it important to look at these contexts. Think of all the peer interactions happening at a preschool: the conflicts, friendships and arguments. All of these can challenge children's emotional regulation (Silkenbeumer et al., 2018). Children have to play with others, to understand their own and others' mental states and emotions, to resolve conflict and to manage their own and others' emotions (Efklides & Misailidi, 2019). There is evidence from children aged 3 onwards that they can express awareness of a positive or a negative experience (e.g. saying 'it's a bit sad'), they can monitor their emotional reactions (e.g. saying 'that wasn't very nice'), they can self-encourage and encourage others. In addition, all these might be expressed verbally or in non-verbal ways (Whitebread et al., 2009b; Zachariou & Whitebread, 2015, 2017, 2019).

ACTIVITY: EMOTIONAL REGULATION

When working with young children, try to identify situations that challenge children's emotional regulation. These might be, for example, a conflict, an argument, or a friendship. Observe closely:

1. Is the children's emotional regulation evident? If yes, how?

   - Do they express awareness of positive or negative experience? (verbally or non-verbally)

   - Do they encourage themselves or others?

   - Do they persist in the face of difficulty?

2. If the children seem to be struggling with their emotional regulation, consider:

   - Is there anything that you could do to support the development of their emotional regulation?

   - Could you model for them how to deal with a challenging situation?

   - Could another child become an example/model for the child who is struggling?

   - Would discussing the child's feelings help?

Emotional regulation development links to behavioural self-regulation development

What seems to be clear is that the development of emotional regulation affects behavioural regulation (and vice-versa) in early childhood (Edossa et al., 2018). The better that children become at regulating their emotions, the easier it is for them to regulate their behaviour (Edossa et al., 2018). In fact, emotional regulation appears to affect behavioural regulation more strongly in early childhood (ages 3–5) than in older children.

Why does this happen? This seems to be based on the early connections that are created in children's brains. Because a young child's brain is high in plasticity (the capacity of the brain to be affected by experience), what a child experiences forges connections between the parts of the brain that are linked to emotional and behavioural regulation (Blair, 2002; Blair & Diamond, 2008).

Behavioural self-regulation: how does it develop?

First of all, it is very important to keep in mind that, even though the majority of children develop behavioural self-regulation rapidly during early childhood (see Table 2.2 for a summary), not all children develop in the same way (Allan et al., 2019; Montroy et al., 2016b), or at the same rate. In practice, this means that practitioners will need to adjust what they do to take account of each child's current ability to regulate their behaviour. Table 2.2 sets out a brief trajectory of development.

Age	What does the child do in terms of behavioural self-regulation?	Where can we find evidence?
12 months to 3 years	Children can listen to, process and follow directions (simple directions when younger, more complex when older)	Kochanska et al. (2001) Allan et al. (2019)
3 years	Evidence of behavioural self-regulation. Children can regulate their behaviour in changing situations	Kopp (1982)
3–7 years	Move from reactive behaviours and co-regulation to more advanced behavioural regulation	Montroy et al. (2016)
7 years	Children perform similarly to adults on behavioural self-regulation tasks	Ponitz et al. (2008)

Table 2.2   Trajectory of development for behavioural self-regulation

As with all other aspects of self-regulation, initial indications of behavioural self-regulation (mainly in the form of executive function, such as attentional control, inhibition and effortful control) become evident through co-regulation, particularly regulation from a caregiver (Allan et al., 2019). A key aspect of behavioural self-regulation is compliance (which we would classify as the child being co-regulated) in young children. This has an upward trend between 12 and 18 months, as children's comprehension skills develop (Kaler & Kopp, 1990). Committed compliance (when the child embraces their caregiver's agenda) also improves significantly up to the age of 3, with the main gains happening in the second year of life (Kochanska et al., 2001). Researchers describe how children can listen to, process and follow simple directions given by their caregivers (e.g. to put a toy away). Directions or instructions become more complicated as the child develops, for example, from just having to put away a toy, to having to complete different steps, such as 'put your toys away, then tidy up your table'. Gradually, the child moves from being 'other-regulated' by the caregiver, to guiding themselves based on the caregiver's instructions, to internalising those instructions, and thus self-regulating (Allan et al., 2019).

At around 3 years of age, children show more consistent evidence of being capable of behavioural regulation, that is, regulating their behaviours when situations are changing (Kopp, 1982). Between 3 and 7, we observe a change in behavioural regulation, in the form of moving from co-regulation or more reactive behaviours to more advanced types of behavioural regulation which incorporate executive functions (Montroy et al., 2016). A child younger than 3 who has to coordinate different executive function aspects for a behaviour might find it difficult (Carlson et al., 2002; Diamond, 2002; Zelazo et al., 2003). For example, they may find it difficult to act based on instructions they have in mind and at the same time ensure that they will not deviate from those instructions to follow their natural inclination (Diamond, 2002). Between ages 3 and 7, behavioural regulation and the skills that support it develop rapidly. Children's behavioural regulation seems to improve considerably between 4 and 6 years old, and by age 7 children perform similarly to adults (Ponitz et al., 2008; Rothbart et al., 2006; Rueda et al., 2004).

WHAT DOES RESEARCH TELL US?

The development of behavioural self-regulation across early childhood

Montroy and colleagues (2016b) look at the development of behavioural regulation in children aged from 3 to 7 years. They assess 1,386 children's behavioural regulation from preschool through first grade, with each child being assessed at least twice between the ages of 3 and 7.

The Head-Toes-Knees-Shoulders (HTKS) task was used to measure children's self-regulation. The children are given the instruction that they should do the opposite of what they are told. For instance, if the experimenter asks them to touch their head, they should touch their toes. This measure collects information about children's attention, working memory and inhibition. It is clear, then, that the task is using executive functions as a proxy for behavioural self-regulation.

Their results suggest that children develop behavioural self-regulation rapidly during early childhood. For example, a three-year-old child would, on average, score 3/20 on the HTKS task, a 3.5-year-old would score approximately 4/20, and a 4-year-old would score on average at around 10/20. Then, at every 6 months older, children seem to improve at around 2/20. A child aged 6.5 would score on average 19/20. This indicates rapid gains in behavioural regulation by age 4 and then slightly slower gains until age 7.

(Montroy et al., 2016b)

Self-regulation, executive function and effortful control development

Reading up to now you will notice that, whether we are exploring cognitive, emotional or behavioural regulation, two terms that come up a lot and which seem to be implicated in their development are effortful control (EC) and executive function (EF). There is no consensus as to whether these two should be viewed separately or together. On the one hand, researchers such as Razza et al. (2015) separate executive function from effortful control and suggest that neuroscientific evidence supports that each of the two is related to different areas of the brain, with EC coordinating emotional processing and EF coordinating cognitive processing. On the other hand, Gagne et al. (2021) propose that EF and EC perspectives are connected, support each other and should be integrated. The simplest explanation of the distinction between the two comes from Neale and Whitebread (2019: 266): EC is related to inhibitory control, which is an aspect of EF. However, 'inhibitory control can be a reflexive, automatic process', whereas effortful control is volitional and involves effort. As in Chapter 1, we take the approach of looking separately at these two constructs which affect self-regulation development.

Executive function development

Executive function is considered a key aspect of self-regulation (see Chapter 1). Emotional, cognitive and behavioural regulation share underlying mechanisms such as executive functions. In early childhood, major changes happen in our brain that link to the development of our executive function, which in turn make self-regulation possible (Efklidis & Misailidi, 2019). As we have already seen in previous sections, executive function measures have very often been used as a proxy for self-regulation (Grau & Preiss, 2019).

According to Roebers (2017), executive function seems to develop in similar timing to metacognition. Executive function is thought to start becoming evident towards the end of the child's first year of life. For example, most children at 16 months old would be able to pass the A-not-B task (Diamond, 2006). In this task, the child is shown a toy which is then repeatedly hidden at location A. The child will then reach for the toy at location A. If the experimenter then hides the toy under location B, most children of a younger age will typically look for the toy under location A, even though they have seen the researcher hide it under location B. By 16 months, Diamond (2006) showed that most children are able to reach for location B. This indicates that two of the components of executive function, that is working memory and inhibition (the child can inhibit their immediate response which would be to reach for the toy at location A as they have done in all previous trials), have emerged.

Children aged 2.5 years will perform even better at more challenging trials (ones with more choices). Similarly, EF tasks that are very challenging for 3-year-olds are feasible for most 4-year-olds (Zelazo et al., 2003). An example of this is the Dimensional Change Card Sort, where children are asked to sort cards in one way (for example, according to colour) and then they are asked to sort the same cards in a new way (for example, according to shape). The pattern of development is very rapid between 2 and 6 years. Executive function development continues through childhood and later in adolescence.

As always, it is very important to remember that not all children develop in the same way or at the same pace. For example, as we saw in Chapter 1, autism spectrum disorder (ASD) and attention deficit/hyperactivity disorder (ADHD) have been frequently linked to different-than-typical executive function development. When looking at executive functions (e.g. inhibition and working memory), these improved over time for children on the autistic spectrum (e.g. Pellicano, 2010), albeit at a slower pace compared to typically developing children (Luna et al., 2007). Similarly, Bergen et al. (2018) report that the brain region linked to inhibition and planning was less mature in children with ADHD. Each child, then, develops at their own pace and practitioners should always start from the child's current abilities and enable the child to work in their Zone of Proximal Development.

What drives the development of executive function?

In a review of the literature on development of executive function, Roebers (2017) concludes that children's interactions with the environment drive its development. More specifically, she proposes that these factors play a role in executive function development:

- Interactions with parents: the quality of parent-child interactions. Even for very young children, the quality of parents' behaviour (e.g. if they support their children's autonomy and if they are sensitive to the child's needs) has a role to play in EF development (e.g. Bernier et al., 2010).

- Interactions in schools and nurseries: children who have attended school for longer show better EF skills than children of the same age who have spent fewer years at school (Burrage et al., 2008). When a child goes to school, they have to follow classroom rituals (e.g. circle time), and requests, and this seems to foster EF.

- Interactions with siblings: children who have a sibling have to practice their executive functions. For example, the child might have to wait for their parent's attention while they deal with the other child (Backer-Grøndahl & Nærde, 2017).

Executive function and the curriculum

Certain approaches to curriculum in early childhood may be beneficial for development of executive function. The quality of interactions between student and teacher and the type of classroom activities seem to matter for EF development. Below we look at two approaches. While the data suggest that these programmes have positive effects on EF development, it is important to be tentative about these results, either because more studies are needed or because the effect sizes of these interventions are small.

Tools of the Mind (Bodrova et al., 2011)

This preschool and kindergarten children curriculum approach was inspired by Vygotsky and highlights the importance of social interactions. It focuses on sociodramatic play and the teacher scaffolding children's problem-solving. When implemented at kindergarten, this had positive effects on EF (but it should be noted that these were small effects).

Playworlds approach (Fleer et al., 2020)

The Playworlds approach is a model of play and educational practice where children are engaged in joint play with adults to dramatise children's literature. Dramatisation involves a dramatic collision which is followed by group activities in an attempt to resolve the collision. The teachers embed executive function activities when interacting with children. For example, the researchers describe an activity where the teacher, through the activity, introduced a rule that in order to resolve a collision, you have to move in the opposite direction to the directions drawn on the map that was given to the children. This, according to the researchers, supports EF development in the children.

It is important to note that the effects of programmes on EF development may be greater in children who are brought up in adverse environments, such as poverty (Blair & Raver, 2014).

Effortful control development

Effortful control (EC) is seen as a behavioural system which is a key facet of self-regulation (Razza et al., 2015). EC is the ability to inhibit a dominant (pressing) response, in order to carry out a less salient (less pressing) response (Rothbart & Bates, 2006). A child exhibits EC when they withhold their urge to taste the birthday cake in front of them until an adult cuts the cake. The dominant response would be the urge to taste the birthday cake, the first response that comes to a child. The less salient response is when the child waits for the adult to cut the cake. EC begins developing in late infancy and continues developing in the early years. It is EC which enables children to intentionally control their emotion and behaviour (Gagne et al., 2021; Rothbart et al., 2004), which illustrates just how important EC is for self-regulation in childhood.

In the first 3 years of life, EC is rudimentary, but rapid development takes place between 3 and 4 years of age. An early-appearing aspect of EC is children's ability to focus attention. By 10 months of age, infants can sustain their attention and, by the time they have reached 18 months, their attention has become more voluntary. The older children get the more sustained attention they show and the better able they are to concentrate for longer (for a review, see Eisenberg et al., 2010b). There is also evidence that, between 22 and 48 months, children's ability to effortfully inhibit behaviour develops. For example, children become better at delaying, slowing down, or suppressing activity, and at effortful attention (Kochanska et al., 2000). This is followed by further improvement in EC, with children becoming better at managing their attention and inhibiting their salient responses (Rueda et al., 2004). EC development continues into the school years and may continue developing into adulthood.

Self-regulation, co-regulation and socially shared regulation development

As we saw in Chapter 1, more recently we have started exploring not just self-regulation, but interpersonal regulation too. Research on regulation now crosses the boundaries of the individual (Vauras & Volet, 2013). We move from focusing on individuals to attempting to understand regulation as dynamic and developing processes influenced by not only personal but also social and contextual factors (Butler, 2011; Perry & Rahim, 2011). We still have a lot to learn about how co-regulation and socially shared regulation develop (Perry & Winne, 2013), but the box below presents one of the first studies that have explored how co-regulation and socially shared regulation develop with age, together with looking at self-regulatory development.

WHAT DOES RESEARCH TELL US?

The development of self-regulation, co-regulation and socially shared regulation: Developmental differences in young children's self-regulation skills

Zachariou and Whitebread (2019) explored self-regulatory development in young children. Because most of the research in this area focuses on very young children's (under 5) or older children's (aged 9+) self-regulation during academic tasks, this project took an innovative approach and investigated self-regulatory development

(Continued)

in children aged 6 and 8 years, in a developmentally appropriate and natural context: musical play.

The research looked at all aspects of regulation. In addition to cognitive monitoring and control, it explored metacognitive knowledge, planning, evaluation, emotional/motivational monitoring and control. It also looked at developmental differences between self-regulation, co-regulation and socially shared regulation.

The research compared a group of 18 children aged 6 to a group of 18 children aged 8. Children were video-recorded while engaging in five musical play sessions which took place during their regular school time. Each instance of regulation was coded as to the type of regulation, using the C.Ind.Le coding framework (see Chapter 5). Each regulatory instance was also coded as to whether it showed self-, co-, or socially shared regulation behaviour.

What were the findings?

- There was a quantitative increase in regulatory behaviours with age. Older children showed significantly more regulatory behaviours compared to younger children.

- The difference between younger and older children was significant in monitoring, planning and emotional/motivational monitoring behaviours compared to other regulatory behaviours.

- This agrees with other research suggesting that regulatory abilities develop with time.

Given that most studies so far have focused solely on control and monitoring, it is important to highlight that this was the first study with results on the remainder specific regulatory behaviours. It thus appears that not only monitoring (as has been highlighted in the literature so far) but also planning and emotional/motivational monitoring behaviours develop between 6 and 8 years of age compared to all other specific regulatory behaviours.

This study was also the first to attempt to explore how co- and socially shared regulation develop. The findings indicate that:

- All self-, co- and socially shared regulation develop with age.

- Socially shared regulation (the ability to share regulation between group members) showed steeper development between the ages of 6 and 8, compared to self-regulation and co-regulation. This finding could be particularly important for practice.

(Zachariou & Whitebread, 2019)

The study on developmental differences in young children's self-regulation skills by Zachariou and Whitebread (2019) established that monitoring, planning and emotional/motivational monitoring behaviours develop between ages 6 and 8, and that socially shared regulation abilities develop impressively from age 6 to age 8.

What implications can this have for practitioners working with children? Think about:

1. When should we start trying to support self- and socially shared regulation skills in children?

2. Should practitioners focus on supporting self-regulation, or socially shared regulation?

3. In what contexts should this take place? In specially organised activities or in naturalistic and meaningful activities? Why?

How can practitioners support children's self-regulation development?

The development of self-regulation is significantly influenced by children's experiences (Blair & Ursache, 2011). The first years of life are very important for children's self-regulatory development. This is especially the case because EC and EF, both closely linked to self-regulation, develop rapidly in the preschool period (Diamond, 2002; Kochanska et al., 2000). What can practitioners do to support children's self-regulatory development?

- Ensure children's opportunities for play. According to Vygotsky (1978), children set their own level of challenge during their play so that it is always developmentally appropriate for them. In play children act 'a head taller than themselves', always above their average age, their daily behaviour (Vygotsky, 1966/2016: 18). In play children 'integrate wants and desires with planning, problem-solving and cognitive abilities in the active shaping and control of their own experience' (Blair et al., 2010: 79). This provides opportunities that foster their self-regulation.

- Classroom routines and activities such as small group play, pretend play, games with rules and musical play foster children's self-regulation (Robson, 2016a; Savina, 2014; Timmons et al., 2016; Zachariou & Whitebread, 2017). In play, children learn to inhibit impulsive behaviours and use language to resolve disagreements or conflicting goals with their peers. They also agree on rules or invent new ones, thus exercising intrapersonal and interpersonal regulation (Efklidis & Misailidi, 2019).

- Scaffold children's work/play/activities (only) when needed. Ensure that either you or a more knowledgeable other (peer or adult) provide effective support, in a child's Zone of Proximal Development. This support can be gradually removed as the child masters a task (Wood et al., 1976). This helps the child move from being co-regulated by another to being self-regulated (Silkenbeumer et al., 2018).

- Use metacognitive prompts such as questions which encourage a child to explain how they have done something, to foster self-regulation (Silkenbeumer et al., 2018).

- Create a positive emotional environment and support children's autonomy, relatedness and competence (Whitebread, 2013).

- Establish a secure emotional environment for children: smile, show affection, be supportive in your talk (Ahn, 2005). Validate, label and discuss emotions. This is related to emotion regulation (Silkenbeumer et al., 2018).

- Allow children the autonomy to make choices between and within tasks (Boekaerts, 2011; Perry & VandeKampe, 2000).

- Encourage a mastery-oriented approach: foster children's positive feelings towards challenge, in which they monitor personal progress and view mistakes as opportunities for learning (Boekaerts, 2011; Perry & VandeKampe, 2000).

- Foster intrinsic motivation (from within) in children (Stefanou et al., 2004).

- Tasks for children should build on what children know, be meaningful, open-ended and complex but at the right level of challenge to stimulate effort and curiosity and also allow children to control challenge (Perry & Rahim, 2011; Perry, 2013).

- Give children opportunities to collaborate with peers, to co-regulate and socially share the regulation (Walker et al., 2004).

OBSERVING HEYI: TEACHER-PROVIDED SCAFFOLDING AND SELF-REGULATION DEVELOPMENT

Heyi (age 6) is learning to play the cello with her cello teacher.

TEACHER: Now, can you bow (play) for me (in a singing voice): 'D, D, A, A, A, A, A'?

Heyi plays the notes, but not smoothly. Her eyes are focused on the cello rather than on the bow.

TEACHER: Good. Now I think you can make that sound even more calm and gentle (touches the bow and guides the child's hand to make the bow movements again,

(Continued)

smoothly). How did I make that sound? (plays the notes again, this time a bit more smoothly).

Heyi is now looking at the bow and monitoring her bow movements.

TEACHER: Fantastic. Now do the same thing (with the bow). I don't want you to do the fingers.

The teacher is scaffolding Heyi's playing very closely. He is asking Heyi to focus only on her right hand, which is the one making the bowing movements, and he takes over the responsibility for playing what the left hand plays.

Heyi plays again. She is now looking at the bow very closely, monitoring her movements and evaluating her sound as she goes (this is evident from her facial expressions).

TEACHER: There we are.

Heyi plays the musical piece much more smoothly, with much more control over her movements.

TEACHER: Now, can you do it from the beginning, and do the fingers too, and get that same lovely sound?

Heyi starts playing and is playing much more smoothly, monitoring her bow movements very closely and controlling her sound so that it sounds smooth.

TEACHER: (as Heyi is playing): Lovely sound.

This is a lovely example of a teacher scaffolding a child's attempts. He is increasing his support when Heyi needs it, removing some of the challenging aspects of the task so that she can focus on the one aspect which is her goal for the day (playing smoothly). Then, as Heyi progresses and can achieve the goal independently, the teacher is gradually withdrawing his support. In the example it is also evident how the child moves from being regulated by the teacher to self-regulating.

Working with parents to support children's self-regulatory development

We know from research that contingent scaffolding (adjusting the level of support according to the child's needs) from parents of children as young as 12 months old can have beneficial effects for aspects of children's self-regulation (Neale & Whitebread, 2019; Zhang & Whitebread, 2017). Practitioners, then, can encourage parents to adopt behaviours that support self-regulation development, for example, scaffolding their children's problem-solving and play, and modelling thinking (Neale & Whitebread, 2019). In addition to contingent scaffolding, Pino-Pasternak and Whitebread (2010) suggest that parents can:

- Encourage metacognitive talk, for example, by giving opportunities to their children to talk about their thinking (e.g. how did you work this out?);

- Encourage active participation in tasks/problem-solving/play;

- Promote an internal understanding of control, which means that the children will learn to be independent and understand that they are in control of their learning/play/behaviour;

- Promote shifts in responsibility between adult and child. This will allow the child to progress within their ZPD;

- Show emotional responsiveness, be emotionally available and attuned to the child's feelings;

- Provide contingent scaffolding.

Conclusion

Self-regulation is significant for young children's development and influences their trajectory in life. We know that self-regulation can be learnt. In this chapter, we have explored how self-regulation develops because this helps us to think about ways of supporting children's self-regulation. Traditionally, it was thought that young children (below the age of 8) cannot self-regulate. However, when researchers found more appropriate ways to measure children's self-regulation, particularly observation, it became evident that even very young children can self-regulate.

The first indicators of self-regulation emerge in the first months of life. Children's cognitive self-regulation or metacognition develops from being able to make simple plans to achieve a goal (at around 6 months old) to monitoring their problem-solving (3 years old), using strategies in problem-solving (4 years old) and continues developing further. In terms of emotional self-regulation, we see rudimentary signs in infancy, when infants engage in self-soothing behaviours and later on in self-distraction. The better children become at using language, the more they start talking about their emotions, monitoring and controlling them. Homes and settings are full of emotionally challenging situations for young children, giving children opportunities to gradually became more adept at self-regulating their emotions. In behavioural self-regulation, rudimentary signs are evident when children listen to and follow directions (from 12 months) and then gradually move from these more reactive behaviours to more advanced, internalised behavioural self-regulation between the ages of 3–7. All of these self-regulation developments are closely linked to EF and EC developments.

More generally, in this trajectory of development, children move from being co-regulated by a more knowledgeable other to becoming self-regulated. We explored the crucial steps practitioners and parents can take in fostering young children's self-regulation development and will return to many of these themes in following chapters.

Key further reading

Grau, V., & Preiss, D. (2019). Supporting young children's self-regulation development. In **D. Whitebread V. Grau** & **K. Kumpulainen** (Eds.), *The SAGE handbook of developmental psychology and early childhood education* (pp. 535–553). London: SAGE Publications Ltd.

Montroy, J. J., Bowles, R. P., Skibbe, L. E., McClelland, M. M., & Morrison, F. J. (2016). The development of self-regulation across early childhood. *Developmental Psychology*, 52(11), 1744–1762.

Robson, S. (2019). *Developing thinking and understanding in young children: An introduction for students.* Chapter 5. Abingdon: Routledge.

Roebers, C. M., Schmid, C., & Roderer, T. (2009). Metacognitive monitoring and control processes involved in primary school children's test performance. *British Journal of Educational Psychology*, 79(4), 749–767.

Zachariou, A., & Whitebread, D. (2019). Developmental differences in young children's self-regulation. *Journal of Applied Developmental Psychology*, 62, 282–293.

3 Where can we find self-regulation in policy and curriculum frameworks?

In this chapter, we look at:

- Policy and curriculum frameworks in the nations of the United Kingdom and a range of international contexts;

- Whether the significance of self-regulation is reflected in policy statements and curriculum frameworks;

- How different curriculum frameworks include aspects of self-regulation;

- What guidance these frameworks give for practitioners supporting young children's self-regulation.

Keywords: policy, curriculum framework, curriculum change, practitioner guidance.

Introduction

Self-regulation is increasingly evident in national and local policies and curriculum frameworks, as well as in global initiatives such as the International Early Learning and Child Well-Being Study (IELS) from the Organisation for Economic Co-operation and Development (OECD). Developments such as these make it vital for practitioners to be able to understand and interpret policies and frameworks – in many cases they are statutory, and have implications for what adults and children do in Early Years settings.

In this chapter, we look at policy in the four nations of the United Kingdom – England, Northern Ireland, Scotland and Wales – alongside a number of countries across the world, as well as the OECD. Looking at what is happening in a range of national and international contexts like this can help us to more fully understand why and how policy and curriculum change has come about, as well as helping us to be informed and reflective about the particular contexts in which we are working.

The increased interest in young children's self-regulation in policy and curriculum frameworks raises a number of questions. First, is the importance of self-regulation reflected in policy and curricula? Following that, do these different frameworks use the term self-regulation explicitly, or are features of what we have come to see as self-regulation implicit in what they set out? Third, do they share a similar view of what self-regulation is, or do they differ in what they emphasise? It is also important to then consider how these different documents support practitioners in developing young children's self-regulation.

Is the significance of self-regulation reflected in policy statements and curriculum frameworks?

In Chapter 1, we identified self-regulation as significant for all aspects of young children's development. We also looked at how it has become of increasing interest to researchers from a number of different fields. Has this increased interest been reflected in policy? If self-regulation is so important for children's development, we could expect that policymakers, nationally and internationally, would want to ensure its inclusion in policies and curriculum frameworks for young children. The inclusion of self-regulation in the IELS from the OECD seems to suggest that self-regulation is increasingly recognised as significant. IELS is an assessment framework which seeks to 'identify factors that promote or hinder children's early learning' (OECD, 2018: 2) in children aged 5. Here, self-regulation is identified as one of four early learning domains for assessment, along with literacy, numeracy and social and emotional skills. While a number of concerns have been expressed about the use of such an approach globally (Moss et al., 2016; Urban & Swadener, 2016), the intention of the OECD is that IELS can be used across the world to provide information to aid the provision of experiences that better support young children's overall development and well-being. For practitioners, it is important to bear in mind that IELS uses specific tablet-based tasks, alongside information from parents and teachers. In this it differs, for example, from the English Early Years Foundation Stage (EYFS) (Department for Education [DfE], England, 2021), where the expectation is that self-regulation will be assessed mainly by teacher observation (DfE, England, 2020a). As we shall see in Chapter 5, there is evidence that young children's self-regulation may be most effectively assessed in naturalistic contexts such as play, rather than through less naturalistically occurring tablet-based assessments.

Where can we find self-regulation in curriculum frameworks?

In a number of policy statements and curriculum frameworks, the term 'self-regulation' is used explicitly. In the United Kingdom, both England and Northern Ireland explicitly refer to self-regulation. In Northern Ireland it appears in the

Pre-School curriculum (a non-compulsory year for children aged 3–4 which pre-cedes the Foundation Stage). Here it is linked to executive function (discussed in Chapters 1 and 2), as well as featuring in the Personal, Social and Emotional area of learning, with a focus on children learning how to self-regulate and to self-regulate their emotions (Council for the Curriculum Examinations and Assessment [CCEA], 2018). As we saw in Chapter 1, in England it is included in the EYFS as an Early Learning Goal for Personal, Social and Emotional Development (Department for Education, 2021). Defining self-regulation in this way, as largely a social and emotional construct, is something which Early Education believes 'will not help the sector to understand what self-regulation is, why it matters, or how it develops' (Early Education, 2019: 9). A little confusingly, it also differs somewhat from *Development Matters*, the non-statutory curriculum guidance written to accom-pany the EYFS in England, published by the DfE (2020b), where it is described using terms drawn from executive function.

It is also valuable to consider whether what is being assessed is always *self*-regulation. The expectation that children will 'Give focused attention to what the teacher says, responding appropriately even when engaged in an activity, and show an ability to follow instructions involving several ideas or actions' in the EYFS, while valuable, is possibly closer to *other*-regulation, seen by Vygotsky (1978) as a developmental process that contributes to self-regulation. In this, there is some similarity with the *Curriculum for Wales: Foundation Phase Framework* which includes as an outcome that children 'usually respond to regulation from a familiar adult' (Welsh Govern-ment, 2015: 50). As we shall see below, there are also statements in the guidance from all four nations that reflect a much wider range of important aspects of self-regulation without always being named as such.

Self-regulation in curriculum frameworks around the world: a holistic perspective

Where else can we look for early childhood frameworks that specifically highlight the importance of self-regulation? In America, curricula and frameworks for the Early Years are not decided at national level, and there is no one set of statements, goals or curriculum content. However, the National Association for the Education of Young Children (NAEYC) is a nationwide professional association, with over 60,000 members across the USA, connecting practice, research and policy and accrediting programmes in Early Years settings. Their *Position Statement* draws on some of the research we looked at in Chapters 1 and 2, emphasising the impor-tance of self-regulation as 'a prime developmental goal for the early years' (NAEYC, 2009: 7), and of particular value for children from challenging circumstances. The NAEYC emphasises the holistic, integrating importance of self-regulation, with important synergies between cognitive, social, emotional and behavioural aspects of development. The Australian Early Years Learning Framework, *Belonging, Being and Becoming*, seems to have a similarly integrating emphasis, with children's increasing capacity for self-regulation contributing to their 'emerging autonomy, inter-dependence, resilience and sense of agency' (Australian Government Department of Education, Employment and Workplace Relations, 2009: 25). This more holistic view of self-regulation is also present in some of the documentation in England. In particular, in the report prepared for the Department for Education on the trial of IELS in England, it is defined as being 'characterised by a child's ability to think before acting, persist at an activity, follow directions, remain calm, and control their impulses'(Kettlewell et al., 2020: 11), and includes regulation of thoughts, emotions and behaviour.

In the NAEYC *Position Statement* (2009) and *Early Learning Program Accreditation Standards and Assessment Items* (2019) and the Singapore Kindergarten curriculum (Ministry of Education Republic of Singapore, 2013a, 2013b), the crucial role of the teacher – as guide, model and provider – is highlighted in this integrated emphasis. The Singapore curriculum stresses the role of the adult in teaching children 'to regulate and manage their feelings, thoughts and behaviour' (Ministry of Education Republic of Singapore, 2013b: 4). The value of this overarching emphasis may be in helping us to notice and appreciate the significance of self-regulation across all aspects of young children's activity.

Social and emotional self-regulation in international frameworks

Common to most of the frameworks we look at here is a focus on young children's social and emotional self-regulation, often as an aspect of their well-being, for example in *Te Whāriki* (Ministry of Education, New Zealand, 2017) where it is highlighted in the Well-being/Mana Atua Strand, and in Australia, where it features in Outcome 3: Children have a strong sense of well-being (Australian Government Department of Education, Employment and Workplace Relations, 2009). Characteristic of many of the frameworks is a recognition that young children are learning to manage often intense feelings and strong emotions (see, for example, Ministry of Education, New Zealand, 2017; NAEYC, 2009) and are developing skills of collaboration, cooperation and turn-taking in their play (Ministry of Education Republic of Singapore, 2013b). These are often linked explicitly with behavioural aspects of self-regulation (it is often hard to draw clear distinctions between them). In Singapore, the Learning Goal 'Manage their own emotions and behaviour' identifies 'Self-regulate their behaviour' as a key knowledge/skill/disposition (Ministry of Education Republic of Singapore, 2013b).

Cognitive self-regulation in international frameworks

There is also some explicit reference to more cognitive aspects of self-regulation, for example, in the Australian Early Years Learning Framework, Outcome 4: Children are confident and involved learners (Australian Government Department of Education, Employment and Workplace Relations, 2009), and as part of the general emphasis on self-regulation across all aspects of young children's activity in frameworks such as the NAEYC *Position Statement* (2009), and *Te Whāriki* (Ministry of Education, New Zealand, 2017), which talks of the importance of supporting toddlers' identity, self-knowledge and self-regulation. Perhaps it is most clearly seen in the IELS, the assessment measure developed by the OECD for use across the world. IELS identifies and assesses three key skills which the OECD (2020) defines as the cognitive component of self-regulation: inhibition, mental flexibility and working memory. These three components reflect those generally accepted as comprising executive function, as we saw in Chapter 1. While the OECD talks of these components as being only a part of self-regulation (Shuey & Kankaraš, 2018), it is also worth noting that in places the OECD substitutes the term 'executive function' for 'self-regulation' (OECD, n.d.). Similarly, *Development Matters*, the non-statutory curriculum guidance for the EYFS in England, published by the DfE (2020b), conflates self-regulation and executive function as one of 'seven key features of effective practice' and identifies four aspects of a child's 'ability': hold information in mind, focus their attention, regulate their behaviour and plan what to do next. As we have seen already, in the EYFS framework, self-regulation is identified as a learning goal for children's Personal, Social and Emotional Development, rather than emphasising the more cognitive competences of executive function. In so doing, these different documents are potentially adding to confusion and uncertainty about what self-regulation is and how different aspects – cognitive, social, emotional and behavioural – contribute to children's overall self-regulatory development.

ACTIVITY: THINKING ABOUT ASSESSING SELF-REGULATION

The OECD *IELS* is designed to be used across the world, in many different contexts. What do you see as the implications of this? Should self-regulation be assessed in the same way and using the same content everywhere, or should such assessment be more local and context-specific?

A summary of some of the key references to self-regulation in the frameworks discussed here, highlighting the different aspects of self-regulation they each emphasise			
	Appears in:	**Is linked to:**	**Features in:**
Australia	*Belonging, Being and Becoming – The Early Years Learning Framework for Australia (EYLF)*	Emerging autonomy, inter-dependence, resilience and sense of agency Social and emotional well-being	Outcome 1: Children have a strong sense of identity Outcome 3: Children have a strong sense of well-being Outcome 4: Children are confident and involved learners
England	*Statutory Framework for the early years foundation stage*	Personal, Social and Emotional Development	Early Learning Goal: Self-Regulation
New Zealand	*Te Whāriki: Early Childhood Curriculum.*	Health and well-being A sense of belonging	Strand 1 Well-being/Mana atua Strand 2 Belonging/Mana whenua
Northern Ireland	*Curricular Guidance for Pre-School Education*	Personal, Social and Emotional Development Executive Function	Personal Social and Emotional Development Area of Learning

Table 3.1   (Continued)

A summary of some of the key references to self-regulation in the frameworks discussed here, highlighting the different aspects of self-regulation they each emphasise			
	Appears in:	Is linked to:	Features in:
United States of America (NAEYC)	*Developmentally Appropriate Practice in Early Childhood Programs Serving Children from Birth through Age 8: Position Statement*, and *NAEYC Early Learning Program Accreditation Standards and Assessment Items*	Synergies between cognitive, social, emotional and behavioural aspects of development	Various, chiefly: Principle of child development 6 Development proceeds towards greater complexity, self-regulation, and symbolic or representational capacities Topic 1F Promoting Self-Regulation Topic 2B Social and Emotional Development
Singapore	*Nurturing Early Learners: A curriculum framework for kindergartens in Singapore*	Regulating and managing feelings, thoughts and behaviour	Learning Goal 2: Manage their own emotions and behaviours

Table 3.1   Self-regulation in a sample of curriculum frameworks around the world

Can we find indirect reference to aspects of self-regulation in frameworks and policies?

So far we have looked at examples from frameworks and policies which specifically use the term self-regulation. Can we also find examples of statements that seem to refer, indirectly, to the kinds of features identified in Chapters 1 and 2 as comprising self-regulation? The answer is a clear yes. While the term itself may not be used, we can see aspects and qualities that relate very clearly to it, with reference to terms such as metacognition, managing and self-management, self-control, self-discipline, self-awareness and self-knowledge, some of which are looked at below.

Metacognition

In Chapter 1, we looked at metacognition as a key element of self-regulation. Both New Zealand (Ministry of Education, New Zealand, 2017) and Singapore highlight the importance of developing metacognitive skills. The Singapore curriculum identifies three specific ways in which educators might promote children's metacognitive skills, supported by questions which are aimed at children:

- Becoming aware of one's thinking processes (e.g. How did you know ...?)

- Comparing one's thinking with the thinking of others (e.g. How is your ... different from your friend's?)

- Expressing emotion and making personal connections (e.g. What do you like about ...?)

(Ministry of Education Republic of Singapore, 2013a: 62)

They set these metacognitive skills within a wider group of higher-level thinking skills, including being able to organise and analyse information and being able to generate new information and make connections. This emphasis on the importance of children's thinking skills is common to the majority of the curricula and frameworks looked at here. In Wales, developing thinking, including processes such as planning, developing, reflecting, analysis and evaluation is recognised as a skill that goes across the curriculum (Welsh Government, 2015). The Northern Ireland Primary curriculum states that thinking skills and a range of personal capabilities, many of which are related to self-regulation, 'underpin success in all aspects of life' (CCEA, Northern Ireland, 2007: 8). They are a useful list to refer back to and to compare with the skills and competences looked at in Chapters 1 and 2.

WHAT DOES POLICY TELL US?

Thinking skills and personal capabilities in the Northern Ireland curriculum: primary

Children should be given worthwhile experiences across the curriculum which allow them to develop skills in:

Thinking, problem-solving and decision-making, such as:

- sequencing, ordering, classifying, making comparisons;

- making predictions, examining evidence, distinguishing fact from opinion;

- making links between cause and effect;

- justifying methods, opinions and conclusions;

- generating possible solutions, trying out alternative approaches, evaluating outcomes;

- examining options, weighing up pros and cons;

- using different types of questions;

- making connections between learning in different contexts.

Self-management, such as:

- being aware of personal strengths, limitations and interests;

- setting personal targets and reviewing them;

(Continued)

- managing behaviour in a range of situations;
- organising and planning how to go about a task;
- focusing, sustaining attention and persisting with tasks;
- reviewing learning and some aspect that might be improved;
- learning ways to manage own time;
- seeking advice when necessary;
- comparing own approach with others and in different contexts.

Working with others, such as:

- listening actively and sharing opinions;
- developing routines of turn-taking, sharing and co-operating;
- giving and responding to feedback;
- understanding how actions and words affect others;
- adapting behaviour and language to suit different people and situations;
- taking personal responsibility for working with others and evaluating own contribution to the group;
- being fair;
- respecting the views and opinions of others, reaching agreements using negotiation and compromise;
- suggesting ways of improving their approach to working collaboratively.

Managing information, such as:

- asking focused questions;
- planning and setting goals, breaking a task into sub-tasks;
- using own and others' ideas to locate sources of information;
- selecting, classifying, comparing and evaluating information;
- selecting most appropriate method for a task;
- using a range of methods for collating, recording and representing information;
- communicating with a sense of audience and purpose.

(Continued)

Being creative, such as:

- seeking out questions to explore and problems to solve;
- experimenting with ideas and questions;
- making new connections between ideas/information;
- learning from and valuing other people's ideas;
- making ideas real by experimenting with different designs, actions, outcomes;
- challenging the routine method;
- valuing the unexpected or surprising;
- seeing opportunities in mistakes and failures;
- taking risks for learning.

(Council for the Curriculum Examinations and Assessment, Northern Ireland, 2007)

Emotional and motivational qualities

In England, the EYFS includes a range of features in the 'characteristics of effective teaching and learning', notably:

- having and developing your own ideas,
- making links between ideas,
- developing strategies for doing things, 'having a go',
- concentrating,
- keeping on trying in the face of difficulties.

(DfE, 2021)

These latter features, in particular, link to emotional and motivational qualities of self-regulation such as risk-taking and persistence. For both Ireland (National Council for Curriculum and Assessment, 2009) and Sweden, these qualities are linked to children's opportunities to develop a positive sense of who they are and 'a positive perception of themselves as learning, creative individuals' (Skolverket, 2019: 10). The NAEYC (2009) identifies the importance of providing experiences for children where they can be both challenged and achieve success, if they are to strengthen their motivation to persist and their willingness to take risks. Other key emotional and motivational elements commonly referred to are ideas of control and self-control, particularly in managing feelings, as in the *Curriculum for Excellence* (Scottish Government, 2009), and coping with disappointment (Welsh Government, 2015).

ACTIVITY: THINKING ABOUT THE SCOPE OF SELF-REGULATION

The documents looked at here often have different interpretations of the scope and content of self-regulation. Does this matter? What, in your view, might be the consequences of this for practice?

INTERNATIONAL EARLY LEARNING AND CHILD WELL-BEING STUDY: ARE THERE DIFFERENCES IN SELF-REGULATION ACCORDING TO GENDER, AND WHAT ARE PARENTS' AND TEACHERS' PERCEPTIONS?

The *Early Learning and Child Well-being: A Study of Five-year-Olds in England, Estonia and the United States* (OECD, 2020) reports on the 2018 IELS Study. This was conducted on 7,000 5-year-old children in England, Estonia and United States. It comprised parent and teacher questionnaires as well as tablet-based assessments. Parents and teachers were asked to rate the children's self-regulation as below average, average or above average (Figure 3.1). Both parents and teachers reported girls as having better self-regulation than boys:

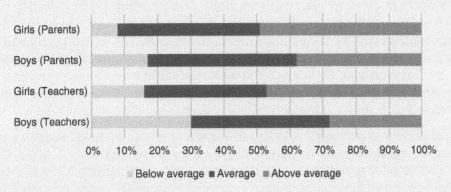

Figure 3.1   Parents and teachers reporting on their children's self-regulation

The results of the direct assessments of the children across the three countries did not, though, bear this out entirely. While girls scored more highly when the results from the three countries were combined, there were also different gender patterns in each country. In Estonia, girls did better than boys across all three subdomains. In the United States, girls were stronger than boys in inhibition and working memory, while in England boys did better on inhibition (OECD, 2020).

Guidance in the frameworks for supporting young children's self-regulation

We saw in Chapters 1 and 2 that strong links have been made between self-regulation and independent learning (e.g. Whitebread et al., 2007, 2009b), and many of the frameworks and curricula here highlight the importance of children's sense of agency, independent learning, and opportunities to make choices and decisions. *Te Whāriki* (Ministry of Education, New Zealand, 2017) emphasises the importance of children's agency and opportunities for independence, choice and autonomy. In Ireland the opportunity to exercise choice and to use initiative is central to the first Standard of Quality, on the Rights of the Child (Department of Education and Skills, Ireland, 2017). Play is identified as a context for such initiative-taking and decision-making in the Northern Ireland Pre-School curricular guidance (CCEA, Northern Ireland, 2018). Practitioners are also advised to involve children in the wider decision-making of the setting (see, for example, Department of Education and Skills, Ireland, 2017), including in curriculum design (Ministry of Education, New Zealand, 2017), the development of rules and routines for behaviour (Ministry of Education Republic of Singapore, 2013b), and in self- and peer-assessment (Scottish Government, 2011).

Developing and supporting self-regulation

What further guidance do frameworks and curriculum statements give about the ways in which all of these aspects of self-regulation can be supported? What is significant here is a view, both implicitly and in many places explicitly, that self-regulatory skills can be actively developed and supported. In effect, self-regulation can be taught and learned. For example, the NAEYC (2019) and the Australian Framework (Australian Government Department of Education, Employment and Workplace Relations, 2009) both highlight the active role of practitioners in directly helping children to develop emotion regulation skills, through actively teaching such skills and through talking with children about their emotions.

Guidance for practitioners includes ideas about the ways in which teachers might interact with children, for example, acting as a model of self-regulation (NAEYC, 2009), and in supporting and motivating children to persist, and showing 'delight, encouragement and enthusiasm for children's attempts' (Australian Government Department of Education, Employment and Workplace Relations, 2009: 25). In *Te Whāriki* (Ministry of Education, New Zealand, 2017) practitioners are asked to look for opportunities to develop aspects such as self-help skills and children's sense of self-efficacy. Similarly, in Singapore practitioners are asked to look for opportunities to use routines and transitions as ways of developing children's self-regulation (Ministry of Education Republic of Singapore, 2013b). They also emphasise the ways in which practitioners should look for opportunities to infuse higher-level thinking skills, including metacognition, across the curriculum (Ministry of Education Republic of Singapore, 2013a). It has been suggested that this kind of 'infusion' approach (see, for example, McGuinness, 1999; Taggart et al., 2005), may be more likely than others to support the development of thinking skills, including children's capacity for transferring their knowledge, skills and understanding from one context to another.

A key way in which practitioners are recommended to support and develop children's self-regulation is through pretence and dramatic play. Drawing on a variety of research evidence, the NAEYC (2009) advocates active teacher scaffolding of imaginative play as a significant contribution to the development of self-regulation. The Singapore Kindergarten Curriculum (Ministry of Education Republic of Singapore, 2013b) suggests that practitioners could set up specific role-play scenarios, for example, receiving a birthday present, or a friend accidentally knocking down their blocks, as opportunities to engage children in discussion which supports their emotion regulation.

OBSERVING PRETEND PLAY: SRIJA, AMAYA AND RAKESH

The two extracts here are from a much longer episode of pretence. As we see throughout the book, pretend play is a rich context in which children develop and display their self-regulation. All three children (age 5) stay in role throughout, while also commenting on the progress of the play. This episode highlights a range of aspects of self-regulation and also provides examples of how they interlink. It also shows the ways in which cognitive and emotional regulation influence behavioural regulation.

SRIJA: Baby, it's your birthday…baby (reaches out and touches Amaya on her knee) I know you're not feeling well (turning to Rakesh, shaking her head) Baby's not feeling well. I'll feed baby. Srija puts her hand out and pushes Amaya gently onto her knees.	*Cognitive: Srija plans the activity, and allocates roles*
SRIJA: You sit down, baby, you sit there – no arguments (walks back to cupboard, Amaya waits, on her knees). Srija walks over to Rakesh and puts her bowl next to him. He looks at it, walks over to the cupboard and takes out a wooden spoon, slapping it on the table next to her.	*Cognitive: Srija demonstrates her knowledge – baby needs to sit and wait, and babies do not like that*
RAKESH: No, you need that one. I'm going. SRIJA: (to Amaya) Say 'bye, baby. Amaya smiles and waves at Rakesh, with a baby look on her face. …	*Cognitive: Rakesh monitors and corrects Srija's choice*
SRIJA: It's been a long day and I'm going to read you a story. They continue to disagree, Srija makes to leave. SRIJA: I'm not playing (turns around, but comes back) Okay maybe. Amaya gets up and walks away. Srija jumps down and grabs hold of her and pulls her back. Amaya stands at the cupboard, 'cooking', then brings over	*Cognitive: Srija knows that stories are read to babies at the end of the day, and announces her plan. She also knows that the game cannot continue if she says she is not playing*

(Continued)

2 bowls and a wooden spoon. Amaya allows Srija to hold the big bowl, but rests the smaller full bowl in her lap, and spoons food into Srija's mouth. Srija makes eating and swallowing gestures. Amaya makes scraping movements as if the food has all gone, stands up with the spoon and bowl and puts it on the table.	
SRIJA: (holds onto Amaya's arm) Okay, it's my turn to be a mummy. Amaya walks away, putting her hands up to her head in a gesture of exasperation.	*Emotional: Srija's gesture is used to appeal to Amaya, who demonstrates her emotional response*
SRIJA: (holding onto her) No, no, no. We both be the mums (holding arms out in front of her in a supplicatory gesture). AMAYA: (shouting) Yeah! SRIJA: We both be the mummy and we haven't got a baby, okay? Let's play.	*Cognitive and Emotional: Srija uses a cognitive strategy for managing the emotion of the situation*

WHAT DOES RESEARCH TELL US?

Is there a link between fine and gross motor skills and self-regulation?: Singapore Kindergarten Impact Project – Fine and gross motor skills are important for self-regulation and early academic skills

The Singapore Kindergarten Impact Project looked at the finding from other research* that young children with better motor skills demonstrate better self-regulation of thoughts, emotions and behaviour. Over 1,200 children participated during the first 6 months of their K1 year (approximate age 4–5).

What did they find?

1. Children with better motor skills have better cognitive and socio-emotional self-regulation and early academic skills.

   • Better fine motor skills were related to better mathematical, reading and writing skills;

(Continued)

- Better fine motor skills were also related to better cognitive and socio-emotional self-regulation, which in turn were related to better mathematical, reading and writing skills.

2. Better gross motor skills were related to better socio-emotional self-regulation.

3. Better gross motor skills were related to better cognitive self-regulation, which, in turn, was related to better early mathematical skills.

(Ministry of Education Republic of Singapore, n.d.)

What we cannot know is whether better fine and gross motor skills contribute to the development of self-regulatory skills. This research tells us that they seem to be related. Interestingly, the report on the pilot for IELS in England (Kettlewell et al., 2020) reaches a similar conclusion. They found that working memory and mental flexibility (two of the skills being measured in the self-regulation strand) relate to children's physical development, as well as their early literacy, numeracy. This may be important for policy. If there is a relationship between the two then we could expect that curriculum frameworks for young children might highlight this relationship. At present, the frameworks looked at here do not really do so, and this may represent a lost opportunity to draw attention to the ways in which motor skills might be related to self-regulation.

*(Cameron et al., 2012; Cameron et al., 2016; Pagani & Messier, 2012)

In your view, should training and professional development programmes for early childhood practitioners do more to support trainees and existing practitioners in knowing about self-regulation, how to develop it in children and how to interpret it in curriculum frameworks?

Conclusion

In this chapter, we have looked at policy and curriculum frameworks in the United Kingdom and in a range of countries across the world, and at the IELS approach of the OECD. Some of these frameworks use the term self-regulation explicitly, while in others it is more implicit, and it is clear that there is no real consensus across these frameworks about what self-regulation is, with different policies emphasising different aspects. In England, at least, this is further complicated by the ways in which different documents around government policy seem to variously highlight different aspects.

We have also seen how these different documents try to support practitioners in developing young children's self-regulation, often highlighting the importance of choice, independent learning and children's agency. Play, particularly socio-dramatic play, is suggested as a key context, as well as the use of routines, and infusing the development of aspects such as metacognition across the curriculum.

Key further reading

For this chapter, the most useful further reading is to look directly at some of the curriculum frameworks discussed here. In addition, you could look at:

Early Years Coalition (2021). *Birth to 5 matters: Non-statutory guidance for the early years foundation stage*. St Albans: Early Education. (Sector-written guidance drawn up by 16 early years organisations.)

Kettlewell, K., Sharp, C., Lucas, M., Gambhir, G., Classick, R., Hope, C., ..., National Foundation for Educational Research (2020). *International early learning and well-being study (IELS): National report for England*. England: Department for Education (available online) https://assets.publishing.service.gov.uk/government/uploads/system/uploads/attachment_data/file/939718/IELS_national_report_Dec_2020.pdf.

Robson, S. (2020). Self-regulation in early childhood policy and practice in England. In **W. Pink** (Ed.), *Oxford encyclopedia of school reform*. New York, NY: Oxford University Press. Available online: https://doi.org/10.1093/acrefore/9780190264093.013.1599.

Shuey, E., & **Kankaraš, M.** (2018). *The power and promise of early learning: OECD education working paper No. 186*. Available online: https://dx.doi.org/10.1787/f9b2e53f-en.

Websites

Early Years Coalition, https://www.birthto5matters.org.uk.

Ministry of Education, New Zealand *Te Whāriki online: Self management and regulation*. https://tewhariki.tki.org.nz/en/teaching-strategies-and-resources/self-management-and-regulation/.

Organisation for Economic Co-operation and Development, https://www.oecd.org/education/school/early-learning-and-child-well-being-study/.

4 Relationships and self-regulation

In this chapter, we look at:

- How parent-child interactions affect self-regulation;
- Parental scaffolding;
- Parental support for children's autonomy;
- Children's peer interactions and self-regulation;
- Children playing and working in groups or alone and their self-regulation;
- Friendship and self-regulation.

Keywords: parent and child relationships, peer relationships, friendship, groups, individual, scaffolding, autonomy support, social, emotional and behavioural regulation.

Introduction

In this chapter, we look at young children's relationships, particularly with family and friends, and the ways in which these may contribute to their social, emotional and behavioural regulation. Peer interactions, parental practices and relationships, and the wider cultural context, are all influential in the development of young children's social understanding and social and behavioural regulation (Miller & Aloise-Young, 2018). In Chapter 8, we focus particularly on relationships between teachers/practitioners and children, and you will also find it useful to look back at some of the ideas discussed here when you read that chapter.

In Chapter 1, we looked at the work of Vygotsky (1978) and his view that children develop their self-regulation in their Zone of Proximal Development (ZPD). As we saw there, the ZPD is defined as:

> *the distance between the actual developmental level as determined by independent problem solving and the level of potential development as*

determined through problem solving under adult guidance or in collaboration with more capable peers.

(Vygotsky, 1978: 86)

What is clear from this definition is that adults and peers both play a pivotal role in children's development of self-regulation.

We begin this chapter by looking at the first, and potentially longest-lasting, relationships children have, namely those with parents, and at how parent–child interactions can influence self-regulation. We focus on the role of parental scaffolding and autonomy support for young children's self-regulation development. We follow this by looking at interactions between children. In particular, we look at how peer relationships affect self-regulation, the possible effects of children playing and working in groups or individually and at the role of friendship. It is also valuable to look at this from the other direction, so we also look at how self-regulation affects peer relationships and what practitioners can do to support peer relationships and thus self-regulation.

WHAT DOES POLICY TELL US?

Statutory framework for the early years foundation stage in England

Self-regulation is included in the English Early Years Foundation Stage (EYFS) in the Early Learning Goals (ELG) for Personal, Social and Emotional Development. This element of the ELG highlights the connections between children's relationships and their affective and behavioural self-regulation:

Children at the expected level of development will:

- Show an understanding of their own feelings and those of others and begin to regulate their behaviour accordingly

(Department for Education, 2021: 12)

Parent–child interactions and self-regulation

The everyday life of the family is a context in which children develop their social understanding and affective self-regulation. Conversation, shared events, play, jokes, disputes, and social rules and routines afford children early opportunities to see how other family members feel and to begin to get inside another person's mind. Here we look specifically at how parents' interactions with their children are linked to their children's self-regulation development. It is useful to look at this alongside all of the 'Working with parents' sections throughout the book.

Deborah Pino-Pasternak has looked in particular at how parenting behaviours affect children's self-regulation (Pino-Pasternak & Whitebread, 2010; Pino-Pasternak et al.,

2010). Pino-Pasternak and David Whitebread (2010) identify three parenting dimensions which affect self-regulation:

| CHALLENGE | CONTINGENCY | AUTONOMY |

Challenge

Challenge refers to how much parents encourage and expose children to high-level cognitive and metacognitive demands as part of their support during, for example, problem-solving tasks (Sigel, 2002). A parental behaviour that is categorised as providing challenge is parents' encouragement of metacognitive talk. This kind of encouragement has positive effects on metacognitive aspects of children's self-regulation, such as higher levels of sophistication in children's planning behaviours and task definition, more verbalisation of their cognitive strategies and more frequent and sophisticated engagement in strategically solving problems (Gauvain & Rogoff, 1989; Moss & Strayer, 1990; Radziszewska & Rogoff, 1988). We look in more detail at metacognitive talk in Chapter 6, and it is worth following up this area there.

What about contingency and autonomy? *Contingency* describes how attentive parents are to their children's cognitive and emotional needs and whether they respond to these needs appropriately and in a timely way (Pino-Pasternak et al., 2010). Below, we look at contingency by focusing on contingent scaffolding and its importance for self-regulation. Finally, *autonomy* is defined as the behaviours that parents value and employ in order to encourage children's independent efforts and decision-making (Mattanah, 2001). Below we explore how both autonomy-supportive, and the opposite, controlling parenting, can affect children's self-regulatory development.

Contingency: parental scaffolding and self-regulation

In Chapter 1, we looked at the idea of scaffolding as the effective support provided by a more skilled person which is gradually relinquished as a child masters a task and the role it plays in children moving from being co-regulated by a more knowledgeable other to becoming self-regulated. Unsurprisingly, parents play an important scaffolding role for children. We look here particularly at aspects of self-regulation such as effortful control, self-regulated learning and inhibitory control. As we saw in Chapters 1 and 2, these are vital aspects of self-regulation.

This parental scaffolding role begins very early in life and seems to have an impact on children's later self-regulation. Neale and Whitebread (2019) found that scaffolding by a mother when a child was 12 months old predicted how much effortful control they would show a year later, at 24 months. Studying playful interactions that involved scaffolding, such as support and modelling for problem-solving and learning during play, they found that maternal contingent scaffolding (adjusting the level of support according to a child's needs) was linked to later higher levels of self-regulation. In particular, it was exactly when mothers contingently intervened, and their intervention led to successful actions by the children, that was the critical element in effortful control later. This shows how interactions between mother and child during play could be foundational for the development of children's self-regulation.

This relationship between parental contingent scaffolding and self-regulation seems to continue over time. Zhang and Whitebread (2017) observed parents and their 6-year-old children completing a task together and looked at (1) parental levels of cognitive support, (2) emotional support and (3) contingency. They then observed the same children completing tasks independently and measured their self-regulated learning. Of all the three aspects, contingency was again the one that stood out as supporting and enabling the children's use of self-regulated learning strategies.

OBSERVING CONTINGENT AND NON-CONTINGENT SCAFFOLDING BY PARENTS

The extracts below feature two observations from Pino-Pasternak et al. (2010).

The first observation is an example of contingent scaffolding by a parent while they engage in an activity with their child. In this example you will see that the level of cognitive demand that the parent poses for the child changes according to the child's understanding. It decreases when the child does not understand something and increases after the child succeeds in an element of the task.

Parent: 'So what calculation do we need to do here?'

Child: 'I don't know'

Parent: 'Let's see… How many marbles did you have on Saturday?'

Child: 'I had 45'

Parent: 'Great! How many did you lose while playing with Mike?'

Child: '22'

Parent: 'So what do you need to do to know how many you have left?'

Child: '45–22, take away!'

Parent: 'Well done!'

The second example illustrates non-contingent scaffolding. In this case, the cognitive demands that the parent poses for their child exceed the child's level of understanding.

Adult: 'Let's see this one (showing a poem) "The Poppy" What type of text is this?'

Child: 'It's about poppies'

Parent: 'Yes but read it. What type of text is it?'

Child: 'Clare Brown, that's the writer'

Parent: 'Yes but look at the text! What kind of text is it?'

(Pino-Pasternak et al., 2010: 241)

Contingent scaffolding by parents, then, seems to be a very important aspect in children's developing self-regulation. What also seems to matter is the affective content of this scaffolding (Gärtner et al., 2018; Lobo & Lunkenheimer, 2020; Sun & Tang, 2019). In the three studies below, what appears to matter is whether the emotional feedback or the affective climate during scaffolding is positive, negative or neutral. Parent scaffolding patterns can have different impacts on a child's self-regulation, depending upon the content of the interaction, with positive feedback and affective content showing links to self-regulatory development, while negative affective content is linked to lower levels of self-regulation by the child.

WHAT DOES RESEARCH TELL US?

The role of emotional feedback and affective climate during scaffolding

The three studies we look at here are valuable in highlighting the significance of the emotional climate between parents and children for children's developing self-regulation.

Study 1: When looking at 3-year-olds and the co-regulation processes when completing a task with their parents, Lobo and Lunkenheimer (2020) found that more flexible and contingent affective parent–child interactions were linked to higher levels of child self-regulation in the same children at the age of 4. While this finding is similar to previous studies, what they also showed was that, in order for there to be a link between contingent scaffolding and higher self-regulation, the affective content of parent–child interactions had to be mainly positive or neutral. In the cases where interactions between parent and child had more negative affective content, this was linked to lower levels of self-regulation at age 4.

(Lobo & Lunkenheimer, 2020)

Study 2: Sun and Tang (2019) also looked at maternal scaffolding in young children aged 3–5. They distinguished between:

- elaborative vs directive cognitive assistance by the mother;
- positive vs negative emotional feedback;
- adult or child responsibility.

They measured children's self-regulation through a tapping task which is closer to executive function measures (rather than the full self-regulation definition as we have adopted it in this book). They found that mothers who showed more elaborative cognitive assistance, and positive feedback, had children with higher levels of self-regulation.

(Sun & Tang, 2019)

(Continued)

WHAT DOES RESEARCH TELL US? *continued*

Study 3: Gärtner et al. (2018), with children aged 24–35 months, looked at parental co-regulation, as reported by parents in a questionnaire. They found that negative co-regulation from the parents (in the form of harsh, controlling, hostile and intrusive parenting such as threatening, frowning or shouting) was linked to lower levels of inhibitory control in the children.

(Gärtner et al., 2018)

ACTIVITY: THINKING ABOUT THE AFFECTIVE CONTENT OF INTERACTIONS BETWEEN PARENTS AND CHILDREN

It is clear that emotion plays an important part in the relationship between parent–child interactions and self-regulation. Think about:

1. What effect do positive emotional feedback/affective interactions have on the child's self-regulation?

2. What effect do negative emotional feedback/affective interactions have on the child's self-regulation?

Discuss with colleagues how you might work with parents to support positive emotional feedback and affective interactions between themselves and their children.

Autonomy: Parental support for children's autonomy and how this links to self-regulation

Autonomy is the third dimension identified by Pino-Pasternak and Whitebread (2010). Parents who support their children's autonomy tend to have children who are better at self-regulation (Grolnick, 2009). This seems to be apparent from the first year of life and continues throughout childhood.

Grolnick et al. (1984) observed mothers and their one-year-old children while problem-solving. Some of the mothers were more supportive of their child's autonomy, while others were more controlling. Autonomy-supportive mothers had children who persisted longer when trying to solve tasks on their own. The effects of autonomy support by parents became even clearer when, 8 months later, not only were the children of autonomy-supportive mothers still more persistent at solving tasks but they were also more competent. Similarly, Bernier et al. (2010) found that autonomy support by a mother when the child was 12–15 months old could predict the level of the child's executive function abilities (working memory, inhibitory control and cognitive flexibility) at ages 18 and 26 months, and this was the case irrespective of the child's general cognitive ability or the mother's education. Importantly, this highlights that parents from all backgrounds and socioeconomic contexts can help their children develop their self-regulation, by being supportive of their autonomy.

This kind of autonomy support from parents seems to continue to have beneficial effects on children's self-regulation later in childhood (Deci et al., 1993; Piotrowski et al., 2013). Kallia and Dermitzaki (2017) found that, when mothers encouraged their child's autonomy, supporting their independent problem-solving and using hints and prompts to enable a child to discover their next step or move towards a solution, the children (aged 4–6 years) were more likely to use self-regulatory skill such as planning and monitoring when working on problem-solving independently. This was in contrast to mothers who were over-controlling, interfering even when a child could work independently. Importantly, autonomy support may also influence children's motivation. Deci et al. (1993) found that parents who were more autonomy-supportive during play had children (in this case, aged 6) who were more intrinsically motivated to face challenges when playing individually. The converse was also true: children of controlling parents showed less intrinsic motivation when challenges came up while playing.

Playing and working with peers: interactions between children and their self-regulation

Peers have a significant role to play in children's general development. The same also seems to be true for the development of self-regulation (Pahigiannis & Glos, 2020), albeit that this is an area of research which is still developing. Looking at the definition of the ZPD (above), Vygotsky explicitly identifies peers as potentially responsible for helping a child develop and reach their own potential developmental level. It is, then, vital to look at how relationships with peers can affect children's self-regulation development, and vice versa, if we are to create environments that foster self-regulatory development.

How do peer relationships affect self-regulation?

For a child, the children they spend time with affect the development of their self-regulation, both in and out of school. Montroy et al. (2016a), for example, found that higher levels of classroom peers' self-regulation was linked to higher self-regulation in individual children (in this case, aged 36–65 months). Specifically, it was those children who had lower levels of self-regulation who seemed to be more positively impacted by peer self-regulation. What might this mean for practice? At school or year group level, it could be worth considering placing children who have lower levels of self-regulation in a class or group in which the overall level of self-regulation is high, to potentially facilitate opportunities for them to further develop their self-regulation. Within a class or group, similarly, organising groups to ensure a mix of self-regulation development may be valuable.

Looking at social context: Does the size of a group matter?

Given that relationships with peers have a role in the development of self-regulation, what happens when those relationships are in different types of social context? Does it matter if a child is playing/working/creating individually, in pairs, in a group or in a whole-class context?

The picture here is not altogether clear. On the one hand, there is evidence that working in groups is important for self-regulation development and that young children respond to opportunities for self-regulation significantly more often in small group contexts rather than larger, or whole group activities (Timmons et al., 2016). Working in groups gives children opportunities for co-regulation and shared-regulation (see Chapter 1 for a reminder of these terms), their individual cognitive load is reduced and their thinking made visible (Iiskala et al., 2004; Whitebread et al., 2009b). Playing and working in a small group or pair can provide opportunities for children to learn self-regulating behaviour by observing others and by supporting one another (Perry, 2013; Perry & Rahim, 2011). For example, explaining a task to another child, and talking them through it, can mean children use more metacognitive language than if they just describe what they did (Desautel, 2009). Palincsar and Brown's (1984) 'reciprocal teaching' approach uses this idea, beginning with adult modelling of a task to children who are then, in turn, asked to teach the activity to their peers.

Whitebread et al. (2009a) observed young children (aged 3–5) playing in different social contexts showing more self-regulatory behaviours during group play, fewer during individual play and the lowest number during whole-class sessions. In larger groups and whole class activities adults can often spend more time on 'managing' comments and activity, and less time engaging in activity-relevant talk (Frampton et al., 2009).

What about when children play alone? Lloyd and Howe's (2003) research with children aged 4–5 years shows a link between solitary pretence or solitary play with objects and divergent thinking, that is, generating ideas. They speculate that the time and space to think things over and replay experiences, in privacy, may be important. They suggest the importance of creating opportunities and spaces for children to play together, or alone, while also helping 'reticent' children to engage with their physical and social environment.

However, there is also evidence to suggest that group work is not always productive in terms of self-regulation. Webb et al. (2013) claim that children do not always interact in productive ways when encouraged to work in peer-directed small groups. In a meta-analysis (examining data from many studies), Dignath et al. (2008) reported that interventions which provided self-regulation training to children through group work had lower effects. They suggest that perhaps children were not used to doing group work or had not yet developed the necessary competencies for this. Consequently, one implication for practice could be to support more opportunities for children to work in pairs or groups.

It may also be the case that different forms of self-regulation emerge in different social contexts. Whitebread et al. (2007, 2009a) found that children show more evidence of metacognitive regulation, particularly monitoring and control, when working in small groups or pairs, unsupervised by adults, than when they are working alone, or in a larger group supported by an adult. However, emotional/motivational regulation behaviours were more in evidence in individual activities, while metacognitive knowledge behaviour was unaffected by the social context.

Group work and quality of self-regulation

We have looked so far at the importance of the socio-emotional interactions of a group for young children's self-regulation. What about how these interactions potentially shape the quality of social regulation? Interactions that are positive and sustain a shared focus on the task through high-quality regulation of the content can facilitate social regulation (Rogat & Adams-Wiggins, 2014; Rogat & Linnenbrink-Garcia, 2011). By contrast, negative interactions such as discouraging a member's participation, showing disrespect, and low group cohesion can provoke significant off-task behaviour and challenge children's abilities to self-regulate their engagement on a task (Rogat & Linnenbrink-Garcia, 2011; Rogat & Adams-Wiggins, 2014). It is interesting to look at how the self-regulatory processes of groups can be influenced by the positioning among group members. For example, Ljung-Djärf (2008) observed 3- to 6-year-olds during group play on a computer and identified three positions: the owner of the activity, the participant and the spectator. If the owner did not show an interest in sharing the play, then he/she positioned his/her peers as spectators and did not allow them to be actively engaged in it. Robson (2010) found that the benefits of group play could be different for individual participants, especially when one member of the group played a particularly dominant role.

Collaborating and working as a group

As well as being *in* a group, there is also evidence that working *as* a group, collaboratively, can be beneficial for young children's self-regulation. As we saw above, working in a group can mean that the cognitive processing load is reduced for an individual, as it is socially shared (Whitebread et al., 2007). This may particularly be the case when children are collaborating on an activity. Collaboration can also support development of a collective awareness of metacognitive strategies as children negotiate, as well as benefitting individual children's metacognitive processing (Larkin, 2015). In Chapter 7, we look at how collaborative digital play can be supportive of problem-solving, with collaboration supporting achievement of a goal in ways that a child playing alone might not (Danby et al., 2018).

Even though group activities appear to promote regulation in some ways, it should not be taken for granted that they promote socially shared regulation. In the study by Whitebread et al. (2007), the most frequently seen type of regulation was self-regulation, followed by socially shared regulation. Hurme and Järvelä (2005) similarly report a relative absence of socially shared regulation in other studies.

It can be argued that the group nature of tasks is an essential but not sufficient requirement for socially shared regulation to evolve. What may be important is an element of collaboration. Greater affordance for socially shared regulation is provided by tasks which encourage dynamic, coordinated and interdependent work that requires collaborative teams to use the expertise of individuals in achieving a goal that could not be achieved by an individual alone (Perry & Winne, 2013; Winne et al., 2013). Winne et al. (2013) stress the importance of the interdependence which is entailed in collaborative work. The quality of collaborative work, but also each member's participation, depends on coordinated regulation being exercised by all team members. For example, collaborative work is at risk if a member is not calibrated well in regulation or is off-task.

How does self-regulation affect peer relationships?

Having looked at how peer relationships affect self-regulation development, we now look at the converse: how a child's self-regulation, particularly behavioural and emotional self-regulation, can affect their peer relationships.

When looking at behavioural regulation, effortful control is related to how well-adjusted children are, to their social skills, and their relationships with peers among others (Eisenberg et al., 2010a). As we saw in Chapter 2, children become better at behavioural self-regulation, including delaying gratification and adjusting their behaviour according to rules, as they age. This self-regulation development is likely to lead to sharing and co-operative play (Murray et al., 2015), and, because of that, higher quality social relationships with peers. As a result, progress on behavioural self-regulation development has been linked to quality social relationships.

We looked in Chapters 1 and 2 at the importance of children's ability to delay gratification, and their inhibitory control, for behavioural regulation. Paulus et al. (2015) found that children's ability to delay the opening of a gift when they were 24 months old, and their inhibitory control at 30 months, was related to their sharing behaviour at 5 years old. Children who were better at delaying gratification and at inhibitory control showed a greater inclination to share with others. It looks like self-regulation plays a role in the prosocial development of children and therefore also in the development of their relationships.

When looking at emotional regulation, there is evidence from babies and young children to indicate the effects of emotional regulation on peer relationships. Liew et al. (2011) show how the ability to manage arousing situations at 18 months predicted the child's empathy and comforting behaviour towards others at 30 months. This suggests that a child who is good at emotional regulation is also likely to be more pro-socially oriented towards people.

Additionally, successful emotional regulation in early childhood may be related to lower levels of rejection by peers in middle childhood. Trentacosta and Shaw (2009) measured young children's emotional regulation at age 3.5 years. In this study a child had to wait for a desirable outcome (in this case a cookie). If the child actively distracted themselves, this was considered to show adaptive emotion regulation. Peer rejection was measured a few years later during a summer camp where these same children (now aged 8–10 years) completed a confidential interview where they were asked to list the three children they liked most and the three they liked least. Children who demonstrated adaptive emotional regulation strategy use in early childhood were less likely to be rejected by peers in middle childhood.

GUIDANCE FROM THE EARLY YEARS SECTOR: BIRTH TO 5 MATTERS (2021)

Birth to 5 Matters was developed by the Early Years Coalition to support practitioners in implementing the EYFS. The guidance on self-regulation acknowledges the relationship between emotional, cognitive and behavioural regulation:

The foundations of emotional and cognitive self-regulation in the Early Years are integrally tied together, and both are necessary for behavioural self-regulation.

(Early Years Coalition, 2021: 20)

Friendship and self-regulation

One particular peer grouping that it is valuable to think about is children's friendship. Children who are friends, and used to playing together, can often work on an activity effectively and may be more likely to succeed in problem-solving activities than non-friends (Garton, 2004; Löfdahl, 2005). This seems to be related to their willingness to coordinate what they do and to resolve any conflicts. As we shall see throughout this book, problem-solving is a significant activity for the development of self-regulation. Friendship, and playing with friends, is also often a fertile context for talk about thoughts and feelings (de Groot Kim, 2010). However, friends can also find it harder to be critical of one another's ideas (Larkin, 2010).

Ashlyn and Leanne, both aged 5, are friends. Ashlyn has been reading 'My cat likes to hide in boxes' to them both in the book corner. At this point, Leanne has taken the book from Ashlyn and is now reading it to them. Adult S is recording them on video, and they are aware she is there.

LEANNE: (reading) But my cat likes to hide in boxes.

Ashlyn chooses another book, walks towards the camera with it then goes back. Leanne taps her on the arm and shows her a page.

ASHLYN: (look of surprise) Look, oh! Oh look! I forgotted that page! (smiling).

Ashlyn has chosen a book with a fabric hand puppet fixed through it, she has her hand in it and is looking at Leanne's book. She lets go of the book, and Leanne picks it up and puts her hand through the puppet. Leanne stands up, comes over to the camera and mimes eating the camera lens with the hand puppet mouth, laughing.

LEANNE: Hahaha, now you do it Ashlyn (putting book down).

ASHLYN: (picks up book and holds it very close to the camera, miming eating) Ah, I'm going to eat you up!

Leanne laughs.

ASHLYN: ('licks' camera lens with the tongue of the puppet) Yum, lick.

LEANNE: (takes the book and licks the lens with it) Lick lick lick! Yum, yum, yum.

ASHLYN: (to Adult S) You have to do it just like that (puts hand over lens to demonstrate).

Leanne continues 'eating' with the puppet.

ASHLYN: My turn.

LEANNE: (hands her the book) Yeah, your turn.

ASHLYN: (waving the puppet at the camera) Oh, I'm going to eat you up!

This observation is rich in evidence of self-regulation, with the girls' friendship playing a clear part here as they share in their self-chosen activity. Ashlyn shows evidence of metacognitive knowledge, particularly of strategies, as she says to Adult S: 'You have to do it just like that'. The strongest evidence is of both girls' metacognitive regulation. For example, Leanne shows planning: 'Now you do it Ashlyn', and control, as she mimes 'eating' the camera. Ashlyn shows planning: 'My turn', and monitoring: 'I forgotted that page!'. There are also signs of emotional and motivational control, particularly as both girls self-encourage and encourage one another by smiling and laughing. Leanne also keeps Ashlyn involved by tapping her on the arm, and saying 'now you do it Ashley' and 'your turn now'.

One aspect of friendship is its possible effect on effortful control. In Chapter 2, we saw that effortful control is the ability to inhibit a pressing response, in order to carry out a less pressing response; an ability which is inextricably linked to self-regulation. An excellent example comes from Neal et al. (2017) who look at the link between children's emotionality, their social play and their effortful control. They observed 3- to 4-year-olds at preschool. Overall, children chose to play with children who were similar to them in terms of their levels of positive emotionality (e.g. their sociability, positive affect). Children who showed more negative emotionality (sadness, anger and/or fear) were less likely to form social play relationships over time. Gradually, during the school year, children's levels of positive emotionality and also their levels of effortful control, changed, becoming more similar to their playmates. This suggests that if a child chose for playmates children whose effortful control was higher than hers, she would be likely to further develop her effortful control to a level similar to her playmates'. We can see here that children's temperament can influence their choice of playmates. In turn, this choice then affects the development of effortful control.

ACTIVITY: OBSERVING FRIENDSHIP AND SELF-REGULATION

Observe children playing in groups. Try to observe at least two groups. One should be a group of friends playing together and the other should be children who do not consider each other friends.

Revisit the definitions for self-regulation, co-regulation and socially shared regulation in Chapter 1. Focus on each of the two groups separately and make notes in response to the questions below:

1. Compare your two groups. In which group did you observe more self-regulation? Where did you see more co-regulation, and where was more socially shared regulation evident?

2. Why do you think this is the case?

Share your thoughts with a colleague and discuss your ideas about:

1. Is friendship important in relation to self-regulation development?

2. What is different in terms of self-regulation/co-regulation/socially shared regulation when children are playing with friends compared to when they are not?

3. What steps can you take in relation to group work/group play to encourage children's self-regulatory development?

Similarly, prosocial behaviour is related to positive aspects of friendships (Rabaglietti et al., 2013). A child who shows consistently high levels of prosocial behaviours is more likely to also be higher in positive quality of friendship and in number of friends compared to a child with lower levels of prosocial behaviour. As we see in the box below, this study also found that a lack of behavioural self-regulation was related to negative quality of friendship.

WHAT DOES RESEARCH TELL US?

Lack of behavioural self-regulation may be linked to negative quality of friendship

Rabaglietti et al. (2013) studied how a lack of behavioural self-regulation can predict the quantity and quality of friendships. The participants in this study were 177 children, aged from 6 to 9 years (on average the children were 7 years old in the first year of the study and 8 in the second year).

The children were asked to fill in a questionnaire once when they were in Year 2 and then again when they were in Year 3. In the questionnaire, lack of behavioural self-regulation was measured through children's responses to 17 items:

I shout,	I stop someone when he/she is talking,	I play noisy games,
I disturb someone,	I do no stay quiet,	I play dangerous games,
I fight (not for fun),	I pull punches and kicks not for fun,	I tease someone,
I hurt my mates,	I threaten someone,	I bite to hurt my mates,
I quarrel with older children,	I talk badly of classmates,	I insult classmates,
I jostle and I do capers with others,	I make fun of classmates.	

Negative quality of friendships, and specifically conflicts was measured through children's responses to four items reflecting feelings about:

frequent fighting,   being angry even after the fight is over,

disagreeing about many things,   reciprocal teasing.

A lack of behavioural self-regulation was positively associated with negative quality of friendship. This means that children who lack in behavioural self-regulation are more likely to show elements of negative quality of friendships, such as conflicts.

(Rabaglietti et al., 2013)

Peer relationships and self-regulation: a bidirectional relationship

What seems to be clear, then, is that relationships and self-regulation are in effect bidirectional, with one impacting the other and vice versa. Holmes et al. (2016) look at executive functions and problems with peers. In their study they measured children's executive functions when they were 4.5 years old and then started looking at children's peer problems from age 6 onwards. It is interesting to note that better executive function reduced the possibility of experiencing peer problems later in childhood (and in adolescence). The direction of the relationship went both ways, because peer problems would then contribute to lower executive function in childhood. Thus, peer relationships have a role to play in the development of executive functions, and executive functions also have a role to play in the development of peer relationships. This also seems to be the case more generally for self-regulation. Stenseng et al. (2015) found that a child who was struggling in their social relationships, specifically a child being rejected and excluded by peers at age 4, might face problems in the development of their self-regulation at age 6. As perhaps we might expect, this relationship goes both ways, with poor self-regulation also then linked to higher levels of exclusion by peers (Stenseng et al., 2015).

To conclude, a child who is still developing their self-regulation and social skills, perhaps at a slower rate than their peers, might find it harder to manage their peer interactions in groups (Pahigiannis & Glos, 2020). At the same time, group contexts can provide many opportunities for the development of these skills.

What can practitioners do to support peer relationships and self-regulation?

- Ensure children have many opportunities for play and activities in small groups, as these are contexts where children exhibit higher self-regulation. This applies throughout the Early Years and across the primary school (Pahigiannis & Glos, 2020);

- Opportunities for children to work in groups in the classroom provide contexts for co-regulation and shared regulation, which facilitates self-regulation (Perry & Rahim, 2011);

- Support children in developing skills in working *in* a group and more collaboratively *as* a group;

- Promote tasks which prompt dynamic, coordinated and interdependent work that requires collaborative teams to use all individuals' unique expertise in achieving a goal that could not be achieved by one individual alone (Perry & Winne, 2013; Winne, Hadwin, & Perry, 2013).

- Focus on children's interpersonal competence and social problem-solving.

- Place emphasis on supporting self-regulation and positive peer experiences. Ensure that the environment of the setting enables positive peer interactions (Pahigiannis & Glos, 2020).

- Support pretend play. Vygotsky (1978) stresses the richness of make-believe play for self-regulating language. Pretend play supports opportunities for children to engage in complex negotiations to create play scenes (Berk, Mann, & Ogan, 2006), with conversations drawing on cultural rules, conventions and models of co-operation (Vygotsky, 1978), supporting their self-regulation.

- Look at ways to support young children's emotion regulation, drawing on the evidence around ideas such as parental scaffolding. Emotion regulation is central to children's overall development and important in the development of cognitive self-regulation.

- Stories, including fairy tales and puppets, are a teaching routine in which emotions can be explored in a sustained way, and children's emotion regulation supported (Fleer & Hammer, 2013).

- Support children in developing the abilities needed to initiate and maintain friendships (Whitebread, 2012).

What about children experiencing emotion regulation difficulties?

Many of the issues discussed here may be particularly heightened for children whose development is atypical. Children with aspects of emotion dysregulation can find it difficult to remain calm, and to calm themselves, they may feel overwhelmed by their emotions, and their behaviour may be unpredictable, including being either aggressive or withdrawn. This can have a negative effect on their social interactions and relationships with peers and adults (Berkovits et al., 2017). Children with attention-deficit/ hyperactivity disorder (ADHD) or autism spectrum disorder (ASD), for example, may have more difficulty in controlling and managing their emotions (Mazefsky et al., 2013; Özbaran et al., 2018). All of these can work against them being accepted as members of a group in play and in developing friendships. In many instances, children with ADHD or ASD will have specific plans in place for support, but it is also useful to think about some general strategies that particularly relate to self-regulation and emotion regulation here, which run alongside the bullet points above:

- Support children in having experience of what it is to feel calm and in control – this will be different for each child.

- Comment when you see a child is calm, or in control, so that they can recognise this in themselves.

- Support children in finding and developing ways to calm themselves, and control their emotions, including self-soothing, self-distraction etc.

- Try to co-regulate a child at times of stress or anxiety, engaging in a calming activity together, for example, relaxed breathing, stroking etc.

- Model emotion regulation, describing your own feelings and showing children how you calm yourself down.

- Help a child to develop a vocabulary about feelings and states and begin to relate these to situations. For example, in conversation name a child's emotions: 'I can see you are upset'.

- Help children to be more aware of the needs and feelings of others, for example, through talk, using photographs, and stories.

Conclusion

In this chapter we have looked at how relationships affect self-regulation and vice-versa. We focused on parent–child interactions and child–child interactions. First we looked at how parents affect children's self-regulation, through three parenting dimensions: challenge, contingency and autonomy. We explored the role of parental scaffolding, particularly contingent scaffolding, and the role of autonomy support from parents in the development of children's self-regulation. Then we looked at how children's interactions with peers affect their self-regulation, but also at how self-regulation affects children's relationships with peers. More positive relationships and interactions with peers lead to better self-regulation, and this is a bidirectional relationship. We also investigated whether playing/working in groups or individually affects self-regulation. While it seems that playing in groups is important for self-regulation development, there is also evidence to suggest the same for playing alone. We also explored friendship as a context for self-regulatory development: positive quality friendships are related to better self-regulation, and lack of self-regulation is related to negative quality of friendship. Finally, we discussed what practitioners can do to support peer relationships and self-regulation both in typically and atypically developing children.

Key further reading

Bernier, A., Carlson, S. M., & Whipple, N. (2010). From external regulation to self-regulation: Early parenting precursors of young children's executive functioning. *Child Development*, 81(1), 326–339.

Neale, D., & Whitebread, D. (2019). Maternal scaffolding during play with 12- to 24-month-old infants: Stability over time and relations with emerging effortful control. *Metacognition and Learning*, 14(3), 265–289.

Pahigiannis, K., & Glos, M. (2020). Peer influences in self-regulation development and interventions in early childhood. *Early Child Development and Care*, 190(7), 1053–1064.

Pino-Pasternak, D., & Whitebread, D. (2010). The role of parenting in children's self-regulated learning. *Educational Research Review*, 5(3), 220–242.

Pino-Pasternak, D., Whitebread, D., & Tolmie, A. (2010). A multidimensional analysis of parent–child interactions during academic tasks and their relationships with children's self-regulated learning. *Cognition and Instruction*, 28(3), 219–272.

5   Observing and assessing self-regulation in young children

In this chapter, we look at:

- Approaches that enable practitioners and researchers to observe self-regulation in young children;

- Talking with children as a way of finding out about their self-regulation;

- Young children's perspectives and participation when we are observing and assessing their self-regulation;

- The role of documentation in supporting evidence of young children's self-regulation;

- Parents and practitioners working together to support observation and assessment.

Keywords: observation, reflective dialogue, assessment, documentation, children's perspectives.

Introduction

In this chapter, we explore approaches to observing and assessing self-regulation in young children, used in both research and practice. Some approaches may be more suitable for use with older children and adults, for example questionnaires, and are not looked at here. We focus here on observation as the most valuable means of 'seeing' and assessing young children's self-regulation. Most frameworks for assessing self-regulation in children younger than nine are based on observations (Gascoine et al., 2017), for example, the C.Ind.Le coding framework, looked at below (Whitebread et al., 2009b). Some other tools require children to undertake a task, often a problem-solving one, and to be observed and/or interviewed by researchers. An example of this is the Metacognitive Knowledge interview procedure developed by Marulis et al. (2016), also looked at below. As we saw in

Chapter 3, the approach of the OECD in the IELS assessment is similar, with children completing tablet-based tasks, observed by a trained administrator.

The frameworks and ideas we look at here are ones which are consistent with the definition of self-regulation we have adopted throughout this book. We have also placed importance on tools which can be used in naturalistic, everyday environments which are meaningful to the children, based on observations, and do not require laboratory conditions. In particular, this suggests the importance of play as a context for observation. These frameworks aim to maintain high standards of ecological validity; that is that their results can be generalised to natural behaviour in the everyday world or classroom (McClelland & Cameron, 2012).

We also look at the role of documentation for helping us to see young children's self-regulation, and for supporting children's and families' active engagement. Throughout, we emphasise the importance of young children's active participation in the assessment and documenting of their self-regulation. This is not only consistent with a view of children as competent, and capable of voicing their perspectives on their lives, but also because children's own thoughts about their thinking and self-regulation are vital if we want to get as full and as accurate a picture as possible.

WHAT DOES POLICY TELL US?

In both England and Scotland, observation is explicitly linked to the assessment of young children's self-regulation.

England: The foundation stage profile

Self-regulation is an Early Learning Goal in the EYFS, assessed as part of the foundation stage profile. Guidance on administering the profile emphasises:

Teachers' judgements will largely be based on their observations during day-to-day activity in the classroom.

(Department for Education, 2020: 8)

Scotland: National improvement hub: effective observation leading to effective assessment

This web-based resource for practitioners working with young children says:

Close observing of young children allows practitioners to understand the fullest capabilities of children as well as to gain insight into how and where children like to learn... Children will also show through their play, how they are developing as capable and competent learners. They will display important skills for learning such as: perseverance, motivation, self-regulation, concentration and creativity.

(Education Scotland, n.d.)

The importance of observation

Observation, of course, plays a central role in formative and summative assessment practice with young children, but why is it most appropriate in the context of self-regulation? Azevedo identifies five reasons which he believes make observation particularly valuable for adults attempting to understand its emergence in young children:

1. observations record what children actually do;

2. they afford links between behaviour and context;

3. they do not depend on verbal abilities, often problematic for young children;

4. they allow for recording of verbal and non-verbal behaviours (including aspects such as eye gaze);

5. they allow for recording of social processes.

(Azevedo, 2009)

The two main frameworks we look at here fulfil all of these criteria, focusing on children as they play and work alone and with others, in the everyday contexts of nursery and school life.

The Cambridgeshire Independent Learning (C.Ind.Le) coding framework

We start by looking at the C.Ind.Le coding framework (Whitebread et al., 2005, 2007, 2009b), already referred to in earlier chapters. This observational framework was developed for use by researchers. While this might not seem immediately relevant to practitioners, it has been a cornerstone of many self-regulation research projects in the last few years, and identifies behaviours that address all aspects of self-regulation – cognitive, social, emotional, motivational and behavioural. All of these are valuable for supporting our understanding of the breadth of self-regulation, and the ways in which young children might demonstrate it. It is also related to the CHILD 3–5 framework, which was developed for use by practitioners (Whitebread et al., 2009b).

The C.Ind.Le framework identifies behaviours from three areas of self-regulation, each further divided into different types of behaviour (Figure 5.1):

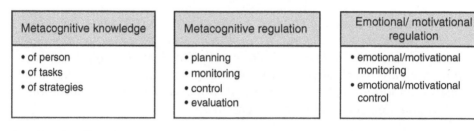

Metacognitive knowledge	Metacognitive regulation	Emotional/ motivational regulation
• of person • of tasks • of strategies	• planning • monitoring • control • evaluation	• emotional/motivational monitoring • emotional/motivational control

Figure 5.1   Three areas of self-regulation as identified in the C.Ind.Le coding framework.

The full C.Ind.Le coding framework, with specific self-regulation behaviours and examples drawn from our recent research projects, is included in Table 5.1.

C.Ind.Le coding scheme: verbal and non-verbal indicators of metacognition and self-regulation		
Category name	**Description of behaviour**	**Examples**
Metacognitive knowledge		
Knowledge of persons		
A verbalisation demonstrating the explicit expression of one's knowledge in relation to cognition or people as cognitive processors. It might include knowledge about cognition in relation to: • *Self*: Refers to own capabilities, strengths and weaknesses, or academic/task preferences; comparative judgements about own abilities • *Others*: Refers to others' processes of thinking or feeling toward cognitive tasks • *Universals*: Refers to universals of people's cognition	Refers to his/her own strengths or difficulties in learning and academic working skills. Refers to others' strengths or difficulties in learning and academic working skills. Talks about general ideas about learning.	*I know how to build a ship by myself.* *I am not good at singing.* *And it was my idea. This was my idea. Look at this, that bit was my idea.* *I don't know how to do this move.* *Do you know why (I am doing this so well)? I have been practising!*
Knowledge of tasks		
A verbalisation demonstrating the explicit expression of one's own long-term memory in relation to elements of the task.	Compares across tasks identifying similarities and differences. Makes a judgement about the level of difficulty of cognitive tasks or rates the tasks on the basis of pre-established criteria or previous knowledge.	Explains what the task lacks in comparison to other ideas. *You have to hold them like this* (gesturing how to carry scissors). Identifies similarities to hand-clapping games they already know.
Knowledge of strategies		
A verbalisation demonstrating the explicit expression of one's own knowledge in relation to strategies used or performing a cognitive task, where a strategy is a cognitive or behavioural activity that is employed so as to enhance performance or achieve a goal.	Defines, explains or teaches others how she/he has done or learnt something. Explains procedures involved in a particular task. Evaluates the effectiveness of one or more strategies in relation to the context or the cognitive task.	*I asked Henry if we needed string, yeah, but Henry said no.* Explaining the game to the rest of the group: *You will be closing the circle when I enter the circle and you will be singing this.*

(Continued)

Table 5.1 (Continued)

C.Ind.Le coding scheme: verbal and non-verbal indicators of metacognition and self-regulation		
Category name	Description of behaviour	Examples
Metacognitive regulation		
Planning		
Any verbalisation or behaviour related to the selection of procedures necessary for performing the task, individually or with others.	Sets or clarifies task demands and expectations. Allocates individual roles and negotiates responsibilities. Sets goals and targets. Decides on ways of proceeding with the task. Seeks and collects necessary resources.	*We have to dig from the other side!* (in sand). Child tries to get the team ready and at the correct position before the start of play. Directs who plays what and when. *We both be the mummy and we haven't got a baby, okay? Let's play.*
Monitoring		
Any verbalisation or behaviour related to the ongoing on-task assessment of the quality of task performance (of self or others) and the degree to which performance is progressing towards a desired goal.	Self-commentates. Reviews progress on task (keeping track of procedures currently being undertaken and those that have been done so far). Rates effort on-task or rates actual performance. Rates or makes comments on current memory retrieval. Checks behaviours or performance, including detection of errors. Self-corrects. Checks and/or corrects performance of peer.	*You know what? They are not enough.* Checking around their peers to make sure they are playing the game correctly. Rylan sees that when he presses one shape down it makes others move. He looks at each joint, assessing the fit of each in turn. He gently lifts the model up, assessing its strength. He holds it up at eye level, making small adjustments to strengthen the joints.
Control		
Any verbalisation or behaviour related to a change in the way a task had been conducted (by self or others), as a result of cognitive monitoring.	Changes strategies as a result of previous monitoring. Suggests and uses strategies in order to solve the task more effectively. Applies a previously learnt strategy to a new situation. Repeats a strategy in order to check the accuracy of the outcome. Seeks help.	Aleah is at the top of the frame. She holds a skipping rope with wooden handles. She ties it round the handrail and pulls on the end, testing to make sure it is secure and will bear someone's weight. Guides another child by demonstration of how the instrument should be used. She moves on the pulse while singing, in this way supporting

Table 5.1   (Continued)

C.Ind.Le coding scheme: verbal and non-verbal indicators of metacognition and self-regulation		
Category name	**Description of behaviour**	**Examples**
	Uses non-verbal gesture as a strategy to support own cognitive activity. Copies from or imitates a model. Helps or guides another child using gesture.	cognitive activity and helping the team to coordinate. *One, two, three*-implementing a known strategy to a new situation.
Evaluation		
Any verbalisation or behaviour related to reviewing task performance and evaluating the quality of performance (by self or others).	Reviews own learning or explains the task. Evaluates the strategies used. Rates the quality of performance. Observes or comments on task progress. Tests the outcome or effectiveness of a strategy in achieving a goal.	*He's too big and he's going to fall over on me.* *We've made a song! It's perfect!* Joshua about his friend: *Taber didn't get the right idea.*
Emotional and motivational regulation		
Emotional/motivational monitoring		
Any verbalisation or behaviour related to the assessment of current emotional and motivational experiences regarding the task.	Express awareness of positive or negative emotional experience of a task. Monitors own emotional reactions while being on a task.	*I don't want to sing.* *No more tricking, because I don't like being tricked.*
Emotional/motivational control		
Any verbalisation or behaviour related to the regulation of one's emotional and motivational experiences while on task.	Controls attention and resists distraction or returns to task after momentary distraction. Self-encourages or encourages others. Persists in the face of difficulty or remains in task without help.	Nods her head encouragingly to make a peer dance. Aashi continues to colour in, focused on her task, while children come barging in past her from outside.

Table 5.1   The C.Ind.Le coding framework

Sources: First two columns from Whitebread et al. (2009b). Right-hand column from Robson (2010, 2016a, 2016b, 2016c), and Zachariou and Whitebread (2017).

Based on observations of young children aged 3–5, The C.Ind.Le framework has been used internationally for observing children up to the age of 9 (Jokić & Whitebread, 2011; Robson, 2016a, 2016b; Whitebread & Cárdenas, 2012; Zachariou & Whitebread, 2019). An important asset of the C.Ind.Le framework is that it supports opportunities to identify both verbal and non-verbal indicators of self-regulation meaning that self-regulation behaviours are not missed if a child has not explicitly verbalised/talked about them.

WHAT DOES RESEARCH TELL US?

Looking at verbal and non-verbal self-regulation behaviour

The Cambridgeshire Independent Learning in the Foundation Stage (C.Ind.Le) project by Whitebread et al. (2007, 2009a, 2009b), focused on observing young children, aged 3–5, during their everyday activities in educational settings. The project lasted 2 years. Its aim was to study whether self-regulation could be observed in young children when sensitive methodologies like observation were employed.

Thirty-two early years teachers and the 3–5-year-old children in their classes participated. The teachers were supported to create learning activities which would encourage self-regulation. The children were video-recorded two or three times per year during activities which were interesting for them. The observations involved different play types, ranging from object-play and construction play to pretence and role-play. Of these observations, 60 events were selected for their richness in self-regulation and were analysed for verbal and non-verbal indicators of self-regulation, using the C.Ind.Le coding framework. In total, approximately seven (6.92) self-regulatory behaviours per minute were observed.

Of the overall 6.92 behaviours observed per minute, 4.31 were verbal behaviours indicating self-regulation and 2.61 were non-verbal behaviours indicating self-regulation.

(Whitebread et al., 2009b)

DEVELOP YOUR UNDERSTANDING: OBSERVING VERBAL AND NON-VERBAL INDICATORS OF SELF-REGULATION

From the research by Whitebread and colleagues (see above) we can see that more than a third of the self-regulation behaviours were non-verbal. This suggests the importance of a tool which can capture both verbal and non-verbal behaviour. If the tool being used to assess children's self-regulation is not sensitive enough to capture non-verbal self-regulation, many of the self-regulatory behaviours will potentially be missed and children's self-regulation may be underestimated.

- What does this mean for you when you are observing and assessing children's self-regulation?

- How can you ensure that you will observe both verbal and non-verbal indications of self-regulation?

- How can this knowledge help you choose a framework/tool to help you observe children's self-regulation?

The Children's Independent Learning Development (CHILD 3–5) checklist: a tool for practitioners

Alongside the C.Ind.Le framework, Whitebread and colleagues developed a framework for observing self-regulation specifically for use by practitioners. The CHILD 3–5 checklist is an observational instrument that was constructed in collaboration with classroom teachers for use in nurseries and classrooms (Whitebread et al., 2009b). Practitioners can observe and assess children's self-regulatory behaviour by scoring 22 statements in prosocial, emotional, cognitive and motivational areas of regulation. Table 5.2 presents the CHILD 3–5 checklist, including all of the statements. A practitioner can score each statement on the CHILD checklist from 0 ('never'), to 3 ('always'). An average score can then be calculated for each area. For example:

Child A is scored as 'usually' (2) in each of the five statements of the emotional self-regulation area.

The sum of these scores (2 + 2 + 2 + 2 + 2) = 10

This is divided by the number of statements in that area (5): 10/5 = 2

So Child A's emotional self-regulation score is 2 ('usually').

The average score for a child's overall self-regulation can be calculated in a similar way.

Checklist of Independent Learning Development (CHILD) 3–5 Name of child:_____ Teacher:_____ Date: _____ School:_____					
	Always	Usually	Some-times	Never	Comment
Emotional					
Can speak about own and others behaviour and consequences					
Tackles new tasks confidently					
Can control attention and resist distraction					
Monitors progress and seeks help appropriately					
Persists in the face of difficulties					
ProSocial					
Negotiates when and how to carry out tasks					
Can resolve social problems with peers					
Shares and takes turns independently					

(Continued)

Table 5.2 (Continued)

Checklist of Independent Learning Development (CHILD) 3–5 Name of child:_____Teacher:_____ Date: _____ School:_____					
	Always	Usually	Some-times	Never	Comment
Engages in independent cooperative activities with peers					
Is aware of the feelings of others and helps and comforts					
Cognitive					
Is aware of own strengths and weaknesses					
Can speak about how they have done something or what they have learnt					
Can speak about future planned activities					
Can make reasoned choices and decisions					
Asks questions and suggests answers					
Uses previously taught strategies					
Adopts previously heard language for own purposes					
Motivational					
Finds own resources without adult help					
Develops own ways of carrying out tasks					
Initiates activities					
Plans own tasks, targets and goals					
Enjoys solving problems					
Other comments:					

Table 5.2   The CHILD 3–5 observational checklist (Whitebread et al., 2009b)

The CHILD 3–5 checklist is one of the first tools to explicitly measure young children's self-regulation, and which practitioners can complete as a result of observing children in their classrooms. CHILD 3–5 was devised for assessing typically developing children.

Observing potential difficulties in developing self-regulation

Both of the frameworks we have looked at here are particularly valuable in giving us insights into what children *can* do, and in providing evidence of their self-regulatory competence. It is also important to explore when and how children's self-regulation fails (Bryce & Whitebread, 2012; Zachariou & Bonneville-Roussy, under review), or when there are potential difficulties in developing self-regulation. The Behavior Rating Inventory of Executive Function (BRIEF) (Gioia et al., 2000), for example, is a questionnaire which can be completed by teachers or parents, and which aims to identify a variety of developmental, neurological, psychiatric and medical conditions in children over 5 years of age. It has also been applied in cases of children with ASD.

Trying to look at when self-regulation falters is *not* in order to encourage a deficit view of young children's self-regulation, but rather so that practitioners can know how to support children. So, even though children are able to self-regulate and there is substantial evidence to support this, below we give an example of a study which looks at young children's failures in self-regulation too.

WHAT DOES RESEARCH TELL US?

What about when there are problems of self-regulation?

In Chapter 2, we looked at a study by Bryce and Whitebread (2012) where children were asked to build a train track to match a predefined shape. The researchers also looked for failures in self-regulation and they used the coding scheme below:

Perseveration behaviours:

- no strategy: when something will not work, uses same strategy over and over or gives up

- not following plan: making a plan and then not following it

- narrow view: a failure to review the whole area or whole array of train track pieces

- focus on join: focusing on joining up the circuit rather than making the shape

- two positives: when child ends up with two sticking out ends, not realising they need to reverse one

- large/small curves: when they run out of small curves, not realising they need to switch to large curves

- finishing error: saying/indicating/suggesting they have finished when they have not (when there is a major discrepancy between their track and the shape)

- goal neglect: showing awareness of the rule/error but not acting accordingly

Distraction behaviours:

- off-task: child seems to have gone completely off-task and forgotten their goal

- distracted: child is distracted (by other people's activity or own thoughts, but works on the task intermittently)

(Bryce & Whitebread, 2012)

First of all, a reminder that the behaviours described in Bryce and Whitbread's study are tailored to the specific task of constructing a train track. The coding scheme was also created for research rather than practice. However, practitioners could keep these behaviours in mind when observing children in their classroom. For example, a child might be indicating a finishing error when they are suggesting they have finished a task when they have clearly not.

The following questions are helpful to consider:

1. Why is this happening? (For example, is it that the task was not interesting or meaningful to the child or is it that the child is not self-regulating their motivation?)

2. What can I do to support the child to self-regulate more effectively next time they are in a similar situation?

When working with children, try to identify instances where you observe one of the above examples of failure in self-regulation. Take note of what the child was doing before, during and after the incident. Try also to note what was happening in the immediate environment of the child. Then consider the two questions above, and aim to come up with a plan for next time you see this child engaging in these behaviours.

Observing and assessing metacognitive knowledge

One important issue when observing and assessing children's self-regulation is that the central cognitive element of self-regulation, that is, the component that C.Ind.Le identifies as metacognitive knowledge (see Table 5.1), often also referred to simply as metacognition, can be more difficult to identify when observing young children in class engaged in an activity. In order to identify metacognitive knowledge, we rely on children's verbalisations, that is, on what children can tell us about their knowledge. This is not necessarily evident while children are working on a task/playing. Children do not always talk out loud at such times. In contrast, metacognitive regulation and emotional/motivational regulation (see C.Ind.Le coding framework above) can both be evidenced through verbal and non-verbal behaviours.

A prevalent approach used to overcome this issue, and to enable fair reporting of young children's metacognitive skills, is the use of metacognitive (or metacognitive knowledge) interviews. Carried out by a researcher (or potentially a practitioner) following the completion of a task, the adult asks targeted questions, which support a child in speaking about their metacognition. In the box below, we present an example of a framework for a metacognitive knowledge interview.

An example of a metacognitive knowledge interview comes from the research of Marulis and Nelson (2021). In their project, they asked children aged 3–5 years to complete a block puzzle. Once the children had completed their final puzzle, the researchers asked them questions to assess their metacognition (Marulis et al., 2016).

Following the model proposed by Whitebread et al. (2009b), they asked questions that target

Metacognitive knowledge of people	Metacognitive knowledge of tasks	Metacognitive knowledge of strategies

The 15 main questions that Marulis and Nelson asked are shown below. Remember that these refer to the specific block puzzle task the children completed in this project, but they may also be useful starting points for your own thinking:

- Do you think you did a good job, an okay job or not so good of a job on the puzzles?
- Did you think anything was hard? Why?/Why not?
- Will the puzzle be harder/easier when you are older? Why?
- Would these puzzles be hard for another child your age? Why?/Why not?
- How did you know you were getting the puzzles right?

The researchers then introduced a finger puppet, named Gogi, who had no idea about puzzles and asked the child to help the puppet learn about these kind of puzzles:

- Would these puzzles be easier for Gogi or you? Why?
- What should Gogi do if they are having trouble with the puzzle?
- Would it be helpful for Gogi to talk to themselves about the puzzle while doing the puzzle?
- Why would/wouldn't that be a helpful thing to do?

Gogi then asked the children:

- Would the puzzle be easier with bigger or smaller pieces? Why?
- Would the puzzle be easier with more or less pieces? Why?

(Continued)

OBSERVING AND ASSESSING METACOGNITION: METACOGNITIVE KNOWLEDGE INTERVIEW continued

- If all of the puzzle pieces were the same colour, would the puzzle be easier? Why?/Why not?

- If I think about how the pieces would fit together before I try, would the puzzle be easier? Why/Why not?

- If I gather the pieces I need first and then build the puzzle, would it be easier? Why?/Why not?

- If I close my eyes while I do the puzzle, would it be easier? Why?/Why not?

The researchers then rated children's responses as shown below:

- 0: not at all metacognitive

- 1: partially metacognitive

- 2: an appropriate metacognitive response.

(Marulis & Nelson, 2021: 224–225)

Using visual methods and reflective dialogues to find out about young children's self-regulation

Here we look at the use of visual methods such as photographs, video and drawings as valuable ways of finding out about, and documenting, young children's self-regulation. These can, of course, be used in different ways. They are valuable records when generated by either children or adults, for assessment and for sharing with others. Here we want to look particularly at their value when used as a focus for discussion about the children's ideas. This has elements in common with the idea of metacognitive knowledge interviews, looked at above. In both cases, the evidence that children themselves can give us about their self-regulation is emphasised. With photographs this kind of discussion is often referred to as photo elicitation (or photo voice when it is the children's own photographs). With video it is often referred to as Video-Stimulated Reflective Dialogue (VSRD). It is increasingly used in research with children (Morgan, 2007; Robson, 2010, 2016c), including children making their own videos (Lewis, 2019). The starting point for both is photograph(s) or a video clip of an episode, used with either an individual child or a small group of children. The discussion that follows is centred on the children's thoughts about their own (and others') learning and thinking, rather than just recall of the episode. The box below includes some useful starting points for questions, used by one of us (Robson, 2010, 2016c).

These questions are not meant to be prescriptive. The most important thing is to use some of the suggestions to stimulate and support discussion, focusing on the children's ideas and thinking.

Reflective dialogue discussion ideas
While we are watching (or looking), please can you tell me about what was happening here? What were you thinking about?

Questions that focus on metacognitive knowledge
1. Did you have an idea about what you wanted to do?
2. What made you choose to go there?
 	
(possible prompts: Did you choose?
                Did …(adult) ask you to go there?
                Were any of your friends there?
                Did a friend suggest it to you/give you the idea?)
 	
3. How did you decide what to do?
4. Did you remember what to do?
5. Have you done anything like (this activity) before?
 	
(if yes: Can you remember what you did then? Did that help you here?)

Questions that focus on metacognitive regulation 6. Do you think you had any good ideas? 7. How did your ideas help you? 8. Why do you think you did…? (possible focus on specific episode in video) 9. What do you think was the best idea you had?
Questions that focus on emotional and motivational regulation 10. Did you like (activity)? 11. Are you pleased with what you did? (Why?) 12. How do you feel when you have finished something that you think you have done well? 13. How do you feel if an idea you have doesn't work? What do you do about that? 14. What do you think you are good at? 15. What do you like doing most of all here?

What might be valuable to bear in mind when using these approaches? We list some ideas below:

- Build trust and rapport with children through involving them, including their familiarisation with the camera, and seeing themselves on camera (Pyle, 2013);

- Think about whether the children can contribute to/decide what video or photographs are being used – moments selected by adults are not always important to children (Morgan, 2007);

- Look carefully at context. Children are more likely to be engaged when the context relates to their interests (Adler et al., 2019);

- Think about the size of the group: individual discussions can be helpful, supporting sustained shared thinking (Robson, 2010, 2016c; Sylva et al., 2010). Pairs of children, including friendship pairs, can be very valuable with young children

(Hill, 2006; Pyle, 2013). Groups of four are really a maximum, but Morgan (2007) highlights the need for children to be familiar with such a format in order to participate most effectively. Hill et al. (1996) suggests that a combination of group discussions and individual interviews may be ideal with young children;

- If you use pairs or small groups, make sure the children are comfortable with one another (Pyle, 2013);

- There is no clear evidence that either single- or mixed-gender groups are better: work with what is best in your own context;

- Try to ensure that questions are open-ended, and that you act in an encouraging way (Ponizovsky-Bergelson et al., 2019), to support richer responses;

- Discussing the photo(s) or video can happen the same day, but is still very effective in following days, up to a maximum of about a week (Morgan, 2007; Robson, 2010).

Why are visual approaches so valuable in the context of self-regulation?

Several features of visual methods, particularly when combined with discussion, may make them very valuable for looking at young children's self-regulation. First, Dockett et al. (2017) suggest that using photographs (and video material) can be interesting and enticing for children's participation. Forman (1999) suggests that video data can be a 'tool of the mind', acting as a visual and oral memory of the event. This, he suggests, frees children's minds to think about what the actions themselves mean. The discussion between adults and children about the shared photographs or video creates opportunities for joint meaning-making and intersubjectivity, an important feature of co-regulation, as we saw in Chapter 1. It can also enrich adults' knowledge of children, and bring to light children's ideas and thinking that are not always visible to an observer of the original activity. For example, one of us watched Bill (aged 5) playing outdoors one afternoon, repeatedly sliding down the slide. He went indoors and found a pillowcase, and came back out with it. However, it was then taken from him by another boy. In discussing the episode later in a VSRD, Bill said he had gone to get the pillowcase because he thought it would help him go faster down the slide.

In Chapter 6, we look at the value of these kinds of reflective dialogues for supporting children's talk about their thinking, and it is useful to also look there. Here, we want to emphasise the way in which they may support children's talk about their metacognitive knowledge, in particular (Robson, 2010, 2016c). As we saw earlier, this can be challenging to elicit through observation alone. Look at the extract from a VSRD below. Throughout, Ashlyn reflected on her own ideas. Here she also considers her friend Simi's:

> *Ashlyn and Adult S are looking at a video of an activity involving children writing on hand-held boards:*
>
> *ASHLYN: And why's Simi looking at my board?*

ADULT: *Why do you think she was looking at your board?*

ASHLYN: *Because she didn't know how to do it.*

(Robson, 2016c: 8)

Children may also be more likely to talk more about their feelings in discussion than when involved in the activity itself (Robson, 2016c), reliving them while looking at photographs or watching a video.

We are not suggesting that these kinds of discussion can always be fitted in to practitioners' busy lives, although the availability of smartphones and tablets helps to make them potentially more achievable. Nevertheless they could valuably be used, or elements of them, even infrequently, to support discussion and documentation.

ACTIVITY: OBSERVING BILL AND NIZAR

Bill (5.5) is outside playing with the wireframe playhouse. He is throwing a skipping rope across the pitched roof. To help him, he has already picked up a large crate and placed it on top of one already there. He adjusts it so that it is secure, then stands on it to help him get hold of the end of the skipping rope, near the apex of the roof. He carries on like this, until Nizar (5.7) walks by, and joins in. They spend 10 minutes throwing ropes over, threading them through, negotiating and working both collaboratively and individually.

(Continued)

The following text has extracts from a VSRD between Bill and Adult S, as they watch a video recording of the activity:

BILL: If Nizar stepped on there and pulled it (rope) tight he'd break it.

ADULT: Why might he break it?

BILL: Because he's big.

ADULT: Oh, there's both of you on the crate now. Oh look, why won't it go over? (in dvd Bill cannot throw end of a rope successfully over the roof of the playhouse)

BILL: Because I'm not throwing it high. Because I'm not, I need another step to step on there (pointing to two crates balanced on top of one another on the screen).

ADULT: Oh, to make you higher?

BILL: (Nods) If you put three steps on there, then it might break. What are we doing now? (high pitch, laughing, watching dvd) Then I can do it.

ADULT: You did it.

BILL: I'm not very high, I need big steps!

...

BILL: I told him not to go on there.

ADULT: Did you?

BILL: He didn't listen to me.

ADULT: Why did you tell him not to go on there?

BILL: Because if there was two, three, if there was three people on there then it would break.

...

BILL: There's Nizar doing it, he can't do it! (on screen Nizar is trying to pull the rope). Oh, that's what I told him to not do that. I didn't tell him to do that, because he was going to climb all the way over, (quietly) he was going to climb all the way over.

Now:

1. Looking at the photographs and the VSRD extracts, identify aspects of self-regulation using either the C.Ind.Le framework or CHILD 3–5 observational checklist. For example, look at how Bill reflects on the usefulness of his strategies, uses mental state vocabulary ('he can't do it!'), and shows emotional and motivational regulation, laughing.

2. What does this tell you about Bill's self-regulation?

3. What might you do next to support Bill's self-regulation?

Documentation and self-regulation

Practitioners have always collected and documented their observations and thoughts about children. Here we want to highlight the ways in which this documentation can support self-regulation, including the development of meta-cognitive skills (Wood, 2013), by making the everyday activities and thoughts of children and adults open to discussion and reflection. Two approaches are especially useful to look at, the structured narrative-style observations in *Learning Stories* from New Zealand (Carr, 2001) and work in Reggio Emilia (Edwards et al., 1998). In Reggio Emilia, children's thinking is made visible through collection, and careful display, of the children's ideas, theories and understandings. These are used in discussion to actively shape thinking. The advantages they identify have clear links to self-regulation:

A broad range of documentation…produced and used *in process* (that is, during the experience) offers the following advantages:

- It makes visible … the nature of the learning processes and strategies used by each child…;

- It enables reading, revisiting and assessment in time and in space, and these actions become an integral part of the knowledge-building process…;

- It seems to be essential for metacognitive processes and for the understanding of children and adults.

> (Project Zero & Reggio Children, 2001: 84; emphasis in the original)

This kind of documentation can include pedagogical documentation panels, videos, photographs, observations, projections, books, written notes, narratives, portfolios and artefacts (Edwards et al., 1998; Knauf, 2017; Picchio, 2014).

Documentation and technology

Increasingly, digital technology, particularly tablets and iPads, is an integral element of documentation. There is a growing range of digital documentation programmes (see, for example, Tapestry, https://tapestry.info/) designed to provide ways of creating, storing and sharing documentation. In common with paper-based approaches, they are intended to serve a variety of functions. The portability of tablets can facilitate the capture of children's experiences in all contexts, throughout the day, which can be viewed, reviewed and reflected on many times (Flewitt & Cowan, 2019). The opportunity to share documents electronically with parents can also support connections between home and setting (Damjanovic et al., 2017). Where children also use the tablets, they can share what is meaningful to them with others, immediately and later (Damjanovic et al., 2017), and create their own documentation (Yelland, 2018).

As with paper-based documentation, this all takes time and commitment, which can be a challenge, given the pressures on practitioners' time. It can be tricky to interact with children and document at the same time (Knauf, 2017). It is also very easy to find yourself with a lot of material to look at and think about – one practitioner said it was 'difficult to know when to stop filming' (Flewitt & Cowan, 2019: 36). It is also important to consider how children themselves can be active participants in this type of documenting (Flewitt & Cowan, 2019).

Children's perspectives and children's participation

Throughout this chapter we have tried to emphasise the importance of children's participation, of hearing their authentic voices, in collecting evidence of their self-regulation. The rationale for eliciting children's perspectives on their lives has been driven by a range of forces, including a concern for children's rights, recognised and enshrined in the United Nations' *Convention on the Rights of the Child* (UNCRC) (United Nations, 1989). The kinds of photo elicitation discussions and VSRD described above and in Chapter 6, are important in their own right, but also because they foreground children's own perspectives, supporting their active participation in their own learning. In a similar way, approaches to documentation which emphasise the centrality of children's roles in both generating the documentation and in reflecting on it, support both children's self-regulation and their personal agency. In this respect, it is important to look at the advantages and drawbacks of digital documentation. On the one hand, it can provide opportunities for children to be directly involved, but, at the same time, some approaches are targeted more at practitioners and parents. In addition, it may also be less immediately accessible to children than, for example, paper-based memory books.

The rationales for children's participation include ethical as well as practical and pedagogical ones. Palaiologou suggests that we need to ask ourselves two questions, if we are to act ethically:

- How do we know that we act with children?

- How do we respect children's wishes to participate but equally not to participate?

(Palailogou, 2019: 197)

Knowing the 'answers' to these questions will be dependent partly upon children's ages. The very youngest children we work with cannot signal their wishes (or consent) to be observed in the same ways as older children, and we need to be particularly sensitive to aspects such as eye contact and gesture. When children are more orally fluent, they are able to more actively and directly participate in the generation and documentation of evidence about their thinking. As Palailogou (2019) emphasises, play can be the best context for this.

How can practitioners better observe and assess young children's self-regulation?

In this chapter, by presenting different approaches to observing and assessing self-regulation in young children, our aim is to provide an overview of how self-regulation is assessed, so that you can tailor your practice to enable you to observe self-regulation in the children in your settings. We are not suggesting that practitioners should use all of the tools we discuss. Some of them are not intended for use by practitioners in the classroom. However, using ideas from these tools, alongside the rest of the discussion here, we summarise some ideas about practitioner interactions and behaviour to support the gathering of evidence of young children's self-regulation:

- Ensure that you observe children during activities that are meaningful and interesting to them. Usually, child-initiated, playful activities provide a wealth of self-regulation evidence (Robson, 2016b, 2016c; Whitebread et al., 2005, 2007, 2009a, 2009b);

- Spend substantial periods of time observing each child carefully before you start making decisions about a child's self-regulation;

- Observe the child in different environments and playing/interacting with different peers or adults, or even by themselves (Whitebread et al., 2005, 2007, 2009b);

- Keep in mind that the environment in which a child is working/playing might have a role to play in the child's self-regulation as you observe it each time (McClelland et al., 2015). This means that you should try to make a note of the specific environment in which you observed the child each time;

- Look at the metacognitive knowledge interviews and VSRD presented above, for ideas of questions that can be used to help children to show their metacognition (e.g. How do you think you did? How did you work it out?);

- Look for ways to ensure that children are participants in observations, choosing what is looked at and discussed, selecting what and how to document their thinking;

- Always aim to listen to the child's perspective. Give them the space, time and multiple opportunities to express this.

Working with parents

The Early Years Coalition (2021) reflect long-held views in early childhood about the crucial role of parents and families in their children's lives in settings, when they emphasise that involving parents is the most significant factor in enabling children to do well despite disadvantage, with their knowledge and experience of their children 'knitted into' daily practice. Parents, grandparents and other family members have, of course, been observing their children from the moment they were born. Involving them in planning and collecting observations, both at home and in the setting, can help them to feel comfortable and valued, as well as deepening practitioners' knowledge and understanding of the children.

Flewitt and Cowan (2019) found that parents particularly appreciated documentation in all forms, and valued it as a way of keeping them informed as well as providing a lasting record of their child's time. In Reggio Emilia, for example, documentation is displayed as projects develop, giving parents opportunities to see the children's thinking in progress. Given the emphasis we have placed upon the value of visual approaches, practitioners in Flewitt and Cowan's (2019) study identified video as having valuable potential for documenting children's play, and, in sharing the video with parents, letting them know that play, a vital context for children's self-regulation, is valued.

As we noted above, digital formats can create opportunities to share documents electronically between home and setting, and some parents may find this more accessible than paper-based formats (Flewitt & Cowan, 2019). However, they also found that, whatever the format, most parents did not contribute to the documentation. This suggests that one important task is to look at reasons why this might be the case (they may be many, of course, including lack of time and lack of confidence), and try to work with families to encourage their active contribution. In the case of self-regulation, as we have already seen, there is a range of terms which may be unfamiliar to parents. This may also be a barrier to parental involvement, if they are unsure of what these mean, and what they look like in their children. Trying to ensure their understanding of these is important, if we are hoping that they will be actively involved in contributing to the observational evidence about their children.

Conclusion

In this chapter, we have focused on introducing approaches that enable practitioners and researchers to observe self-regulation in young children. Observation is central to practice when working with young children, and we have looked at two frameworks which foreground the use of observation in everyday contexts: the C.Ind.Le coding framework and the CHILD 3–5 checklist. We also look at the problems children may face when they try to self-regulate, and a framework that can help us identify difficulties in that process.

We have emphasised that in order to obtain the fullest picture of young children's self-regulation, and one which best reflects their competences, we need to know not just about what they can do by observing them, but also about their thoughts, by hearing what they say about their thinking. So, we have explored the use of metacognitive knowledge interviews, where the adult asks the child questions about their metacognitive process, alongside visual methods (such as photographs and videos) such as Video-Stimulated Reflective Dialogue (VSRD). In so doing, we have also stressed the central importance of valuing young children's own perspectives, and their active participation in evidencing and documenting their self-regulation. We see documentation in all forms as both a way of evidencing young children's self-regulation and supporting its development. In this, technology has a role to play, alongside more traditional tools. Tablets and iPads can help to make the use of visual methods and reflective dialogues much more accessible to all practitioners, and to parents. Finally, we have reviewed how parents and practitioners can work together to support observation and assessment: parents observe their children continuously and practitioners can deepen their knowledge of the children, through involving parents at all stages, and in all ways.

Key further reading

Bryce, D., & Whitebread, D. (2012). The development of metacognitive skills: Evidence from observational analysis of young children's behaviour during problem-solving. *Metacognition and Learning*, 7(3), 197–217.

Gascoine, L., Higgins, S., & Wall, K. (2017). The assessment of metacognition in children aged 4–16 years: A systematic review. *Review of Education*, 5(1), 3–57.

Marulis, L. M., & Nelson, L. J. (2021). Metacognitive processes and associations to executive function and motivation during a problem-solving task in 3–5 year olds. *Metacognition and Learning*, 16(1), 207–231.

Robson, S. (2016a). Self-regulation, metacognition and child- and adult-initiated activity: Does it matter who initiates the task? *Early Child Development and Care*, 186(5), 764–784.

Robson, S. (2016c). Are there differences between children's display of self-regulation and metacognition when engaged in an activity and when later reflecting on it?: The complementary roles of observation and reflective dialogue. *Early Years*, 36(2), 179–194.

Whitebread, D., Coltman, P., Pasternak, D. P., Sangster, C., Grau, V., Bingham, S., …, Demetriou, D. (2009b). The development of two observational tools for assessing metacognition and self-regulated learning in young children. *Metacognition and Learning*, 4(1), 63–85.

6 Communication and language for self-regulation

In this chapter, we look at:

- The links between oral language and self-regulation;

- Gesture and self-regulation;

- Talking to ourselves: private speech;

- Talking about feeling, thinking and knowing;

- Narrative and pretend play;

- Social contexts for talk which supports self-regulation;

- What practitioners can do to support self-regulation through communication and talk;

- Working with parents to support the development of self-regulation through communication and talk.

Keywords: talk, gesture, private speech, narrative, pretend play, metacommunication.

Introduction

The ability to use language to communicate, and to make sense of our experiences, is uniquely human. Though, as Fernyhough (2008) points out, it is not just the fact that we can communicate in this way which separates us from other animals; it is what that language allows us to do. For Vygotsky (1978: 125), 'thought is not merely expressed in words, it comes into existence through them', and, crucially, it provides us with a way of sharing those thoughts with others, in a process which Littleton and Mercer (2013) call 'interthinking'. This sharing begins in the earliest moments of life, in the early 'protoconversations' (Trevarthen, 1995) that babies have with their carers, which bring together gesture, eye contact and speech sounds in a joint endeavour to communicate and connect with one another.

The focus of this chapter is on communication and oral language, which underpin all areas of young children's learning and development (Department for Education [DfE], England, 2021). This includes communication with others, but also communication with the self – and how this can support young children's self-regulation. In particular, the place of what is called 'private speech' is explored, along with the ways in which talk about feelings and thoughts can support and develop young children's self-regulation. Narrative and pretend play, social contexts, and the roles of practitioners are also looked at for the vital part they play in supporting young children's self-regulation through talk. Much of the chapter concentrates on spoken language, but we also look at the role of gesture and embodied cognition in self-regulation.

Talk and self-regulation

Are there particular features of language which help young children to develop their self-regulatory skills and knowledge? The work of Vygotsky has been hugely influential in our understanding of the relationship between self-regulation and language. In his view, language is the pre-eminent tool for young children's development of control of behaviour (behavioural self-regulation) and cognition (cognitive self-regulation) (Vygotsky, 1962). In the years since his work first came to be known outside his native Russia, many others have looked at this relationship, and there is good evidence to show that, among other things, language is central to the development of young children's social understanding, and hence their theory of mind (see Chapters 1 and 2) (Goswami, 2008). In addition, there is an association between language skills in general and self-regulation (Vallotton & Ayoub, 2011). It is useful to bear in mind that gender may have an influence here, with girls ready to use language as a tool for self-regulation earlier than boys (Lagattuta et al., 1997; Vallotton & Ayoub, 2011).

WHAT DOES POLICY TELL US?

Development Matters: non-statutory curriculum guidance for the early years foundation stage

In *Development Matters*, the non-statutory guidance Early Years Foundation Stage (EYFS) in England, self-regulation is identified as one of seven 'key features of effective practice', and the role of language is emphasised:

> *Language development is central to self-regulation: children use language to guide their actions and plans.*

(Department for Education, England, 2020b: 11)

The importance of gesture and movement

Before we look at these ideas in more detail, it is helpful to look at the part played by non-verbal communication, particularly gesture, in support of self-regulation. Piaget's earliest developmental stage, the sensorimotor stage, describes how, in his view, very young children come to know about the world by the physical acts, including gestures, which they can perform (Piaget, 1950). For Piaget, this is a stage that children develop out of, but in recent years there has been more emphasis on the idea that gesture, and embodied cognition, remain important for cognition, and higher-level thinking processes such as self-regulation, throughout life. Gabbard (2015: 229) believes that 'cognitive processes, including thinking, are deeply grounded in our bodily interactions with the environment'.

Gesture and self-regulation

What is the evidence that gesture can aid self-regulation? Perhaps a useful starting point is to look at the ways in which we typically use gesture when we talk to one another. Watch most people and it is clear that they accompany their talk with gestures that seem to play a range of roles: supporting explanations, engaging others, highlighting ideas and feelings, and even facilitating the processing of oral language (Wilson & Foglia, 2015). Gestures that accompany speech can support working memory, an important element of executive function (Wilson & Foglia, 2015). Hattie and Yates conclude that:

> when students use their hands as they speak, their understanding of what they are saying can move to a deeper level, and their overall performance on academic tasks can be enhanced.

(Hattie & Yates, 2014: 141)

Importantly, however, there is clear evidence that gesture also supports self-regulation independent of talk. This can be the case when children are already competent speakers. For example, O'Neill and Miller (2013) found that in a sorting task looking at executive function in children aged between 2.5 and 6 years, the children who gestured more were more accurate and efficient when shifting to a new sorting rule. It may also be that very young children, who are not yet skilled talkers, use gesture as a tool for thought in much the same way as their older peers use speech (Kuhn et al., 2014). In a study with children aged 14–18 months, Basilio and Rodriguez (2017) found that all of the children used gestures and non-verbal means to regulate both their actions and their behaviour, including important self-regulatory processes such as planning, monitoring, controlling and evaluating what they did. These gestures were used to communicate with their parents, but they also seemed to be used for more personal purposes, to 'think' in gestures, perhaps as precursors to private speech, which we look at later in this chapter.

What goes for gesture may also be the same for other body movement. Gesture accompanied by body movements can help with remembering (Aranda & Tytler, 2017), and activities such as problem-solving (Gabbard, 2015), and the physical nature of acting out socio-dramatic play themes can have a positive effect on young children's memory for stories (Lillard et al., 2013).

OBSERVING GESTURE AND SELF-REGULATION: ASHLEY

This extract from a discussion between Ashley and Adult S shows some of the ways in which gesture is related to self-regulation. Ashley's talk and gestures provide examples of her metacognitive knowledge (about the task, and about her own and Adult S's knowledge) and metacognitive regulation (particularly planning, strategy use and controlling the activity).

Before the discussion, Ashley (5.0) and her friend Suhani had been playing a treasure map game involving coordinates:

Later that day Ashley and Adult S watch a video recording of the game. Ashley explains to Adult S what they were doing:

(Continued)

OBSERVING GESTURE AND SELF-REGULATION: ASHLEY *continued*

ASHLEY: Yes, we need a map (gesturing with hands held out in front of her). So, you know when I played that game when I win I just flicked the coin (looks at Adult S, smiling, gestures 'flicking' with hand).

ADULT S: Right.

ASHLEY: (smiling) Um, we have to have a piece of paper, like that (points to paper on table in front of her), and because this is my piece of paper with squares on it ('draws' square shape in the air with fingers), and, um, we need a cover, um, like that book (looks at video and points at book standing up) so you can't see. Um, if they see that means they will know what it is (claps hands together and holds them against her chest).

Ashley begins by explaining what is needed for the game – her comment 'we need a map' and her gesture representing a 'map' shape show her memory and knowledge of the task, key aspects of self-regulation. She follows this with a flicking gesture to accompany her words, which not only shows her knowledge of a strategy for playing the game, but also demonstrates her awareness that this gesture may help adult A to better understand what she did. Her next comment, that they needed a piece of paper 'like that', and the accompanying pointing gesture, demonstrates her understanding of planning for the activity, and the resources needed. Her gestures of 'drawing' a square, and pointing at the book in the video, are ones which she seems to know will help Adult A understand what she and Suhani were doing, and demonstrate her metacognitive knowledge. Throughout, her gestures match her talk, and in places are used to further explain her points.

What can practitioners do to support gesture and movement for self-regulation?

The implication of what we have already talked about here is the value of encouraging young children to use gesture and body movements as they engage in activities. Goldin-Meadow (2015) highlights the value of parents and practitioners supporting gesture in babyhood and early childhood in support of spoken vocabulary. Differences in the size of children's spoken vocabulary are already well established before children begin school, with children and family socioeconomic status (SES) being a particular factor (Goldin-Meadow, 2015). Practitioners can support the acquisition of children's oral vocabulary, and more complex linguistic constructions such as sentence use, by focusing on an early-developing skill like gesture use, and by encouraging parents to do the same.

Children may also be more daring or creative in their gestures than they might be with their speech (Claxton, 2012), and gestures can sometimes reveal more knowledge and understanding than children's words alone may do (Elia & Evangelou, 2014). Claxton (2012: 81) suggests that practitioners who are more sensitive to the kinds of meanings children are making as their gesture may be 'more likely to sense when a student is on the cusp of learning something new, and to intervene productively'.

Gesture and movement may be particularly valuable in working with children with special educational needs. Using, and modelling, gesture can be an invaluable tool for practitioners and parents with all children, but particularly those whose use of gesture is limited as a result of a specific need. Goldin-Meadow (2015) identifies two key ways in which gesture is valuable in working with children with potential language delay, for example. First, she suggests, practitioners can be looking to see whether a child is producing gestures in a timely fashion, similar to their peers. This can serve as a diagnostic tool for pinpointing subsequent difficulties with spoken language, given the links we know there are between gesture and oral language. Second, as we have seen, gesture can facilitate oral language learning, and is thus a valuable tool for intervention. This is valuable in itself, but as we shall see below, oral language is a vital element of self-regulation, and identifying potential language delay can also help practitioners to be alert to the possible difficulties children may face in developing and displaying self-regulation, and to look at how to intervene in order to support them.

Practitioners' own use of gestures in their interactions with children can be very valuable in supporting the development of self-regulation. One important area is memory, a vital aspect of self-regulation. So et al. (2012), for example, found that 4–5-year-olds were more likely to remember the word 'stack' if the practitioner made a 'stacking' gesture with his hands when saying the word, rather than if he used the word alone. In a review of research, Novack and Goldin-Meadow (2015) suggest that teachers' gestures can also lead to increased gesturing in children. They suggest that practitioners' gestures can guide children's attention and scaffold verbal information:

- Gesture can support learning when children *see* a teacher gesture during instruction without making gestures of their own;

- Seeing gesture can support children's learning in the absence of physical objects;

- Including gesture with speech can enhance learning. For example, toddlers are more likely to learn the concept of 'under' if the practitioner uses speech and gesture rather than just words or pictures;

- Including gesture with speech allows practitioners to provide children with multiple strategies *at the same time*, for example, presenting two useful strategies for an activity, one in speech and another in gesture.

The importance of parents' use of gestures: how toddlers think with their hands – social and private gestures as evidence of cognitive self-regulation in guided play with objects

We looked earlier at the evidence from this study about the importance of children's own gestures for their developing self-regulation. This study also found that adults' uses of gestures are valuable.

Sixteen children attending Early Years Schools in Madrid, Spain, were video-recorded at the ages of 14, 16 and 18 months engaging in a) independent play where parents sat next to their child and did not intervene, and b) guided play, in which parents were instructed to 'play with the child and help him/her to use the toy (a shape sorter or wooden hammer toy) by him/herself'.

They found that a range of parent actions, including demonstrating actions using the objects in their play and being responsive to their children's gestures, supported children's self-regulation. They conclude that:

Self-regulatory skills, which are crucial for school readiness and later educational attainment, seem to emerge and be influenced by parental mediation very early in life.

(Basilio & Rodriguez, 2017: 1984)

Private speech: talking to ourselves

Children (and adults!) often talk to themselves as they go about their lives. When Piaget (1959) looked at this he concluded that, when young children did engage in self-talk, this was an unsuccessful attempt at social speech, which had had no effect on their thinking. Vygotsky came to a very different conclusion. In his view, young children's self-talk is an instrument of thought. Rather than Piaget's egocentric speech, this talk is what Vygotsky (1962) calls private speech, and it plays a crucial role in young children's developing self-regulation. For Vygotsky, the interpersonal process of talking with others helps children in developing their understanding of the world. In this, they are essentially being regulated by others. They then gradually learn to use talk for themselves, intrapersonally, as self-commentary (private speech). This private speech is eventually verbalised internally, becoming silent, inner speech, and signifying the ability to fully self-regulate. This view is very much supported by research carried out since Piaget and Vygotsky were formulating their ideas in the

1920s and 1930s (Fernyhough, 2008; Mead & Winsler, 2015) and strengthens the idea that private speech is critical to the development of self-regulation.

Private speech peaks in early childhood (Elias & Berk, 2002), but it is still evident in older children, and in adults, particularly when an activity is new, or the context is challenging, either cognitively or emotionally (Mead & Winsler, 2015). Think about when you first set up a new mobile phone: you probably find you are muttering to yourself, thinking aloud and rehearsing what needs to be done. The kind of self-commentary that children engage in as they play and work may include comments and questions about what they are doing, descriptions, remarks aimed at self-encouragement and supporting concentration, and clarifying one's thinking, all of which can help to regulate both thoughts and behaviour. It may also not just be talk. In a Reception class in England, Taber (aged 5), for example, accompanied his time at the computer with song. Playing a game he knew well, he sang confidently and loudly, nodding his head in time as he did so. When he started a new, more challenging game, his singing slowed significantly, and was quieter, but still formed a running commentary to his actions.

What is so important about private speech?

Private speech may have a number of advantages for young children. These are set out in Figure 6.1. These features are advantageous for all, but they may be particularly important for children who typically have more difficulty developing aspects of self-regulation such as behavioural control and executive functioning. Among these are children with attention deficit hyperactivity disorder (ADHD) and autism spectrum disorder (ASD). Encouraging and supporting private speech with children with ADHD and ASD may be valuable in supporting their self-regulation, and in helping them to internalise their speech, and develop inner speech (Mead & Winsler, 2015).

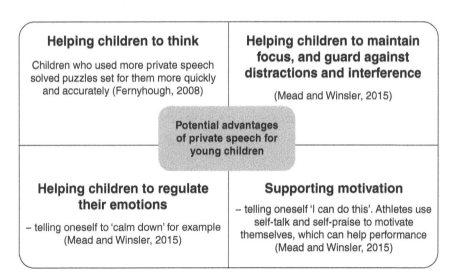

Figure 6.1   Potential advantages of private speech for young children

What is the role of practitioners in young children's private speech?

Perhaps the most important thing adults can do is to support and encourage young children to talk to themselves – the evidence is that such talk may not be disturbing to others, unless it is very loud (Mead & Winsler, 2015). The kinds of self-scaffolding which private speech affords children may be invaluable. Lambert (2005), for example, concludes that self-talk as children draw and paint can help them in thinking in more abstract, sophisticated ways. Asking children to be very quiet can even have a negative effect on their performance (Mead & Winsler, 2015). In the *Tools of the Mind* curriculum (Bodrova & Leong, 2006), children are particularly encouraged to use private speech when they are learning new things, or when they encounter challenge.

Diagnostically, listening to young children's private speech can be very helpful for practitioners. As we have seen, private speech may be most prevalent when activities are at an appropriate level of challenge for children, and this can be a useful indicator that planning is appropriate. In addition, listening to young children's self-commentary can reveal aspects of their thinking that either observation, or looking at a 'product' may not. Think, for example, of the ways in which children talk to themselves as they draw and paint. These representations often change and evolve, with ideas developed as the activity progresses, and new meanings made. Coates and Coates (2015) highlight how the self-talk children engage in as they draw and paint can shape their thinking and mark-making, as well as reflecting it.

Child-initiated and adult-directed activities and private speech

Are there also particular contexts which are helpful for supporting and max-imising children's self-regulation through their self-talk? Both adult-directed and child-initiated activities can be rich contexts for private speech (Robson, 2016a), but open-ended activities including construction, problem-solving, and particu-larly pretend play, may be especially valuable (Krafft & Berk, 1998; Whitebread, 2012). More closed-ended, highly teacher-directed activities can often be asso-ciated with less private speech (Krafft & Berk, 1998), possibly because children hand over more control to adults, and there is less need for *self*-regulation at such times. However, what may be important is the level of teacher direction: Winsler and Diaz (1995) found that an 'intermediate' level of practitioner direction – neither very little nor very high – actually maximised levels of private speech. Robson (2016b) found little difference between the levels of private speech regardless of whether adults were present (but not necessarily directing an activity) or absent. All of this suggests that what may be most important for private speech, as in other aspects of practice, is careful consideration by prac-titioners about the roles they take up, and their interactions with young children. The activity below explores some of the things we might look for in young chil-dren's private speech in practice.

Observe children using private speech as they play, and try to find examples of the different uses identified earlier, in helping children to:

- think;
- maintain focus;
- regulate their emotions;
- motivate themselves.

    1. Do you see some of these more than others?
    2. Do different children use self-talk in different ways?
    3. Do you see it as helpful to them?

Talking about feeling, thinking and knowing

In order to talk about our feelings and thoughts, we all need to have the vocabulary to do so, and this acquisition of language about the mind, and about mental and emotional states, is vital for the development of both theory of mind, and meta-cognition, a fundamental aspect of self-regulation. Metacognition means 'thinking about thinking': putting those thoughts about our thinking into words, in both private speech and in dialogue with others, requires us to have the right tools – the words – to do so.

When do children begin to talk about their feelings and thoughts?

Children's exposure to talk about mental and emotional states begins long before they are able to use such vocabulary for themselves. Meins (1999) describes how mothers who are 'mind-minded', that is, they talk both *about* and *with* their children using mental state terms such as 'know' and 'try', can be important for secure attachment, but also for scaffolding very young children's early growth of understanding that mental states underlie behaviour, and that these can be talked about. Degotardi (2015) suggests that practitioners' mind-mindedness also plays a vital part in this process of children's developing understanding of the mind. For example, in helping young children to resolve conflicts in their play, practitioners who encourage perspective-taking in children, using terms that relate to emotional states – 'how would you feel if...' – may be helping children to develop emotional and social self-regulation (Bingham & Whitebread, 2009).

Children themselves start using language that refers to feelings and desires – happy, sad, want – sometime during their second year, and by the time they are 2 they are using these kinds of terms in ways that show they are aware that these are mental states (Bartsch & Wellman, 1995). This talk about feelings seems to be important both for itself and in supporting children's later talk about cognitive states such as thinking and knowing.

As with other aspects of language, girls may outperform boys (Lagattuta et al., 1997), possibly because parents may talk about emotions more with daughters than sons. Looking at the type of emotion expression, girls may be more likely to express positive emotions such as happiness and surprise. Boys, on the other hand, may be more likely to express negative emotions such as anger (Chaplin, 2015). Chaplin believes that these differences emerge as a result of a combination of factors – biological difference (girls tend to have greater language capability earlier than boys), socialisation, and the influence of 'in-the-moment social context and societal expectations within a culture' (Chaplin, 2015: 16). This last factor may be especially important to think about: while there may be some general gender differences, the expectations and practices of the particular social and cultural contexts children grow up in will also influence their acquisition and use of the language of feelings. All of this makes it important that practitioners ensure that they are sensitive to these potential differences, and that they are also using emotion-rich talk (of both positive and negative emotions) with boys and girls.

Talk about cognitive states typically develops by the age of about three years (Bretherton & Beeghly, 1982). Most common are words such as 'know' (including 'I don't know'), 'remember', 'forget', 'think' and 'understand', but development of children's knowledge and use of terms continues throughout childhood and into adolescence.

OBSERVING TALK ABOUT KNOWING AND THINKING: SAFI AND SOHAL

Safi (5.5) has led this self-chosen activity. He has been wrapping a small cardboard box in paper. His best friend, Sohal (5.2), is following his lead, but he is not as competent at it. At this point in the observation, Safi is trying to help Sohal wrap his box. He tries to decide how to place and fold the paper around. He scrunches ends, adjusts positioning, then the box falls out of his grasp.

(Continued)

SAFI: Aah! Ooh, ah! (picks box up and holds it up to Sohal) you can leave it like this.

Sohal shakes his head.

SAFI: Okay, I know what to do.

Sohal leans over and flattens the paper, smoothing it with his hand.

SAFI: (starts to walk over to the shelves, dancing backwards and forwards, hand on his chin, then puts his hand up in the air) I know! (turns round, and repeats the dancing) I know! I know! (laughing).

Sohal watches.

Safi walks back to the table, shaking the box and talking.

Sohal picks the box up and stands it on the table.

SOHAL: How about if I do this – let me do this.

Safi picks up his own box, and, talking to himself, unwraps it completely.

SOHAL: (picks up a pen and starts writing on his box with it) It's easy Safi (looking up at Safi) See what you need to do.

Safi: (walking over to look at Sohal's box) I don't know, I don't know where.

At the age of five, Safi and Sohal clearly understand and can use vocabulary that describes their mental states. They also seem to appreciate that other people's mental states are different to their own, as they try to explain ideas to one another. Safi, in particular, confidently uses 'know', along with 'I don't know', two of the commonest and earliest terms children use. Interestingly, he also uses a gesture, putting his hand up in the air, to signal and accompany 'I know', as if to emphasise his point. Safi also uses the word 'can': 'you can leave it like this'.

Sohal's statements also show his understanding. He speculates to Safi, using 'do': 'How about if I do this – let me do this', along with 'need': 'See what you need to do'. His use of the word 'easy' here also suggests he is making a judgement about the activity.

How can practitioners support talk about mental and emotional states?

Practitioners are ideally placed to support the development of children's emotional and mental state vocabulary in a number of ways, including encouraging perspective-taking, as we saw earlier. They can also use and model it themselves. Engaging children in conversation and language games that involve mental and emotional state terms can help children to understand the meanings of the words being used. In a study with children aged 3–5 years, Grazzani Gavazzi and Ornaghi (2011) found that this was particularly valuable for the children aged four and over, probably because their conversational skills were well developed, and because they already had some understanding of the existence of mental states in both them-selves and others. Making opportunities to talk about and reflect with children on what they have been doing, for example focusing on metacognitive terms – 'what have you learnt?', 'what made you think that?', 'that was good thinking' – can help this process of becoming more aware of the language of feeling and thinking, and support children's understanding of talk as a powerful tool for thinking (Littleton & Mercer, 2013). It may be especially helpful for developing and observing children's metacognitive knowledge (Robson, 2016c).

Narratives and pretend play

The Early Years Foundation Stage (DfE, 2021) highlights both story and role play as significant contexts in which children can share ideas, and develop both their vocabulary and repertoire of language structures. In the context of self-regulation, narratives, both written and oral, and pretend play are particularly valuable resources.

Stories often feature mental state vocabulary, as well as providing opportunities for practitioners to discuss events in the story, and aspects such as why a character has behaved the way they did. This kind of 'dialogic' reading can help children to develop their own narrative skills, and use of mental state language (Lever & Sénéchal, 2011). Likewise, children's own narratives provide opportunities for them to develop internal state language, and to think about things from another per-son's perspective. Curenton and Gardner-Neblett (2015) highlight the strong oral narrative traditions in African culture, and the ways in which, as a result of their exposure to oral traditions at home, African-ancestral children may use internal state vocabulary like want, need, scared and know, before their European heritage peers. These narratives may not only be oral. There are, for example, an increasing number of narrative digital apps. Fleer (2017) found that the creation of narratives on a tablet led to perspective-taking on the part of the children.

Finally, practitioners can support play in which children use the terms as part of their play. Think, for example, of the ways in which talk about feelings and thoughts proliferates in shared pretend play, as children talk about roles and negotiate ideas. This aspect is looked at in more detail in Chapter 7, but it is useful to highlight the role of language here. Dockett (1998) draws a distinction between two types of language use in socio-dramatic play:

- pretend communication – children's talk in role. Children take on another person's ways of speaking, tone of voice, even vocabulary, demonstrating their ability to take on another's perspective, and to think about how that person might act, and what they might say.

- metacommunication – children's talk about the play – 'let's pretend you're a mummy and you're happy I'm here', 'put the dog's bowl under the table'.

These messages help co-players to know 'this is pretend', and demonstrate children's ability to put themselves in another's place, to understand that their thoughts about the play may be different, and to create shared meanings.

Bredikyte and Hakkarainen (2017) argue that this kind of social role play is the best space for developing young children's self-regulation. The playworlds approach, which we first looked at in Chapter 2, is underpinned by the idea of adult facilitation in creating an imaginary world, in which the players develop shared ideas and co-construct a storyline together. Bredikyte and Hakkarainen (2017) outline different types of adult support at different ages:

- 'At the beginning of the play age (around 2–3 years)' – adult initiative in modelling play behaviours;

- Between 3 and 5 years – children's own initiative is crucial. The adult has a secondary role, as a play partner, helping to co-construct a storyline and implementing children's ideas;

- After 5 years – children are independent players and the adult observes and supports, enriching and supporting symbolic thinking.

(Adapted from Bredikyte & Hakkarainen, 2017: 249–250)

It is, though, important to bear in mind that the outcomes will not be the same for all children. As with other perspective-taking capabilities, children with ASD may behave atypically, more rarely engaging in pretend play, particularly shared pretence, than other children. Douglas and Stirling (2012) believe that this has its roots in the impairments in social cognition characteristic of ASD. In particular, areas of metacommunication difficulty for children with ASD can be an understanding that you need to clearly signal that you want to engage in pretend play, and also need to clearly articulate your ideas to negotiate the pretence, as well as understanding that shared pretence is a joint activity in which your ideas need to be shared with others.

TALK IN NARRATIVE AND PRETEND PLAY FOR SUPPORTING SELF-REGULATION: VIVIAN GUSSIN PALEY

Vivian Gussin Paley is particularly associated with the use of children's own narratives and their fantasy play in ways which support their thinking. She explains:

'Let's pretend' was a stronger glue than any preplanned list of topics, and the need to make friends, assuage jealousy, and gain a sense of one's own destiny provided better reasons for self-control than all my disciplinary devices.

(Paley, 1986: 124)

(Continued)

Her approach embodies a routine of children telling their stories to the practitioner, and these then forming the basis of co-constructed narratives, acted out by the children. Underpinning many of these are three themes of friendship, fairness and fantasy. In this extract from *Wally's Stories*, Paley is asking the children about Wally's lion story, and his comment that he is going to be a mother lion when he grows up:

Eddie and Lisa are in the doll corner when I bring up the subject. 'Wally has decided to become a lion when he grows up'. They look up and laugh hesitantly. 'He intends to learn magic', I add.

> 'Oh, that way', says Eddie. 'It depends how hard he studies. That's the hardest thing to do'.
> 'It's impossible', Lisa argues. 'You can't turn into a lion. That's too big. Maybe a mouse or a cat'. She pauses. 'But he can dress up to look like a lion'.
> I turn to Earl. 'Do you suppose a boy could become a mother?'
> 'He can put on a dress and a wig', Earl answers.

(Paley, 1981: 8)

Astington (1994) believes that, in Paley's comments on the children's narratives, her use of words and expressions *about* thinking – 'oh, I think I know what reminded you of that' or 'are you wondering … ?', is important. She comments:

> In Paley's classroom the talk is not just about things in the world, it is also about the children's thoughts about things in the world.

(Astington, 1994: 185)

Talking about thinking and feeling: reflective dialogues

In Chapter 5, we look at the idea of reflective, or metacognitive, dialogues, as a tool for observing and assessing self-regulation. Here it is useful to think about them as a tool for encouraging and supporting self-regulation, through their very explicit focus on thoughts and feelings. The starting point is a dialogue between a child, or children, and an adult, usually about something the children have done. The focus is on thoughts and feelings, and the children's reflections on these, and on what they know about themselves as learners and thinkers. The dialogue may or may not use aids such as photographs or video material. Wall and Higgins (2006) have also used cartoons which feature a number of templates of classroom life – a group activity, circle time, individual activity – and include empty speech and thought bubbles. Practitioners and children discuss an activity the children have been engaged in, and the ideas discussed are recorded in the bubbles.

In these reflective dialogues, questions such as 'How would you go about teaching other people all you have learned about…' (Pramling, 1988: 271) or 'What do you think was the best idea you had?' can help children to become more consciously aware of their own thinking. These kinds of dialogues can be particularly valuable for the development of young children's metacognitive knowledge, and their expressions of emotional and motivational regulation (Robson, 2016c). They can also help to support children in reflecting on their knowledge. One afternoon, watching a video in which he was trying to retrieve a ball from the low roof over an outdoor area, Safi (age 5.2) pointed at the screen and said 'That's how I couldn't do it!'.

This kind of reflective dialogue can provide children with opportunities to comment and reflect on their own, and others', knowledge and feelings, and features such as strategy use, that are not as evident during the hurly burly of engaging with the activity itself. Look back at the observation earlier in this chapter of Ashley and her account of the coordinates game during a reflective dialogue. Ashley's verbal commentary is rich with evidence of her metacognitive knowledge and regulation. The evidence is that the more children engage with this kind of activity, the richer the talk about their thinking and learning becomes (Robson, 2016c). Look at the activity below, as a way of exploring young children's (and practitioners'!) use of words about mental and emotional states.

ACTIVITY: ENCOURAGING TALK ABOUT MENTAL AND EMOTIONAL STATES

We have looked at the importance of young children's talk about mental and emotional states for their developing self-regulation, and at some of the earliest terms children start using, such as:

happy, sad, think, know, remember, forget.

1. Think now, and discuss with colleagues, what other words would be helpful here, for example, what about words like idea, guess, believe, imagine and pretend?

2. Look for opportunities to use these words with children, and try to observe and record whether children start using these words more in their play and talk. Are they using them with an understanding of their meaning?

Social contexts for talk

The importance of social context is looked at in more detail in Chapters 4 and 8, but here we look in particular at the way in which talk in these contexts plays a vital part in the development of young children's self-regulation. Social interactions, involving talk and communication between children and adults, and between children and children, are central to the development of self-regulation (Vygotsky, 1978).

Talk between adults and children

We have looked throughout this chapter at the importance of dialogue and discussion between adults and children, for children's perspective-taking, for their understanding of internal states, and for their understanding of themselves as thinkers and knowers. Practitioners with a positive interaction style have also been shown to use more metacognitive language with young children (Frampton et al., 2009).

GUIDANCE FROM THE EARLY YEARS SECTOR: BIRTH TO 5 MATTERS (2021)

Birth to 5 Matters was developed by the Early Years Coalition to support practitioner in implementing the EYFS. The guidance on self-regulation acknowledges the vital role of practitioners in talking with children about thoughts and feelings:

> *For young children, co-regulation also has both emotional and cognitive aspects. It includes the adult modelling calming strategies and naming and talking about feelings and ways to manage. This helps children learn to recognise their feelings and builds their cognitive awareness of strategies to reduce or manage extremes of emotion. At the same time, adults scaffold cognitive self-regulation by talking with children about thinking and learning.*

> (Early Years Coalition, 2021: 20)

Ideas such as 'interthinking', with its emphasis on collective thinking processes and exploratory talk, put practitioners in the role of co-regulator, gradually supporting children's move to self-regulation through their talk and communication (Littleton & Mercer, 2013). This has similarities with Sustained Shared Thinking (SST), a term developed during the Researching Effective Pedagogy in the Early Years (REPEY) project (Siraj-Blatchford et al., 2002) to describe interactions in pre-school settings that are effective in sharing thinking, and which contribute to the development of higher order thinking. They identify the types of adult–child interaction which support SST, including:

- *Scaffolding* to extend children's knowledge and understanding through the use of strategies such as open-ended questioning;

- *Extending* by making a suggestion that helps a child to see other possibilities;

- *Discussing* which supports the interchange of information or ideas;

- *Modelling* which includes demonstration of activities and verbal commentary from the adult;

- *Playing* when the adult uses humour or plays with a child.

Sylva et al. (2010) found that episodes of SST happened most often in talk between a child and an adult, or between an adult and a child pair. The larger the group, the more likely it was that adult talk would be monitoring, or directly teaching, leaving fewer opportunities for children to extend their thinking. SST is included in the Sustained Shared Thinking and Emotional Well-being (SSTEW) Scale, and also includes non-verbal interactions, particularly between adults and young children and babies, or children with English as an additional language (Siraj et al., 2015).

WHAT DOES RESEARCH TELL US?

Making learning visible: the role of language in the development of metacognition and self-regulation in young children

The aim of the Children Articulating Thinking (ChAT) project was to see whether young children's (5–6-year-olds) self-regulated learning could be enhanced, not by direct teaching but by supporting their ability to use talk productively in group problem-solving activities, and to articulate their thinking. Practitioners began by introducing key talk vocabulary, like 'agree', 'take turns' and 'negotiate', and modelled this in their talk with children, in role play and using puppets. Then, building on the work of Mercer and the *Thinking Together* approach (2000), they devised 'rules for talk' with the children, including ideas like taking turns to speak, listening to one another, and trying to agree. They also used metacognitive vocabulary like 'think', 'describe', 'explain', 'learning' and 'know', and encouraged the children to use these as they cooperated together in an activity.

What did they find?

- All of the children's self-regulatory skills were improved;

- The biggest improvements in self-regulatory skills were made by a child who was assessed initially as having low self-regulation;

- The more that children engaged in discussions together that encouraged their shared thinking and use of strategies and rules for talk, the higher the quality of their dialogues became.

(Whitebread et al., 2015)

In 2019, the Education Endowment Foundation looked at other research in this area (a 'meta-analysis' of research) and concluded that dialogic interventions like *ChAT* and *Thinking Together*, with their emphasis on spoken language and verbal interaction, consistently show positive impact on learning.

Talk between children

What about talk and interactions between children? Playing and working together can provide important opportunities for children to learn self-regulating behaviour by observing and talking with others. Children engaged in an activity as a pair or in a small group, unsupervised by adults, may use talk that shows more diverse expressions of task and strategy knowledge (Robson, 2016a), and more meta-cognitive monitoring and control (Whitebread et al., 2007). If the children are interacting not just *in* a group but *as* a group, in a collaborative activity, there may be further benefits. Working together can reduce the 'thinking' load for individual children, as well as supporting the development of a collective awareness of metacognitive strategies, as children negotiate in an activity (Larkin, 2015).

As we noted in Chapter 4, explaining an activity to another child, and talking them through it, can involve children in using more metacognitive knowledge than if they just describe what they did (Desautel, 2009). Siegler and Lin (2010) found that 4- and 5-year-old children also benefitted more from explaining other people's answers in a task than explaining their own, and that explaining both why correct answers were correct and incorrect ones were incorrect was better for learning than only explaining correct answers.

What can practitioners do to support young children's self-regulation through communication?

Throughout this chapter we have looked at implications for adults working with young children. Importantly, Whitebread (2012) concludes that self-regulation can be taught and learnt through the kinds of social interactions involving talk that we have looked at throughout. It is useful to summarise and add to the implications for practitioners here:

- Encourage children's use of gesture and body movement to aid their thinking, and use gestures yourself;

- Encourage children's self-talk and private speech – 'Talking out loud helps young children to think better' (Fernyhough, 2008: 106);

- Be alert to the need to particularly support private speech in children with ADHD and ASD (Mead & Winsler, 2015);

- Listen closely to children's private speech as a useful guide to how they are thinking about things, and how challenging an activity might be;

- Think about how and when to get involved in what children are doing. Being nearby rather than leading can be a support to children in talking things through, and may encourage children to support one another (McInnes et al., 2010; Robson & Rowe, 2012);

- Encourage perspective-taking in children to help them to become aware of others' thoughts and feelings;

- Model mental and emotional state vocabulary and metacognitive language, to support children in becoming more consciously aware of their thinking;

- Look at the potential which contexts such as stories and narratives, problem-solving and pretend play have for children to use mental and emotional state vocabulary, and to take the perspective of others;

- Support children with ASD in engaging in pretend play, developing their understanding of shared pretence as a joint activity, and their skills in articulating their ideas (Douglas & Stirling, 2012);

- Look at the potential of child-initiated activities (often where adults are not involved) for children's private speech, greater diversity of expressions of task and strategy knowledge, and joint communication between children (Robson, 2016a);

- Provide for and encourage collaborative activities in which children have opportunities to talk with peers about their thinking, and to be reflective about their learning;

- Give children enough time to think about and make comments in group talk;

- Invite children to comment on each other's ideas;

- Encourage children to explain a task or activity to another child (Desautel, 2009; Palincsar & Brown, 1984);

- Make time to revisit and review children's activities and ideas with them, using dialogue, and prompts like photographs and video (Robson, 2016c);

- Encourage children to self-evaluate (Carr, 2011);

- When giving children feedback, emphasise processes, strategy use, and perseverance, which can help support children's self-efficacy and emotional and motivational regulation (Zimmerman, 1994).

HOW DOES THIS RELATE TO POLICY?

Statutory Framework for the early years foundation stage: Setting the standards for learning, development and care for children from birth to 5

Many of the implications for practice identified here also reflect key elements of the Early Learning Goals for Communication and Language in England, and can be helpful in identifying evidence of children's competence. These include:

(Continued)

ELG: Listening, Attention and Understanding

Children at the expected level of development will:

- Listen attentively and respond to what they hear with relevant questions, comments and actions...;

- Make comments about what they have heard and ask questions to clarify their understanding;

- Hold conversation engaged in back-and-forth exchanges with their teacher and peers.

ELG: Speaking

Children at the expected level of development will:

- Participate in small group, class and one-to-one discussions, offering their own ideas, using recently introduced vocabulary;

- Offer explanations for why things might happen...;

- Express their ideas and feelings about their experiences ... with modelling and support from their teacher.

(Extracts from DfE, 2021: 11)

Working with parents

We have seen earlier the value of parents' use of gestures, and their responsiveness to their own toddlers' use of gestures, as important supports for the emergence of self-regulation. In addition, there seems to be a lot of evidence which points to the use of gesture by practitioners, for children's conceptual understanding, and their ability to attend to strategies for dealing with things. So, encouraging parents to use gestures, with their children, and to continue doing so, both accompanying speech and also by themselves, will be valuable.

Many of the suggestions here for practitioners in supporting young children's talk are valuable in working with parents. Family life is rich in opportunities for conflict resolution, often between siblings, meaning that parental encouragement to think about how someone else might feel can happen readily. As well as this, practitioners can emphasise the value of talking with children, and reflecting on, something they have done, focusing on terms that explore thoughts and feelings. We have also seen the role played by narrative in developing young children's self-regulation. In settings it is useful to identify picture books that may be particularly valuable, which can be used with the children, as well as lent out for home use. Think, for example, of books in which two different narratives may be happening at the same time, one in the pictures and one in the text, and the opportunities this gives for discussion about the characters' thoughts and ideas. In John Burningham's 'Come away from the water, Shirley', for example, Shirley's thoughts about what is happening on her day at the seaside are contrasted in pictures with the reality, giving rise to rich opportunities to think and talk about Shirley's thinking.

Conclusion

Communication – in all forms – is central to the development of young children's self-regulation. In this chapter we have looked at the ways in which verbal and non-verbal communication can support this development. We have seen how valuable it can be to pay close attention to the gestures and movements that children make, both as a way of 'seeing' self-regulation and for supporting it. Looking at oral language, the crucial importance of private speech is highlighted, along with the importance of helping children to develop an understanding of themselves as thinkers, particularly by aiding the development of mental and emotional state language.

Some key contexts for communication and talk that supports self-regulation are looked at, particularly encouraging perspective-taking, narratives of all kinds, open-ended activities, pretend play, problem-solving and opportunities for children to collaborate, including without an adult being involved. At the same time, we have also seen that these contexts may not afford all children the same opportunities, and that children with specific needs, including those with ADHD and ASD, may require particular support.

Finally, it is important to remember the crucial role of the practitioner. This includes the kinds of gestures and talk they use themselves, the support they give to young children's private speech, and the ways in which they talk about thoughts and feelings with children.

Key further reading

Early Years Coalition (2021). *Birth to 5 matters: Non-statutory guidance for the early years foundation stage*, Early Education. https://www.birthto5matters.org.uk/wp-content/uploads/2021/04/Birthto5Matters-download.pdf, (especially sections on Communication and Language and Physical Development).

Gabbard, C. (2015). Embodied cognition in children: Developing mental representations for action. In **S. Robson** & **S. Flannery Quinn** (Eds.), *The Routledge international handbook of young children's thinking and understanding* (pp. 229–237). Abingdon: Routledge.

Krafft, K. C., & **Berk, L. E.** (1998). Private speech in two preschools: Significance of open-ended activities and make-believe play for verbal self-regulation. *Early Childhood Research Quarterly*, 13(4), 637–658.

Mead, D., & **Winsler, A.** (2015). Children's private speech. In **S. Robson** & **S. Flannery Quinn** (Eds.), *The Routledge international handbook of young children's thinking and understanding* (pp. 150–162). Abingdon: Routledge.

Novack, M., & Goldin-Meadow, S. (2015). Learning from gesture: How our hands change our minds. *Educational Psychology Review*, 27(3), 405–412.

Vallotton, C., & Ayoub, C. (2011). Use your words: The role of language in the development of toddlers' self-regulation. *Early Childhood Research Quarterly*, 26, 169–181.

Whitebread, D., Pino-Pasternak, D., & Coltman, P. (2015). Making learning visible: The role of language in the development of metacognition and self-regulation in young children. In **S. Robson & S. Flannery Quinn** (Eds.), *The Routledge international handbook of young children's thinking and understanding* (pp. 199–214). Abingdon: Routledge.

7   Contexts for self-regulation

> In this chapter, we look at:
>
> - Contexts that foster self-regulation;
>
> - How play can promote self-regulation;
>
> - Pretend play and self-regulation;
>
> - Music and musical play contexts and self-regulation;
>
> - Problem-solving and self-regulation;
>
> - Self-regulation across the early childhood curriculum;
>
> - Working with parents.
>
> *Keywords:* play, playfulness, pretend play, musical play, problem-solving, curriculum, framework.

Introduction

In this chapter, we focus on what kinds of contexts might be especially supportive of the development of young children's self-regulation. In particular, these include play – of all kinds, but especially pretence – and problem-solving. Play and playfulness are, of course, central to all aspects of young children's lives, and there are countless books about play already. Here we are focusing on how play supports young children's self-regulation and at how playful contexts can help adults develop and see self-regulation. Drawing on an original and important approach with clear implications for practice, we look at the potential of music and musical play as fertile contexts for self-regulatory development. We also look at young children's problem-solving, both in itself, and at the ways in which play and problem-solving are often linked in children's activity and self-regulation.

The chapter then looks at self-regulation across the curriculum. While we want to highlight the central importance of play and problem-solving, we also look at the wider context of young children's self-regulatory development, particularly in settings, and at how this relates to the early childhood curriculum. As we saw in

Chapter 1, there is now strong evidence that self-regulation is foundational to young children's development, and that aspects of self-regulation predict long-term school achievement. This seems to be apparent from as early as three years of age (Blair & Razza, 2007). We conclude the chapter with discussion about working with parents to support their children's self-regulation.

Play and self-regulation

The importance of play

The Early Years Foundation Stage (EYFS) emphasises the importance of play for young children. In so doing, it also highlights a number of key characteristics of self-regulation, including exploration, goal-setting, problem-solving and relationships:

Play is essential for children's development, building their confidence as they learn to explore, relate to others, set their own goals and solve problems. Children learn by leading their own play and by taking part in play which is guided by adults.

(Department for Education, 2021: 16)

Why is play important for self-regulation?

The importance of play, and playful contexts, for self-regulation is reflected in the long history of research and practice in the area. Jerome Bruner's pioneering research (1972) suggested that the extended period of human childhood and the opportunities it offered for children to engage in playful activities support the development of higher order cognitive skills (or flexibility of thought) that are closely linked to self-regulation. However, as far back as the 1930s Lev Vygotsky (1978) had articulated a cognitive mechanism through which play contributed to children's intentional learning, creativity and problem-solving (all contexts where self-regulation is needed). This mechanism is the Zone of Proximal Development (ZPD), first looked at in Chapter 1. Go back, now, to the definition there, in which Vygotsky clearly links play and problem-solving. For Vygotsky, children set their own level of challenge during their play so that it is always developmentally appropriate for them (Vygotsky, 1978).

The ZPD is created through two communicative ingredients:

- intersubjectivity (shared understanding between participants);

- scaffolding (effective support by a more skilled person, gradually relinquished as the child masters a task).

For practitioners, then, this points to the value of play in which adults are involved, as well as children's self-initiated and self-directed play. Ensuring that children have opportunities to engage in both child-initiated and adult-guided play is important in supporting children's development and display of self-regulation and meta-cognition (Robson, 2016a).

What do studies about play and self-regulation show?

Vygotsky's ideas inspired much research investigating the relationship between play and the development of self-regulation. Early studies were often experimental. Sylva et al. (1976) investigated the effects of a play or taught condition on the problem-solving abilities of children. In one study, for example, children were asked to solve the problem of how to retrieve some food that was out of their reach, with two sticks, neither of which was long enough individually to reach the food. The solution is to join the two sticks together with a clamp, also given to the children. One group of children had the opportunity to play freely with the objects. The other group of children were taught how to use the sticks and clamp in ways that would help them solve the problem. Both groups of children solved the problem equally well, but the play group appeared to persevere more when their first attempts to solve the problem did not work. They also employed more strategies in their efforts to find a solution. So, in this experiment at least, children who had an opportunity to play were more likely to engage in successful self-regulation during their attempts to solve the task.

Observing young children's play

This experimental approach is complemented, particularly in recent years, by studies which have relied on direct observations of children as they play. For example, Elias and Berk's (2002) observational study suggested a correlation between children's play in the classroom and their socially shared behaviour/responsibility during circle time and cleaning-up time – two instances where self-regulation is required. Karpov (2005) reports a study by Manuilenko (1948) where 3- to 7-year-old children were playing 'standing sentry'. When children did this in a room with their friends, they were able to stand motionless for longer compared to when they were playing standing sentry on their own. They concluded that the friends were monitoring the sentry, supporting Vygotsky's view that a significant factor for the development of self-regulation is children's use of talk to regulate the behaviours of others.

The Cambridge Independent Learning (C.Ind.Le) project found that self-regulation mostly occurred while children were engaged in playful activities (Whitebread et al., 2005, 2007, 2009a, 2009b). In this study, 3- to 5-year-old children were video-recorded over a period of 2 years, during class and play time. Perhaps most importantly, this study has helped us to look in more detail at specific self-regulatory behaviours in play. They found that different areas of self-regulatory behaviours appeared at different rates. During play, metacognitive regulation was most preva-lent, followed by metacognitive knowledge, with emotional/motivational regulation behaviours being the least frequent (Whitebread et al., 2009a, 2009b). In particular, playful situations appeared to mainly promote monitoring, control and planning behaviours (Whitebread et al., 2009b). Robson (2010, 2016a), working with children aged 3–5 years, similarly found that playful activities were particularly valuable for the development and display of metacognitive regulation and skilfulness. In playful activities, children were often clearer about what they were doing, and why, and they generated more ideas and used a wider range of strategies. They were more likely to collaborate and help one another, to comment on what they were doing and to engage in more target setting and monitoring behaviour (Robson, 2016a). Looking at specific self-regulatory behaviours during play can give valuable insights into the affordances of play, which can help to inform practice.

What about older children? Is play still important for their self-regulation? The Play, Learning and Narrative Skills (PLaNS) study explored, among others, the impact of guided play on the development of young children's self-regulatory abilities in the context of writing (Pino-Pasternak et al., 2014). Working in mixed ability groups, children aged 5–10 years in UK primary schools developed ideas for writing across a range of genres and used LEGO to build a construction to help them develop the ideas that they wanted to include in their writing. They also engaged in constructional and pretend play when they were building their ideas with LEGO. The children made very significant progress in their creativity, their independence and perseverance (themselves related to self-regulation) when writing. The children also made significant progress in self-regulation. In addition, the children's playfulness during the building activities was strongly related to the quality of their collaborative skills, involving their use of exploratory talk and socially shared regulation (Whitebread et al., 2015). This suggests not only that play and self-regulation are related in older children but also that playfulness is related to socially shared regulation.

As Whitebread et al. (2019) conclude, the evidence is accumulating to suggest that young children's play experiences foster their self-regulation.

ACTIVITY: THE IMPORTANCE OF PLAY

We should note that children who attend preschools emphasising play rather than academic outcomes achieve higher scores on self-regulation measures (Hyson et al., 2007).

1. How might this piece of knowledge affect your practice?

2. Think whether you might want to make any changes to your practice, given what we know about the importance of play. What might they be?

Pretend play and self-regulation

Play, then, is important for young children's self-regulation. Are there, though, particular types of play that may be especially valuable? Looking back at many of the studies described above, it is pretence, or make-believe play, which comes up time and again. With the exception of a few studies, such as that by Lillard et al. (2013), which focuses mainly on the development of executive function, the evidence suggests that, in early childhood, pretend play is significant in the development of children's emotional, cognitive and behavioural self-regulatory abilities. Elias and Berk (2002) conclude that both the frequency and persistence of complex sociodramatic play are associated with the development of self-regulation.

WHAT DOES POLICY TELL US?

The importance of pretend play

Self-regulation is now included in the EYFS in England. In the non-statutory guidance, *Development Matters*, where self-regulation is identified as one of seven 'key features of effective practice', the role of pretend play is emphasised:

Pretend play gives many opportunities for children to focus their thinking, persist and plan ahead.

(Department for Education, 2020b: 11)

For Vygotsky, pretend play provides children with the ground to create their ZPD. This happens because pretend play provides the roles, rules and scenarios that enable children to perform at levels beyond their ages (Berk et al., 2006). The *rule-based nature* of pretend play encourages children to draw on examples from their environments, and devise and follow social rules in pretence. As Vygotsky (1978) pinpointed, pretend play provides children with opportunities to conquer impulses for the sake of their play, not because they are obliged to but because they feel that they are free to do what they want, to sustain the play. The *Tools of the Mind* curriculum (Bodrova & Leong, 2006) is based on Vygotsky's ideas about the value of pretend play. Bodrova (2011) suggests that make-believe play is an ideal context for self-regulation because it embodies all three elements for self-regulation: being regulated by others, regulating others and engaging in voluntary self-regulation.

Having established the above, we should also keep in mind that not all children show the same levels of self-regulation during pretend play. For example, in a project by Vieillevoye and Nader-Grosbois (2008) children with intellectual disability showed, on average, lower self-regulation than the typically developing group. The authors then go on to suggest that pretend play should be prioritised in both typically developing children and in children with intellectual disability for supporting the emergence and development of self-regulation.

Pretend play and emotion regulation

What is more, pretend play enhances children's abilities in *emotional regulation*. During play, children have the opportunity to enact and modify emotional experiences and to manage their feelings. In a study by Galyer and Evans (2001), children aged 4–5 years and their parents participated in a pretend play game. The children first engaged in a pretend play game using the toys available. Subsequently, a large crocodile puppet who was very hungry and could 'eat' all of the toys was introduced. Galyer and Evans found that children who were effective at keeping their pretend play going, despite this event, had high emotional regulation skills in other contexts. Furthermore, children who engaged in pretend play with their caregivers frequently scored higher on measures of emotional regulation.

WHAT DOES RESEARCH TELL US?

Pretend play and cognitive and emotional self-regulation: preschoolers' cognitive and emotional self-regulation in pretend play

This study by Slot et al. (2017) explored preschoolers' cognitive and emotional self-regulation during pretend play. Involving 95 three-year-old children in a naturalistic play setting, the study focused on guided play situations with realistic-looking kitchen toys.

The researchers observed three indicators of cognitive self-regulation:

Metacognitive knowledge	Metacognitive regulation	Persistence

and four indicators of emotional self-regulation:

Knowledge of emotions	Emotion regulation	Resolving conflicts	Behavioural self-control

The results showed that 3-year-old children are capable of cognitive and emotional self-regulation during pretend play:

- The children displayed metacognitive regulation in the form of planning, monitoring and control, in both verbal and non-verbal episodes;

- Children showed medium to high levels of persistence;

- Metacognitive knowledge was less frequently observed (often the case in research with young children);

- Children could regulate their emotions and manage how to express their emotions if these would be disruptive to their pretend play;

(Continued)

WHAT DOES RESEARCH TELL US? continued

- Children were able to resolve conflicts with peers, sometimes with help from the teacher;
- Children also showed behavioural self-control, for example, by sharing their toys.

Finally, the *quality* of pretend play was strongly related to the observed cognitive and emotional self-regulation. Slot et al. (2017) argue that complex pretend play needs metacognitive regulation and persistence and that one of the features of pretend play is that it requires children to express and modulate their emotions in ways that are socially acceptable.

(Slot et al., 2017)

DEVELOP YOUR UNDERSTANDING: PRETEND PLAY, AND METACOGNITIVE KNOWLEDGE AND META-EMOTIONAL KNOWLEDGE

In the study above by Slot and colleagues (2017), the researchers admit that a limitation of the study was that they only investigated self-regulation and pretend play concurrently. This means that they cannot make claims as to whether, for example, pretend play causes self-regulation.

1. What could be a way to overcome this limitation? How can further studies overcome this? Have you read about any studies which are not concurrent?

   Also, this study reports that metacognitive knowledge and meta-emotional knowledge was not frequently evidenced by children during these pretend play situations.

2. Does this mean that young children are not capable of metacognitive knowledge or meta-emotional knowledge?

3. Why could it be that there was no frequent evidence of metacognitive knowledge and meta-emotional knowledge?

4. What could further research aim to do to ensure that it explores the children's potential for metacognitive knowledge and meta-emotional knowledge? What, in your view, is the role of situations that trigger or elicit these strong emotions?

Pretend play and talk

Pretend play may also be particularly rich in opportunities for *self-regulating language* and private speech (Vygotsky, 1978). In Chapter 6 we looked at young children's talk in pretend play, and at the value placed on children's narratives in pretend play, and it is useful to go back to the discussion there. Here it is important to highlight that during pretend play children engage in complex negotiations to create play scenes (Berk et al., 2006). All their conversations draw on cultural rules, conventions and models of co-operation (Vygotsky, 1978).

In a study reported by Whitebread et al. (2019), the social pretend play of 76 children aged 3–6 years was video-recorded (Whitebread & O'Sullivan, 2012). As well as looking at the children's metacognition and self-regulation in general, the researchers also looked at the children's talk, in particular, their meta-communication. They looked at the talk children made when in role (so-called implicit), and when out of role (explicit). This latter type of talk includes the kinds of comments children make which are aimed at regulating the play's content and direction (metacommunication) – 'you be the dog, and you jump up at me'. Younger children employed mostly in-role metacommunication and 6-year-olds employed mostly out-of-role metacommunication. However, what is perhaps most important here is that for all ages, the children's social pretend play was rich in metacommunicative and self-regulatory incidents. The examples below describe the kinds of metacommunicative comments the children made.

WHAT DOES RESEARCH TELL US?

Preschool children's social pretend play: supporting the development of metacommunication, metacognition and self-regulation

This study by Whitebread and O'Sullivan (2012) looks at how metacommunication becomes evident during pretend play. The authors provide fascinating examples of metacommunication which they observed in young children's pretend play.

Whitebread and O'Sullivan explain that metacommunication can function in a bifold way:

- it helps children clarify their actions for themselves

- it gives their play partner useful information for their play

In the following example, the authors observed a naturally occurring social pre-tence episode in preschool. The two children are C1 (47 months) and C2 (43 months). They are in the home area and C1 is cooking supper.

C1: I'm making supper, you'd like supper... ok, I'll make your food... Da, da da da, da, da, da. Do you like these? (Dried apricots)

C2: Ya, and I'd like some nana (banana) too!

Page 205

In this example, it appears that both functions of metacommunication are at play. C1 is, on the one hand, giving information to C2 about their play, by clarifying to C2 what he is doing. On the other hand, his words and the chanting appear to be supporting him to stay on task.

(Continued)

In the next example, Whitebread and O'Sullivan describe how 'while the play frame was being established metacommunication involved matters such as ensuring the bride, groom and their guests had the appropriate attire'. In the following example, upon realising that they did not have a 'priest' when going to the church for the ceremony, C12 (47 months) and C14 (50 months) needed to step out-of-frame momentarily to solve this problem. Assigning the role to the educator (A2) then allowed the children to continue with their script.

A1 (Hairdresser): Tell us where are you getting married?

C14 (Groom): In the church

C12 (Bride): And we are going to a hotel after!

C12 (to C14): Come on, we must go to the church now, grab your bag!

C14: But where is the church?

C12: We need a church...ok you'll have to be the priest (pointing to A2).

A2: Ok, you want me to be the priest.'

Page 206

Once again, in this example of metacommunication, the children are clarifying their actions for each other and giving useful information to each other about their play. They are deciding where they are 'getting married' and that they have to immediately leave for the church. However, they also realise that they have still not decided where the church is nor have they decided on who will be the priest. In this extract, through their metacommunication, they manage to successfully problem-solve, which allows their play to carry on.

(Whitebread & O'Sullivan, 2012)

Music and self-regulation

There is mounting evidence supporting a link between self-regulation and music. Much of this comes from research looking at the effects of formal musical training. Researchers from different backgrounds agree on potential links between music and self-regulation, and they often regard self-regulation as the mediator between musical training and enhanced performance. For example, in a study comparing children (aged 4–6) who had attended a music training programme, with peers who had attended visual art training, Moreno et al. (2011) reported improvements in the first group's intelligence. The improvements in these children's verbal intelligence were positively associated with changes in functional brain plasticity during an executive function task. We should note here that the majority of the executive functions investigated in this research are those currently considered closely linked to self-regulation (see Chapter 1). Therefore, it could be argued that executive functions, and hence self-regulatory functions, are the central processes strengthened by musical training (Bialystok & DePape, 2009; Degé et al., 2011; Moreno et al., 2011). At the same time, we should acknowledge that there is also research (e.g. Schellenberg, 2011) questioning the role of executive function as mediating between music training and performance (IQ).

It is very important to note the potential that music has for neurodivergent children and children coming from disadvantaged backgrounds. Music might be a route for improving executive functions and self-regulation in children with ADHD (Williams, 2018). Music might also be a route for reaching children with an autistic spectrum disorder even if they lack in communication skills (Särkämö et al., 2013). Similarly, a rhythm and movement intervention has been found to support emotional self-regulation in children from disadvantaged communities (Williams & Berthelsen, 2019).

Self-regulation and musical play

When looking at young children, it is particularly important to discuss what is known about self-regulation in informal music settings. Musical play has been proposed as a fertile informal music context for promoting self-regulatory skills (Winsler et al., 2011; Zachariou & Whitebread, 2017). The importance of looking at musical play comes from the fact that it is a universal phenomenon which plays a major role in children's lives from very early on (Papaeliou & Trevarthen, 2006).

Before exploring the links between musical play and self-regulation, we should explain what musical play is. Musical play consists of activities allowing children to explore, improvise and create with sound (Littleton, as cited in Tarnowski, 1999; Lew & Campbell, 2005) and may include vocalisations, rhythmic movement of the body and play with sound-making objects (Tarnowski, 1999; Young, 2005). The prevalent types of musical play are hand-clapping games (Harwood, 1998), circle games (Lew & Campbell, 2005), movement play (Tarnowski, 1999; Gluschankof and Littleton, as cited in Marsh &Young, 2007), singing play (Young, 2003; Littleton, as cited in Marsh &Young, 2007) and instrumental play (Marsh & Young, 2007; Young, 2004).

Until recently, there was only anecdotal evidence of the potential links between musical play and self-regulation, but research by Winsler et al. (2011) demonstrated the link between self-regulation and musical play. The participants were 3- and 4-year-old children, half of whom were participating in music and movement classes (incorporating musical play), while the rest had not experienced structured early childhood music classes. The children's self-regulation was assessed through laboratory self-regulation tasks. The findings suggested that children who were enrolled in music classes showed better self-regulation and used more self-regulatory language in the form of private speech, a strategy which was positively associated with their performance on a selective attention task. In addition to this, the researchers reported how the children enrolled in music classes were more likely to use singing or humming to themselves as a facilitative strategy while engaging in a delay of gratification task. This strategy was linked to inhibiting their desire to open a gift or call out to the experimenter (this latter strategy was negatively related to performance and self-regulation). So, it could be argued that the children participating in musical play sessions were more likely to successfully engage in strategies that would foster their self-regulation. As Winsler et al. (2011) hypothesised, this could be because children who participate in this form of music engagement might also be able to use song, music and dance as tools for directing their behaviour.

In two more recent studies, one of us explored children's self-regulation during musical play activities (Zachariou & Whitebread, 2015, 2017). The rationale for these studies was that musical play shares many of the characteristics of other playful contexts, such as pretence, that effectively foster self-regulation. Musical play's rule-based nature, reinforcement of self-regulatory language and emotional self-regulation are all consistent with the features of contexts fostering self-regulation, as looked at earlier in this chapter. Furthermore, the opportunities musical play affords for early expertise, social interaction, true co-operation and co-regulatory behaviours to emerge, and the fact that it supports creativity, exploration and problem-solving, suggest that it is a type of play that could potentially be extremely rich in the opportunities it provides for enhancing self-regulation. Bearing in mind that the fundamental characteristics that encourage the creation of the ZPD, such as intersubjectivity and scaffolding, are also evident in musical play, we hypothesised that musical play could be an ideal context for self-regulation to flourish in.

In the first of these studies, children's self-regulation was evident in their musical play (Zachariou & Whitebread, 2015). In this study, the first author observed and video-recorded the musical play of ten children aged 6–7 years, in a primary classroom in Cyprus. Using the C.Ind.Le coding framework (Whitebread et al., 2009b), we found that the most frequently coded self-regulatory behaviours during musical play were children planning, monitoring and controlling their play. The example below provides a glimpse of the types of self-regulation that were evident in musical play activities.

WHAT DOES RESEARCH TELL US?

Musical play and self-regulation: does musical play allow for the emergence of self-regulatory behaviours?

The example of musical play below is full of self-regulation behaviours by the children. It illustrates how self-regulation is evident in verbal behaviour but also in non-verbal behaviour. The column on the right links children's behaviours to self-regulation.

The children are doing movement (musical) play. The children have already had a go at moving to a piece of music as a group. They are now sitting down and the teacher is telling them that they should try this again and they should make an effort to work more as a group. Alkinoos had the idea of dancing using 'Mickey' moves (from a popular children's cartoon show) but Craig and Vasilis have been

(Continued)

agreeing on doing moves from the Zeibekiko (a traditional Greek dance). This is the moment before the music starts playing again and the boys are negotiating how they will move to the music (Table 7.1).

Child	Non-verbal behaviour	Verbal behaviour	Regulatory behaviour
Vasilis	He is pointing with his finger to all of them.	'Guys, we should all play together'.	Metacognitive Regulation-Planning
Alkinoos	Looks slightly disappointed. (He was about to suggest his moves when Vasilis interrupted him.)	'What?' (Meaning: how are we going to dance?)	Metacognitive Regulation-Planning
Craig	Tries to put Alkinoos' and his arms in the correct position for the Zeibekiko method.	'We should be holding hands like this'.	Metacognitive Regulation-Planning
Vasilis	Shows the Zeibekiko moves.		Metacognitive Regulation-Planning
Alkinoos		'Zeibekiko?' He is asking if what they mean is Zeibekiko and tries to clarify the task demands.	Metacognitive Regulation-Planning
Alkinoos		'I don't want to (dance like Zeibekiko)'.	Emotional/Motivational Regulation-Emotional/ Motivational Monitoring
Vasilis	His voice has a persuasive tone.	Tries to encourage Alkinoos: 'Come on! It's very easy!'	Emotional/Motivational Regulation-Emotional/ Motivational Control
Craig	He taps Alkinoos' leg, grabs him by the shoulder and looks him in the eye, frowns and has a serious tone in his voice when saying:	'Errr... Don't play (with us then)!' He is very angry at Alkinoos who is not agreeing with them.	Emotional/Motivational Regulation-Emotional/ Motivational Monitoring
Alkinoos	He has a very calm tone in his voice and he is smiling.	'The teacher doesn't want...' He is trying to explain to the boys that this kind of dance (Zeibekiko) is not what the task/music asks for.	Metacognitive Knowledge-Knowledge of Tasks
Craig	He frowns and looks very disappointed. When he says these words he also nods at the same time, putting emphasis on his words.	Says fiercely: 'She does (want it)'!	Emotional/Motivational Regulation-Emotional/ Motivational Monitoring
Alkinoos	He hesitates for a bit and then calmly says:	'She doesn't want this kind of dancing'	Metacognitive Knowledge-Knowledge of Strategies

(Continued)

Table 7.1 (Continued)

Child	Non-verbal behaviour	Verbal behaviour	Regulatory behaviour
Craig	He is still frowning, looks at Alkinoos in a very intense way and fiercely moves his hand up. He is almost shouting at him:	'Er... Don't play!'	Emotional/Motivational Regulation-Emotional/ Motivational Monitoring
Alkinoos	He hesitates for a second but then stands up, slightly raises his shoulders, gently pulls the boys' arms so that he puts them at the correct position for Zeibekiko. While smiling he says in a very positive way:	'All right!' He decides to step back and do what the other two boys are suggesting.	Metacognitive regulation-Control

Table 7.1 Verbal and non-verbal behaviours indicating specific types of self-regulation during musical play

(Zachariou & Whitebread, 2015)

In Chapter 1, we looked at the distinctions between self-regulation, co-regulation and socially shared regulation. Now look at the box above on 'What does research tell us?' and find at least one example of each:

• Self-regulation

• Co-regulation

• Socially shared regulation

Think and discuss with colleagues:

1. What could be the reason that we can see socially shared regulation in this case study?

2. What aspect of the play is encouraging socially shared regulation?

   Then observe the children you work with:

3. Can you see any socially shared regulation in their musical play or in their pretend play?

4. What changes can you make to enable children to engage in more socially shared regulation?

5. How can you support those children who are already showing socially shared regulation further?

In the second study (Zachariou & Whitebread, 2017), musical play sessions were implemented in 36 children's whole-class music sessions, over 5 weeks. The activities involved singing play, hand-clapping games, circle games, instrumental play and movement play, and each lasted approximately 30 minutes. The tasks contained elements of free play, but mainly afforded 'guided play'. Thus the children's play was most often sensitively and responsively guided by an adult, within a context meaningful for the children. The activities usually required the children (aged 6–8) to work in pairs or groups and to be creative (the children were usually given some initial stimulus by the teacher but then required to develop their own ideas). The video-recordings were coded on the basis of the C.Ind.Le coding framework. We identified more than 15,000 short episodes of self-regulation behaviours which took place during the musical play activities.

The findings indicated that the musical play activities afforded all the children ample opportunities to display and practise their self-, co- and socially shared regulation. Some of the most predominant self-regulation behaviours included checking their efforts, checking whether they were on track and self-correcting when they made a mistake (cognitive monitoring). For example, during a hand-clapping game, a child who is checking whether she and her peer are doing the correct movements, by carefully focusing on the hand movements, is performing cognitive monitoring. Importantly, children showed understanding of their own and others' emotions and monitored their emotional/motivational reactions (emotional/motivational monitoring). An example of this could be a child expressing that they do not want to sing, or a child pulling a long face at the end of a musical play activity that did not go as planned.

An intriguing finding from this study, however, was the clear prevalence of socially shared regulation during musical play activities. Musical play provides ample opportunities for children to share the regulation within a group, by playing interdependently: in musical play children depend on each other. Imagine trying to play a hand-clapping game when your partner does not make the right moves! So musical play could provide a valuable foundation on which these important, collaborative problem-solving and socially shared regulation abilities can be built. Musical play, then, appears to be a fertile context for young children's self-regulation, and, very importantly, for their socially shared regulation too.

How can practitioners support young children's self-regulation in play and playful contexts?

Whether at home or at a setting, children spend a lot of time playing. Below we identify some implications for practice. It is important to keep in mind that even though skilful support by practitioners can be beneficial in young children's self-regulation in play, children also tend to show a lot of self-regulation when engaging in self-initiated and child-led play. Keep in mind that adult involvement can affect play in both directions: positively or negatively. We look at this in more detail in Chapter 8.

- Give children uninterrupted time and space to play.

- Allow children the time and space to engage in child-initiated play that is entirely led by children themselves (Robson, 2016a).

- Include guided play activities (i.e. play under the guidance of an adult). Here you can be goal-oriented but simultaneously provide meaningful contexts for the children (Golinkoff et al., 2008; Hirsh-Pasek et al., 2008). Autonomy is important for fostering productive forms of self-regulation, but should be complemented by instrumental support from practitioners (Perry, 2013).

- In play, support children to articulate their thinking. This stimulates the development of their self-regulation (Pino-Pasternak et al., 2014).

- When engaging in play, avoid taking over and directing. Instead, become genuinely involved. In this way, you will not be reducing children's opportunities to regulate their play, and you then potentially support socially shared regulation of play (Whitebread et al., 2019).

- Offer children opportunities for more open-ended play, opportunities to make choices and control the level of challenge (Perry et al., 2006; Zachariou & Whitebread, 2015).

- Support children's pretend play, which may be particularly rich in opportunities for self-regulating language and private speech (Whitebread & O'Sullivan, 2012).

- When considering how to engage in children's naturally occurring pretend play, consider how you can nurture the play without making it adult-driven. Focus on the children's play needs. This can help enhance their metacognitive abilities (Whitebread & O'Sullivan, 2012).

- Model metacommunication strategies in play. This can support children who are beginning to engage in complex forms of pretend play and stimulate the development of self-regulation (Pino-Pasternak et al., 2014; Whitebread & O'Sullivan, 2012).

- Consider creating spaces for social pretend play where children have a real say in the design of the space (Whitebread & O'Sullivan, 2012).

- Give children opportunities for musical play activities. In these musical play activities, consider adopting free but also guided play (Zachariou & Whitebread, 2017).

- In musical play, give children opportunities for group-work. Here, collaborative problem-solving and socially-shared regulation abilities can be built (Zachariou & Whitebread, 2017).

- Remember that musical activities which are intrinsically interesting to children could encourage them to engage in more self-regulatory behaviours.

Problem-solving and self-regulation

Problem-solving is a goal-directed activity. The goal may be one we have set for ourselves – 'how am I going to reach the biscuit tin on that high shelf?' – or it may be set for us by someone else – 'can you build a house out of Lego?'. Children encounter (and solve) problems constantly, and the kinds of problems they deal with can be physical, cognitive, emotional and social. In all cases, Siegler et al. (2017) suggest that children's cognitive flexibility helps them to attain their goals.

Why is problem-solving important for self-regulation?

There is a lot of evidence to suggest that problem-solving is a very important context for young children to both develop and display their self-regulation (Bronson, 2000; DeLoache & Brown, 1987; Robson, 2016a). We have already seen that Vygotsky (1978) places a lot of emphasis on the importance of problem-solving for the development of young children as self-regulating learners. Why might this be? In attempting to solve any problem, we need to assess the situation, reflect on what we already know, generate ideas that might help us to solve the problem, choose strategies, implement these, make decisions and evaluate whether or not those strategies were successful. As we have seen throughout this book, these kinds of actions and skills are fundamental to self-regulation. They occur as children engage with the world around them, including the digital world, as described in the research below.

WHAT DOES RESEARCH TELL US?

Touchscreens, problem-solving and self-regulation: young children's transfer of learning from a touchscreen device

Digital technology and touchscreens in particular are a feature of most young children's lives. At the same time, there have been concerns expressed about the impact of this on a number of aspects of development in babies and young children, for example, their ability to avoid distraction (a key aspect of self-regulation) (Portugal et al., 2021). In a study with children aged 4–6 years, Huber and her colleagues looked at children's ability to learn how to solve a problem on a touchscreen, and then apply this learning in their interactions with physical objects. The problem-solving activity is called The Tower of Hanoi, and, as demonstrated in the picture below, children are asked to transfer disks from one peg to another, abiding by three rules: they can only move one disk at a time, they cannot put a larger disk on top of a smaller one and disks must always be put on a peg, not another surface. It is a task that has been used extensively with young children, to assess problem-solving, planning ability and executive function (as we have already seen, a vital element of self-regulation).

(Continued)

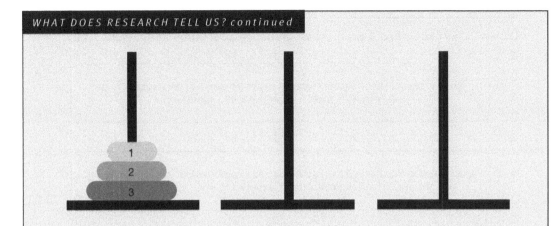

What did they find?

- Children who practised using a touchscreen made as much improvement in learning how to solve the problem as children who practised with the physical objects;

- Children who used the touchscreen were able to transfer their problem-solving skills and strategies to the physical object.

(Huber et al., 2016)

This kind of activity involves very active use of a screen, with children highly engaged. As the authors suggest, this emphasis on the importance of active, as opposed to passive, learning, is significant in all aspects of children's activity. Perhaps what is most important about this study is that it highlights the importance of avoiding over-generalising about the risks (and value) of screen-based activities for young children's development. In a review of research literature in the area, Herodotou (2018) found that the majority of studies she looked at reported a positive effect on children's problem-solving, among other aspects of learning.

How do children's problem-solving skills develop?

Children are busy solving their self-set problems from very early in life – reaching for a comforting toy, trying to attract an adult's attention, working out how they can make things happen. Even from this very young age, they are engaged in making plans for reaching their goal and solving the problem. Often, in young children, that planning and action happens simultaneously (Gura, 1992), but over time they become more skilled at planning in advance of action and in developing more complex plans.

For a long time the accepted view was that a key aspect of the development of young children's problem-solving skills was the ways in which they developed progressively better strategies for correcting their errors, moving beyond a simple strategy such as trial and error. For example, using construction play, DeLoache and Brown (1987) identified a progressive sequence as children age (Figure 7.1):

> Exerting physical force without changing any of the elements: for example, brute force in trying to make a larger cup fit into a smaller one

> Making limited changes in a part of the problem: local correction, for example, taking out one piece of train track and trying to make it fit, whilst ignoring the rest

> Considering and operating on the problem as a whole: for example, standing back and assessing what is happening across all parts of the train track

Figure 7.1   The progressive development of children's problem-solving skills, according to DeLoache and Brown (1987)

However, this may not be the whole story, and more recent evidence shows that the ways in which children attempt to solve a problem may be rather more complex, including thinking about problems in multiple ways at any one time and making decisions about which strategy may be most appropriate given the context. This 'overlapping waves' approach (Siegler et al., 2017) shows children reflecting on their strategy use in previous situations, and how successful that was, and drawing on their knowledge and experience. Look at the example below, of Rylan, to see his use of a range of strategies, as well as how these relate to his self-regulation.

OBSERVING RYLAN: PROBLEM-SOLVING STRATEGIES

This extract from a longer observation illustrates a number of the kinds of strategies that young children use in attempting to solve a problem.

(Continued)

Rylan (aged 4.9) is on the floor in the carpet area of the classroom, with some interlocking plastic blocks. He has joined 3 pieces together to make an L-shape and is trying to fit a piece in to close the shape. He has trouble fitting the shape in. He presses it down, but it will not fit. He takes the shape out, presses the joints of the shapes below it, to make sure they are fitted well, then picks the final piece up and tries to fit it in again. *(Monitoring: reviewing and checking progress)*

He tries rotating it, but it still will not fit, as the outline does not exactly correspond with the shapes either side. *(Control: repeating a strategy to check if it will work)*

He seems to be able to fit it along one edge but not along both. He picks it out again, puts it back in the bin and selects a different piece, in another colour. He tries this piece, rotating it until it fits. He presses it in, with the heel of his hand and his fingers. *(Monitoring: reviews progress and self-corrects)*

RYLAN: (to himself) I made it. *(Evaluating: commenting on his progress)*

He holds it up, stands up and holds it against his face, looking through the central gap and smiling broadly. *(Emotional and motivational control: self-encouraging and persisting)*

Rylan's self-set problem is how to complete the shape he has started. He clearly has a plan, and he uses physical force (pressing the shape down), makes some limited changes (rotating the shape) and also shows that he can consider the problem as a whole (looking at other parts of the construction and checking their fit and then selecting a different piece). DeLoache and Brown (1987) would suggest that these three types of strategy form a developmental sequence, with strategies such as physical force being replaced by more sophisticated ones as children develop. However, Rylan's approach seems more consistent with Siegler et al.'s (2017) model, in which older strategies continue to be used alongside newer, more advanced, ones, with children making appropriate selections in light of the particular problem.

What about self-regulation? How does this problem-solving context reveal aspects of Rylan's developing self-regulation? The notes in italics at the end of sections in the observation highlight particular aspects of self-regulation, especially Rylan's meta-cognitive regulation, as he monitors, controls and evaluates his actions. It is also interesting to see him demonstrating emotional control at the end of the observation.

How can practitioners support young children's self-regulation through problem-solving?

In nurseries and schools, children will be engaging in both their own self-set challenges as well as ones set for them by the adults around them. The implications for practice suggested here are relevant and valuable in both cases. As you can see from the suggestions, there are times when being involved as children problem-solve can be valuable and other times when it can be better to stand back, and for children to play alone, or with others. Often the choices here depend upon what you are trying to achieve.

- Ensure that children have time and opportunity to play with varied resources, so that they learn to use these in creative ways and create their own problems and challenges (Wood, 2013).

- Ensure that children have sufficient, uninterrupted, time to solve their problems, encouraging a trial-and-error approach, which can help children to develop deeper understandings (Shiakalli & Zacharos, 2012).

- Physical movement and action simulation (Gabbard, 2015) and participation in movement and dance (Deans, 2016; Deans & Cohrssen, 2015) can have a positive effect on young children's problem-solving.

- As an adult, think carefully about how and when to get involved: being nearby rather than directly involved or leading an activity can give children opportunities to support one another and talk through and solve problems (including conflict situations) (Robson & Rowe, 2012).

- As an adult, model problem-solving by thinking aloud, and sharing ideas and strategies with children.

- Direct involvement with children as they problem-solve can give adults opportunities for discussion and direct observation, which aids diagnosis of children's problem-solving processes.

- Adult–child joint problem-solving can support young children's metacognition and problem-solving, but sometimes children can be more likely to give up responsibility to an adult when they are involved and even say they cannot do something (Robson, 2016b).

- Talk between adults and children provides opportunities for adults to make meaningful connections between ideas, give examples and model problem-solving strategies (Bronson, 2000; Hattie & Yates, 2014), and supports discussion about how children are thinking about and trying to solve problems (Littleton & Mercer, 2013).

- Pretend play and problem-solving may have a reciprocal, mutually beneficial, relationship with one another. Pretence and role play may be particularly valuable for problem-solving (Hoffmann & Russ, 2016; Robson, 2017).

- Children's collaborative problem-solving can help them to gain confidence, imitating others and drawing on their ideas (Whitebread et al., 2005).

- Children's solitary play can be valuable for supporting problem-solving, by giving them time and space to reflect for themselves, privately (Lloyd & Howe, 2003).

Problem-solving in the EYFS

Development Matters, the non-statutory guidance for the EYFS, includes a range of references to problem-solving. It is useful to look at these, as they highlight how important support for the development of children's problem-solving capabilities is in all areas of the curriculum (Table 7.2).

Non-statutory guidance	Examples of how to support this
Playing and Exploring Children will be learning to: Guide their own thinking and actions by talking to themselves while playing. For example, a child doing a jigsaw might whisper under their breath: 'Where does that one go? – I need to find the big horse next'.	Help children to develop more control over their actions by giving them many opportunities to play freely and find their own ways of solving problems.
Creating and thinking critically Children will be learning to: Solve real problems: for example, to share nine strawberries between three friends, they might put one in front of each, then a second and finally a third. Finally, they might check at the end that everyone has the same number of strawberries.	Suggestion: you could prompt a conversation with questions like: 'Do you remember when...?', 'How would you do that now?' or 'I wonder what you were thinking then?'
Communication and Language Children in reception will be learning to: Use talk to help work out problems and organise thinking and activities, and to explain how things work and why they might happen.	Encourage children to talk about a problem together and come up with ideas for how to solve it. Give children problem solving words and phrases to use in their explanations: 'so that', 'because', 'I think it's...', 'you could...', 'it might be...'
Personal, Social and Emotional development Children in reception will be learning to: Show resilience and perseverance in the face of challenge	Help them to develop problem-solving skills by talking through how they, you and others resolved a problem or difficulty. Show that mistakes are an important part of learning and going back is trial and error not failure.
Children in reception will be learning to: Think about the perspectives of others.	Ask children to explain to others how they thought about a problem or an emotion and how they dealt with it.
Mathematics 3- and 4-year-olds will be learning to: Solve real-world mathematical problems with numbers up to 5.	Discuss mathematical ideas throughout the day, inside and outdoors. Suggestions: • 'I think Adam has got more crackers...' • support children to solve problems using fingers, objects and marks: 'There are four of you, but there aren't enough chairs....'

(Continued)

Table 7.2 (Continued)

Non-statutory guidance	Examples of how to support this
Expressive arts and design Children in reception will be learning to: Explore, use and refine a variety of artistic effects to express their ideas and feelings. Return to and build on their previous learning, refining ideas and developing their ability to represent them. Create collaboratively, sharing ideas, resources and skills.	Discuss problems and how they might be solved as they arise. Reflect with children on how they have achieved their aims.

Table 7.2   Non-statutory guidance

Department for Education (2020b).

Looking across the curriculum

The contexts that we have emphasised here as particularly powerful – especially play and problem-solving – provide very wide-ranging opportunities for the development of young children's self-regulation and can underpin all potential areas of their activity in settings and at home. Here, it is useful to look very briefly at some of those potential areas, in particular in the context of the early childhood curriculum. In Chapter 6, we looked at the links between young children's language and communication and self-regulation, but there is a lot of research evidence that points to the importance of self-regulation in all areas of the curriculum. This includes in mathematics (Fuhs et al., 2014; Larkin, 2010), science (Larkin, 2010; Roebers, 2017), literacy (Becker et al., 2014; Degotardi & Torr, 2008) and physical development (Whitebread, 2012), in particular, but it is easy to see how all aspects of self-regulation can support the curriculum and can be developed as a result of children's engagement with all areas of the curriculum.

In the following pages (Table 7.3) we look at some examples of ways in which self-regulation can be seen across all aspects of young children's activities in settings, using the EYFS (DfE, 2021). The areas of Personal Social and Emotional Development, and Communication and Language are looked at in Chapters 4 and 6, and so are not included here. The Checklist of Independent Learning Development (CHILD) 3–5, looked at in more detail in Chapter 5, is used here to identify aspects of self-regulation. This observational checklist was developed by David Whitebread and colleagues (Whitebread et al., 2009b) for practitioners to use in their classrooms.

Early Years Foundation Stage	Example	How can this relate to self-regulation? – CHILD 3–5
Physical Development		
By creating games and providing opportunities for play both indoors and outdoors, adults can support children to develop their core strength, stability, balance, spatial awareness, co-ordination and agility.	Belle (2.5 years) is sitting in a wooden rocking 'boat', rocking back and forth. Michael (2.5 years) walks up behind her and tries to climb in without saying anything. BELLE: (pointing to seat opposite in the boat) There (points again) there. Michael moves uncertainly and looks nervous. He tries to climb in. Belle takes his wrists, to help him, steadying him. He sits, and Belle starts to rock back and forth to get them going. Michael stops rocking, smiles at Belle and she smiles back. They resume rocking. BELLE: Whee! Whee! They mimic one another, rocking and laughing loudly.	ProSocial: Is aware of the feelings of others and helps and comforts ProSocial: Engages in independent co-operative activity with peers
Gross motor skills provide the foundation for developing healthy bodies and social and emotional well-being.	Three boys (ages 4 and 5) are building a pirate ship using large construction materials, outside. Joshua and Kade are negotiating roles, particularly who is 'boss'. KADE: Are you five, then? JOSHUA: I'm four. KADE: I'm five. JOSHUA: Kade, I'm four. Christian tries to resolve things, suggesting shared leadership. CHRISTIAN: Let me tell you who is it. It's you (pointing to Joshua). KADE: That's not fair. JOSHUA: Okay, there can be two bosses, and we both do the same things, yeah? Yes, we're the two bosses, okay?	ProSocial: Can resolve social problems with peers ProSocial: Can resolve social problems with peers
Fine motor control and precision helps with hand-eye co-ordination, which is later linked to early literacy.	Rosie (age 5) is drawing and colouring in her picture. She turns the paper as she does so, which helps her to colour in more easily and more accurately.	Motivation: Develops own ways of carrying out tasks

(Continued)

143

Table 7.3 (Continued)

Early Years Foundation Stage	Example	How can this relate to self-regulation? – CHILD 3–5
Repeated and varied opportunities to explore and play with small world activities, puzzles, arts and crafts and the practice of using small tools, with feedback and support from adults, allow children to develop proficiency, control and confidence.	Karl (age 3) has been doing woodwork at a bench with Alison, an artist working with the children. He offers the screwdriver to another boy at the table, KARL: (to Alison) I want to another nail in. ALISON: You find another nail then Karl. Karl returns with hammer and nail. ALISON: Where are you going to put it? This is your bit of wood (points to Kyron's construction). KARL: (holds hammer in left hand, with nail in pincer grip in right hand.) Tongue sticking out, he looks at nail and uses hammer confidently. Looks around at others) Frankie, I'm hammering. ALISON: You are hammering. Karl, that's lovely! KARL: (starts hammering again, tongue sticking out, then starts to look around.) He looks at wood, and alternately taps the 2 nails on it with the hammer, competently and focussed) It's like music!	Cognitive: Shares and takes turns independently Motivation: Plans own tasks, targets and goals Motivation: Finds own resources without adult help Emotional: Can control attention and resist distraction
Literacy		
Language comprehension (necessary for both reading and writing) starts from birth. It only develops when adults talk with children about the world around them and the books (stories and non-fiction) they read with them, and enjoy rhymes, poems and songs together.	Four children (age 4 and 5) and their teacher are in a group reading session. MISS S: Okay, have a good look through this book. I want you to think, as you're looking through the book, is this a story book, or do you think it's going to be an information book? The children all look at their books. MALIA: an information book. MISS S: An information book? Why do you think it's an information book? MALIA: It's got hard reading. MISS S: Because it's got hard reading, yeah, maybe. What other things do you have in an information book? SAFI: It's just that there are people doing things (pointing to pictures), it shows what they're doing.	Cognitive: Can make reasoned choices and decisions Cognitive: Can speak about how they have done something or what they have learnt

Skilled word reading, taught later, involves both the speedy working out of the pronunciation of unfamiliar printed words (decoding) and the speedy recognition of familiar printed words.	MISS S: (holding the book up) Yes, they're photographs in here, aren't they? Shall we have a go at reading it? It's a really tricky one, so I hope you've brought your reading brains with you. ALANA: Yes, we can read it because our reading brains are not outside our heads! Omar (4.10) walks over to a table where Kade is drawing. He is carrying a folder. OMAR: Will you write your name, Kade? K A D, K A D, KAD (tapping the table to emphasise each letter). Kade writes his name, stands up and looks at the paper, waiting. OMAR: (looks at what Kade has written) Not K and A and D and E (looking at Kade). KADE: It is (closing folder and walking away). OMAR: (smiling) Okay then, K A D E.	Cognitive: Is aware of own capabilities Motivation: Initiates activities
Writing involves transcription (spelling and handwriting) and composition (articulating ideas and structuring them in speech, before writing).	Sohal is at a writing activity. He has just written 'A spaceship'. TEACHER A: A spaceship. So what's your next word? SOHAL: (thinking) Has. TEACHER A: Has, well done. New word - what do we need to remember? SOHAL: (holding index finger up) A space. He puts his finger on the paper, to make a space to guide him in writing the next word.	Cognitive: Can make reasoned choices and decisions Cognitive: Uses previously taught strategies

Mathematics

Children should be able to count confidently, develop a deep understanding of the numbers to 10, the relationships between them and the patterns within those numbers. By providing frequent and varied opportunities to build and apply this understanding – such as using	Ashlyn and Sohal are painting, when Ashlyn says: ASHLYN: What is six and six? SOHAL: Uh? ASHLYN: What is six and six? SOHAL: (looks at his fingers, smiles) I don't know that (shaking head). ASHLYN: (smiling) I know what it is. SOHAL: What?	Cognitive: Is aware of own capabilities

(Continued)

Table 7.3 (Continued)

Early Years Foundation Stage	Example	How can this relate to self-regulation? – CHILD 3–5
manipulatives, including small pebbles and tens frames for organising counting – children will develop a secure base of knowledge and vocabulary from which mastery of mathematics is built.	ASHLYN: Twelve! SOHAL: I knew that. I know ten and ten, twenty. ASHLYN: (smiling, rinsing her brush) How do you know that? (looks thoughtful) What is five plus five? SOHAL: Ten. ASHLYN: What s five take away five. SOHAL: Five take away... (holding hand out with fingers splayed, wiggling fingers) Four! ASHLYN: No. Five take away five (nodding head and looking at him, speaking clearly). SOHAL: What is that? ASHLYN: Five! (quickly shakes head) It's zero. Five take away five.	Cognitive: Asks questions and suggests answers Cognitive: Uses previously taught strategies
In addition, it is important that the curriculum includes rich opportunities for children to develop their spatial reasoning skills across all areas of mathematics including shape, space and measures. It is important that children develop positive attitudes and interests in mathematics, look for patterns and relationships, spot connections, 'have a go', talk to adults and peers about what they notice and not be afraid to make mistakes.	Amaya (4.1) is in the block area. She goes over to the shelf, and takes a cylinder block and places it upright on a nearby windowsill. She returns and selects another cylinder, a little shorter. She continues this, until she has six cylinders in a row, from tallest to shortest. AMAYA: (to Adult S, nearby) Look! I've built a wall. ADULT S: Is it a wall? AMAYA: (puts fingertip on each cylinder, one by one) That's what it is! A wall.	Emotional: Tackles new tasks confidently Cognitive: Can speak about how they have done something or what they have learnt
Understanding the World		
Understanding the world involves guiding children to make sense of their physical world and their community.	Safi (5.2) and Adult S have been watching a video together on the laptop. SAFI: Let's pause here (presses pad to pause the video).	Cognitive: Adopts previously heard language for own purposes

The frequency and range of children's personal experiences increases their knowledge and sense of the world around them. In addition, listening to a broad selection of stories, non-fiction, rhymes and poems will foster their understanding of our culturally, socially, technologically and ecologically diverse world. As well as building important knowledge, this extends their familiarity with words that support understanding across domains. Enriching and widening children's vocabulary will support later reading comprehension.	Adult W and 3 children (age 5) are using food colour, vinegar, washing up liquid and baking powder, to observe chemical reactions. The children are taking it in turns to mix. MISS W: Omar, have you got your cup ready? Amina picks it up as if to enquire if she can do it. MISS W: Omar's going to do it. Amina and Stuart watch. Later, when it is Stuart's turn Omar turns to him and encourages him to add food colour to another cup. He mimes vigorous shaking. Kamila (5.1) is at the creative table, making a skirt inspired by the DVD the children have watched about an indigenous tribe in South America. She has a long strip of black paper in front of her and is sticking strips of green tissue to it, along the length. She continues, undistracted by what is going on around her, occasionally looking up and smiling. KAMILA: I can do it! (Strokes the paper) I can do it (to herself). Joshua comes and stands next to her and starts to make a skirt. KAMILA: You need loads of glue (smiling, looking at her work as she sticks) Joshua, loads of glue. She holds up her circlet and examines it. KAMILA: (quietly) Simeoni, can you help me? Simeoni does not take notice. KAMILA: (completes her skirt, and walks over to Miss S, smiling) I've finished. MISS S: (looks and smiles) Kamila, that is super. Show us what you've done. How do you put it on? Kamila carefully lowers the circlet down, steps in with one foot, then tries to put the other in, but is unsteady. So she sits down on the floor and pulls it sitting down, carefully pulling it up. She stands up and looks down at the skirt, carefully feeling strips of tissue, smiling.	ProSocial: Shares and takes turns independently Cognitive: Uses previously taught strategies Emotional: Tackles new tasks confidently Emotional: Can control attention and resist distraction Cognitive: Can speak about planned activities Emotional: Monitors progress and seeks help appropriately Motivational: Enjoys solving problems Emotional: Persists in the face of difficulties

Expressive Arts and Design

It is important that children have regular opportunities to engage with the arts, enabling them to explore and	Robbie (4.10) has decided to organise an activity of paper spider making. JOSHUA (4.9): (walks past the table) I want to make a spider. Christian (4.7) looks up and talks about what to do.	Motivation: Initiates activities ProSocial: Negotiates when and how to carry out tasks

(Continued)

Table 7.3 (Continued)

Early Years Foundation Stage	Example	How can this relate to self-regulation? – CHILD 3–5
play with a wide range of media and materials.	JOSHUA: (picking up sheet of paper with spider on it) I would like to make one of these, Robbie. I'm going to scare everyone with this spider. (Goes to pick up scissors from the shelves, and Robbie points him towards the table.) ROBBIE: They're over there. JOSHUA: (walks over there) Where, where...there's no, scissors over there, I need them here. ROBBIE: (walking over to Joshua, then back towards the shelves) I was tricking you, they're still over there, I was tricking you. JOSHUA: Why were you tricking me? ROBBIE: Because I wanted to. JOSHUA: No more tricking, because I don't like being tricked.	Motivational: Plans own tasks, targets and goals Emotional: Can speak about own and others behaviour and consequences
The quality and variety of what children see, hear and participate in is crucial for developing their understanding, self-expression, vocabulary and ability to communicate through the arts. The frequency, repetition and depth of their experiences are fundamental to their progress in interpreting and appreciating what they hear, respond to and observe.	Shami (2.6) and Tamara (3.1) are kneeling, banging rhythmically on drums, using beaters. Adult E walks over and watches. IMMANUEL (2.11): (walking over) I want to play. ADULT E: You want to play as well? All three children play on the drums. Shami goes over and picks up a handbell, and returns ringing it loudly. ADULT E: (leans over and picks up another bell) Shall we sing a song together? What song can we sing? SHAMI: Twinkle Twinkle. ADULT E: Okay. Ready? After three – one, two, three. Twinkle twinkle little star. Immanuel beats a steady rhythmic accompaniment; Shami rings the bell with a steady beat. ADULT E and TAMARA: (singing, Tamara also ringing bell) How I wonder what you are. All children continue using their instruments in time with the tune.	Emotional: Tackles new tasks confidently Motivation: Finds own resources without adult help Cognitive: Can make reasoned choices and decisions Emotional: Tackles new tasks confidently

Table 7.3 Looking across the EYFS and self-regulation

Working with parents

In this chapter, we have looked at different contexts that foster children's self-regulation and at some of the implications this has for practice. It is also important to look at how practitioners can work with parents and families to support children's self-regulation. Displays in the setting, comments in children's learning journals, workshops and home–school communications can show parents how practitioners are supporting the development of self-regulation. They can also provide opportunities for discussion and the development of a shared under-standing about how children develop, both at home and in the setting. Such discussions can give practitioners rich insights into children's experiences and interests, as well as providing opportunities to learn from (and with) the families they work with.

Perhaps most importantly, practitioners can support parents' understanding of the ways that play encourages self-regulation development and reassure them of the importance of time for their child to play at home. When children are playing they are not 'just playing'. They are learning how to monitor and control their emotions, their behaviours, their thoughts. In support of self-regulation, practitioners can also encourage parents to:

- allow children plenty of time to play and to ensure that their play is meaningful and important to the children;

- follow their children's lead, allowing the children to make decisions, and to set their own level of challenge;

- get involved but avoid taking over the play;

- provide time and space (and everyday props!) for pretend play and musical play;

- give children opportunities for self-management, for example, self-care such as putting on their own clothes, as opportunities for problem-solving and the development of strategies for self-regulation;

- look for opportunities for children to solve their own self-set problems in everyday life at home;

- model problem-solving, talking with children and demonstrating strategies.

Conclusion

This has been a long chapter, but it brings together all we have looked at throughout the book. In it, we have looked at a range of contexts that foster self-regulation. We first looked at play, which has long been thought to support children's self-regulation. We explored Vygotsky's ZPD as the mechanism through which play contributes to children's self-regulation. We have looked at the evidence that children's play is full of opportunities for self-regulation, particularly pretend play and musical play. Pretend play provides the roles, rules and scenarios for children to perform at a level beyond their current level of development. Similarly, musical play seems to exhibit all those characteristics that make pretend play a fertile context for self-regulation.

Another key context looked at here which has been linked to self-regulation is problem-solving. Problem-solving requires actions and skills that are fundamental to self-regulation. Finally, we have looked across the curriculum, at the importance of self-regulation in mathematics, science, literacy and physical development.

Key further reading

Robson, S. (2016a). Self-regulation, metacognition and child- and adult-initiated activity: Does it matter who initiates the task? *Early Child Development and Care*, 186(5), 764–784.

Vygotsky, L. S. (1978). In **M. Cole, V. John-Steiner, S. Scribner, & E. Souberman** (Eds.), *Mind and society: The development of higher mental processes*. Cambridge, MA: Harvard University Press.

Whitebread, D., Grau, V., Kumpulainen, K., McClelland, M. M., Perry, N. E., Pino-Pasternak, D., ... Zachariou, A. (2019). The importance of play, oral language and self-regulation in children's development and learning: Implications for quality in early childhood education. In *The SAGE handbook of developmental psychology and early childhood education*. Los Angeles, CA: SAGE. doi:10.4135/9781526470393.n32

Zachariou, A., & Whitebread, D. (2017). A new context affording for regulation: The case of musical play. *International Journal of Educational Psychology*, 6(3), 212–249.

8 Planning – and not planning – for self-regulation

In this chapter, we look at:

- Pedagogical approaches for self-regulation;
- The continuum from child-initiated to adult-led activity: what does this mean for self-regulation?;
- The effects of adult interactions and their involvement and absence on young children's self-regulation;
- The physical environment;
- The 'stuff' of self-regulation: Materials and resources;
- Working with parents.

Keywords: pedagogy, child-initiated, adult-led, guided play, guide, facilitator, interaction, collaboration, environment, indoors, outdoors, toys, resources.

Introduction

In this final chapter, we look at how we can plan – and not plan – for young children's self-regulated learning (SRL). It might seem late in the day to be thinking about planning, but, as always, planning comes about as a result of all that we already know – about what we want children to learn, about the curriculum and about the children themselves. The 'not planning' reflects the idea that what is sometimes called *intentional learning*, that is, what adults plan, is only ever a part of the story, and that much learning and development, including SRL, comes about as children pursue their interests and engage in self-directed activity.

This chapter is about what is often referred to as 'pedagogy', that is, ideas and theories about teaching and learning. Here, we look particularly at the significance for young children's self-regulation of the kinds of pedagogical decisions that practitioners make in settings. As we can see from the way it is described in

Development Matters (DfE, 2020b) (below), pedagogy includes the decisions that practitioners make about the extent to which children are supported in having choice, how much of their time is spent engaging with activities organised and led by adults and the kinds of roles adults take up, as guide, facilitator and teacher. It also includes decisions that adults make about the environment. This chapter builds particularly on Chapter 7, which focused on play, problem-solving and the Early Years curriculum.

WHAT DOES POLICY TELL US?

Development Matters and pedagogy

In *Development Matters*, the non-statutory guidance for the EYFS published by the Department for Education in England, pedagogy is one of seven key features of effective practice:

Pedagogy: helping children to learn

- Children are powerful learners. Every child can make progress in their learning, with the right help.

- Effective pedagogy is a mix of different approaches. Children learn through play, by adults modelling, by observing each other and through guided learning and direct teaching.

- Practitioners carefully organise enabling environments for high-quality play. Sometimes, they make time and space available for children to invent their own play. Sometimes, they join in to sensitively support and extend children's learning.

- Children in the Early Years also learn through group work, when practitioners guide their learning.

- Older children need more of this guided learning.

- A well-planned learning environment, indoors and outside, is an important aspect of pedagogy.

(Department for Education, 2020b: 10)

ACTIVITY: PEDAGOGY AND SELF-REGULATION

1. Look at the list in the policy box above. As you read this chapter, try to identify how self-regulation may be most effectively supported by the kinds of key pedagogical decisions set out here.

2. Can you identify something from this list that you would like to further develop in your own setting?

'Teaching' for self-regulation: pedagogical approaches

In using the term 'teaching' we are not implying a formal, top-down approach. Instead, we use it to refer to the many ways in which adults support young children's learning in settings – guiding, facilitating, modelling, communicating, demonstrating and instructing, in a range of contexts, from child-initiated and free play to adult-led activity, with individual children, and in small and larger groups. In Chapters 1 and 2, we looked at the evidence that self-regulation can be taught and learned, including with young children (Perels et al., 2009), and that interventions targeted at children's self-regulation and metacognition are effective (Education Endowment Foundation, 2019), with a positive impact on learning outcomes, strategy use and motivation (Dignath et al., 2008). As we noted there, this may particularly be so for children with low levels of self-regulatory skill (Tominey & McClelland, 2011), including those at risk because of poverty and income inequality (Raver, 2012).

As we have seen, there are some programmes that target children's self-regulation, such as the Vygotskian-inspired *Tools of the Mind* curriculum (Bodrova & Leong, 2006). Importantly, though, working within existing curriculum frameworks is all that is needed to support and develop young children's self-regulation successfully. Desautel (2009) believes that we can see elements of metacognition in many long-standing routines and practices in nurseries and schools. He suggests that children's learning journals and memory books, for example, involve reflection and discussion about learning and thinking. Think, too, about the common use of acronyms with school-age children, such as 'WALT' ('We are learning to…'), 'WILF' ('What I [the teacher] am looking for…') and 'TIB' ('This is because…'), which draw attention to learning and thinking, including intentions and outcomes.

What might be some of the key underlying principles of a pedagogy that supports the development of self-regulation in young children? The Cambridge Independent Learning (C.Ind.Le) Project (Whitebread, 2012) identify four, shown in Figure 8.1.

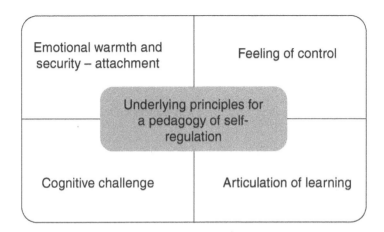

Figure 8.1   The C.Ind.Le project: underlying principles for a pedagogy of self-regulation

Why might these be particularly valuable? First, together they reflect all aspects of self-regulation: affective, cognitive and behavioural. Taking each in turn, we know a lot about the importance of emotional warmth and security, for example, the importance of children's early interactions with caregivers for their later emotional and cognitive development (Miller, 1999). The second principle, feelings of control, needs little explanation – we all like to feel in control, and young children are no different. Think about the ways in which even very young babies move beyond reciprocating an adult gesture like poking the tongue out to taking control by initiating the gesture themselves. As Vygotsky (1978) emphasises, a vital aspect of play is that children are in control of what they are doing. Perry et al. (2002) point to the importance of young children's opportunities to control challenge in activities for their emerging self-regulation. The third principle, cognitive challenge, is closely linked to Vygotsky's (1978) idea that children's learning is most powerful and effective when they are operating within their Zone of Proximal Development (ZPD), that is, what they can do given some support from a more experienced adult or peer. Observation helps us to see what an appropriate level of challenge looks like for a child, including how achievable that might be, both with and without support. The final principle, articulation of learning, reflects all that we know about how talking about our thinking and learning helps us to become more aware of it, and provides us with a way of thinking about it. These principles are also reflected in the conclusions of Nancy Perry, in the research box below.

WHAT DOES RESEARCH TELL US?

Young children's self-regulated learning and contexts that support it

Nancy Perry has spent many years observing children in classrooms, trying to understand how features of tasks, relationships and evaluation practices either support or constrain children's development of SRL and helping practitioners to develop what they do and how they interact with children. Her observations show that children of all ages engage in SRL most often when they:

a. have opportunities to engage in complex, meaningful activities that extend over multiple sessions;

b. are given choices in terms of what to work on, where and with whom;

c. control challenge by deciding, for example, how much to write, at what pace and with what level of support;

d. are involved in setting evaluation criteria and reviewing and reflecting on their learning.

- Children in high-SRL settings were more systematic and strategic in their approach to an activity than children in low-SRL contexts, including being

(Continued)

more flexible and open to seeking help when necessary. They also were more likely to engage in co-regulation and socially shared regulation, working together or soliciting the support of a peer who knew more than they did.

- Children in low-SRL classrooms were more likely to have limited choices and to have more restricted activities. Adults were mainly responsible for evaluation and focused on children's performance.

(Perry, 1998)

How do these principles and findings relate to the ways in which we might organise activities? In particular, what are the implications of the pedagogical decisions we make about the balance between child- and adult-initiated activities, the ways in which adults get involved or stand back and their interactions with children?

Looking at the continuum from child-initiated to adult-led activity: what do these mean for self-regulation?

Throughout this book we have emphasised the importance of play for young children. In Chapter 7, the evidence that play, in particular pretend play, is central to young children's self-regulatory development is set out. At the same time, play is one of a number of ways in which children learn. The EYFS says that 'Children learn by leading their own play, and by taking part in play which is guided by adults' (Department for Education, 2021: 16). So it is against this backdrop that we want to look, in the context of self-regulation, at how young children's time in settings is organised. Sharp distinctions between adult-led and child-initiated activities can often be hard to discern in everyday contexts, and an activity may move in and out of being adult- and child-led, adult guided, and with an adult absent and present.

Birth to 5 Matters sets out a range of ways in which children learn. All of these are relevant for young children's SRL. They also emphasise that activities led by adults may be most effective when they are playful:

Play, while central, is not the only way in which children develop and learn in the early years. Children also have opportunities to learn through first-hand experiences of all sorts, alongside being shown how to do things, having

(Continued)

conversations, and taking part in activities which are planned by adults to introduce or practise particular skills. Such adult-led activities are not play but they are most effective when they use some of the features of play to engage and motivate children, by ensuring that they are playful – with elements of choice, hands-on experience, connections to children's interests, and enjoyment.

(Early Years Coalition, 2021: 11)

It is important to begin here by saying that the evidence is that all types of context support young children's development and display of self-regulation (Robson, 2016a; Whitebread et al., 2007). However, there is also a lot of consensus from classroom-based research that child-initiated activities, particularly ones in which children are playing in small groups, are significantly more likely to support self-regulation. For example, one of us studied young children's musical play in the classroom and found that children showed significantly more self-regulation in activities that were initiated (and then fully led) by children themselves compared to activities that were initiated by the teacher and then led by the children (Zachariou & Whitebread, 2021).

Why might this be? Looking at possible reasons can help us to think about planning to support self-regulation in all contexts:

- when children have choice, and opportunities to control the level of challenge, they may show a range of metacognitive behaviours (Perry et al., 2002; Robson, 2016a). McInnes et al. (2011) found that when the amount of choice in play decreased, children's motivation and engagement were lessened, and they performed more poorly at problem-solving;

- child-initiated activities may be particularly valuable for problem-solving, a key context for developing self-regulation (Ramani, 2012; Robson, 2016a);

- child-initiated play may be valuable for key aspects of metacognitive regulation such as generating and analysing ideas and communicating these with others (Robson, 2015);

- child-initiated activities may be more motivating for children, and motivation is a key aspect of self-regulation (Graue et al. 2004);

- children may show greater persistence in child-initiated activities, an important aspect of emotional and motivational regulation (Robson, 2012);

- self-set learning goals are a central element of SRL (Boekaerts & Niemivirta, 2000). This may lead to higher self-regulation because children are potentially less likely to believe that their learning is controlled by others (Robson, 2010);

- adult-led activities may not capture children's interests as much, making it less likely that they will activate prior knowledge for themselves, and more likely they will rely on adult regulation and support (Boekaerts & Niemivirta, 2000);

- adult-directed involvement and 'closed-ended activities' (Krafft & Berk, 1998: 653) may lead to less use of private speech by children, a significant contributor to the development of self-regulation (see Chapter 6).

This does not mean that adult-initiated activities do not have a place when it comes to developing self-regulation. Children may be more likely to approach and initially engage in an activity when it is led by an adult (Robson & Rowe, 2012), and Vitiello et al. (2012) found that adult-directed activities supported more positive engagements between children and adults. Similarly, Zachariou and Whitebread (2021) found that activities which were fully initiated and led by the teachers provided evidence of children's self-regulation that was comparable to child-initiated play, and more than activities that were teacher-initiated but then child-led. In contrast to the finding from Krafft and Berk (1998), cited above, Winsler and Diaz (1995: 463) found that young children's private speech was most evident during tasks with an 'intermediate degree of teacher regulation'.

Self-regulation, metacognition and child- and adult-initiated activity: does it matter who initiates the task?

In this study of 4–5-year-olds in a London school, video-recorded observations of children engaged in child- and adult-initiated activities in a range of areas, indoors and outdoors, were analysed using the C.Ind.Le framework (Whitebread et al., 2007).

What did the study find?

- Both child- and adult-initiated contexts supported children's self-regulation and metacognition;

- overall, children were significantly more likely to show self-regulation and metacognition in child-initiated rather than adult-initiated activities.

Looking at each major category in more detail:

Metacognitive knowledge

- Metacognitive knowledge provided the lowest frequencies of self-regulatory behaviour, and there were no significant differences between child- and adult-initiated activities;

- in adult-initiated tasks children's expressions of metacognitive knowledge were often procedural (practical, knowing how to do something) and were

(Continued)

important in helping both themselves and their peers in completing a task successfully;

- in child-initiated activities children's expressions of task and strategy knowledge were more diverse, for a wider range of purposes. Comments were often concerned with ensuring successful continuation of an activity, including discussion and negotiation, and often showing knowledge of strategies useful in achieving a goal. These characteristics were much rarer in adult-initiated tasks.

Metacognitive regulation

- Children were much more likely to show metacognitive regulation in child-initiated activities, particularly in planning, monitoring and control.
- In child-chosen activities much of the activity was collaborative.
- Children sought help in relatively few instances. However, they were much more likely to *offer* help to their peers in child-initiated activities.
- This category accounted for the most frequent display of self-regulation, consistent with other findings (Whitebread et al., 2007).

Emotional and motivational regulation

- There were no significant differences between children's emotional and motivational regulation in child-initiated and adult-initiated activities.
- Children were more persistent, including using verbal and non-verbal self-encouragement, in child-initiated activities.

Child-initiated activities very often provided the richest opportunities for children to both develop and display their self-regulation. In part, this could be because adult-initiated activities may demand less *self*-regulation from the children, with adult intentions supporting *other*-regulation. The beneficial outcomes, though, may be many and varied. For example, in child-initiated activities children were clearer about what they were doing, and why, they generated more ideas and used a wider range of strategies. They were more likely to collaborate and help one another, to comment on what they were doing and to engage in more target setting and monitoring behaviour.

In adult-initiated activities children often appeared to give control to adults. Children seemed less interested in the outcomes and were often less sure of what they should do. At the same time, children were keen to display their knowledge to adults and often directed their comments to them, checking that what they were doing was right.

(Robson, 2016a)

Getting involved and standing back: interactions between children and adults

Following on from decisions about adult-led and child-initiated activities it is important to consider the kinds of pedagogic interactions that practitioners have with children and the impact they can have as a result of their presence or absence in children's activities. The ways in which adults interact with children play a vital role in supporting self-regulation. They may do this indirectly, supporting children's interactions with one another, as well as directly, in their own interactions with children. For Vygotsky, practitioners, as more experienced others, support children directly in their interactions with them, including modelling thinking and action. Hakkarainen et al. (2013: 213) emphasise the involvement of adults in young children's play as vital to 'moving the boundaries of the zone of proximal development'. The pressures on practitioners to 'deliver' the curriculum can sometimes mean that they find themselves more often involved in adult-led and adult-directed activities, with less time to engage with children in child-led play. There are also often, of course, many occasions when adults take the pedagogic decision to stay back and support children's independent play.

Initially, an adult being present can influence children's choices of whether or not to get involved in an activity, as we noted above (Robson & Rowe, 2012). Hutt et al. (1989) found that girls were often attracted to activities at which adults were present, while the opposite tended to be true for boys, who also spent least time at an activity if an adult was there. Robson and Rowe (2012), though, did not find such a gender difference. What happens once children are there? The evidence is not clear cut. Hutt et al. (1989), for example, found that young children's activity and attention spans increased with adult presence. In our research, one of us found that children were sometimes more receptive to adult ideas rather than other children's, and that adults were important for supporting children's speculative thinking (Robson & Rowe, 2012) and procedural knowledge (Robson, 2016b). However, adult presence can also lead to a change in control of the activity, with children feeling less involved, giving ownership of the task to the teacher, and potentially losing confidence in their own abilities (McInnes et al., 2010). When they are present, adults can become a focus for children's attention, with children looking to adults to set goals, allocate roles, check and correct progress and resolve disputes (Robson, 2016b; Zachariou & Whitebread, 2021).

Looking more closely at self-regulation, both adult involvement and absence are supportive of young children's self-regulation, but Robson (2016b), Whitebread et al. (2007) and Zachariou and Whitebread (2021) all found that children's self-regulation was significantly more likely when adults were absent. The one area in which this does not seem to be the case is children's metacognitive knowledge – of themselves and others as learners, of tasks and strategies. When they are present, adults seem to be particularly important for supporting children's expressions of metacognitive knowledge (Whitebread et al., 2007), perhaps by helping to focus children's attention, stimulating them to reflect, and to articulate their thinking more.

Metacognitive regulation may be especially more likely when adults are not involved in young children's activities, particularly children's planning, monitoring and controlling (Robson, 2016b; Whitebread et al., 2007). The examples in the box below illustrate the different areas of metacognitive regulation with observations of children's independent play from which adults were absent.

OBSERVING METACOGNITIVE REGULATION: YOUNG CHILDREN IN INDEPENDENT PLAY

Planning

In their pretend play Alyra (age 5) and Subira (age 4) demonstrate a number of aspects of planning, including negotiating, allocating individual roles and responsibilities, and deciding on ways of proceeding with the activity:

SUBIRA: Okay, it's my turn to be a mummy.

Alyra walks away, putting hands to head in a gesture of exasperation.

SUBIRA: (holding onto her) No, no, no. We <u>both</u> be the mums (holding arms out in front of her in a supplicatory gesture).

ALYRA: Yeah!

SUBIRA: We both be the mummy and we haven't got a baby, okay? Let's play.

Monitoring

Rosy (age 4) shows a number of aspects of monitoring behaviour. Her commentary shows her using self-talk to clarify and support her thinking, as she reviews her progress in her self-chosen activity:

Rosy has squirted paint onto a sheet of paper. She folds it in half, presses down on it, then unfolds it, looks at the shapes the paint has made and smiles. She squeezes more paint on, folds the paper again and presses.

ROSY: Press, press, press (pressing each time she says the word, then picking it up she unfolds it to reveal the picture and smiles) Wheheeee!

She squeezes blue paint onto the paper and folds it again.

ROSY: (very quietly) Press, press.

She looks up, smiles, then looks back at the paper and presses on it with her fingertips. She slowly unfolds the paper, looks at it, but does not smile. She frowns slightly, as she assesses her picture.

Control

Aleah (age 5) is on the climbing frame. She applies a number of previously learnt strategies, which she tries in order to solve her self-set problem effectively. These

(Continued)

include knowing how to tie a rope, testing to make sure it will bear someone's weight and throwing the rope part of the skipping rope to Bill (age 4), before the wooden handle. She knows that the task will not be solved effectively if she hits Bill with the handle, as he is likely to be hurt, and the game would have to stop:

Aleah is at the top of the frame, looking down. She holds a skipping rope with wooden handles. She ties it round the handrail and pulls on the end, testing to make sure it is secure.

Zaina swings on the rope.

Bill, next to Aleah, undoes the rope and throws it down.

Talia, on the ground, picks it up and tries to throw it back up but cannot reach.

ALEAH: (pointing at rope) Give me that end, quick!

Talia reaches up, runs off with the rope, comes back with a longer rope and passes the end up to Aleah.

Bill goes down and passes the first rope through a gap in the barrier to Aleah. She holds the ends of both ropes and pulls, walking backwards.

She then passes one rope back to Bill, first throwing over a loop, then the wooden end.

Evaluation

There is evidence of evaluation in Rosy's assessment of her painting, in the Monitoring example above. A second example is of Joshua (age 4), who has been making a hat from paper and found materials and has glued it together after fitting it round his head. He shows evidence of evaluating the strategies he has used and the quality of what he has done:

JOSHUA: It works, it will stay there forever.

Children may also be more likely to regulate their emotions and motivation when they are engaged in independent activities without the presence of adults (Robson, 2016b; Whitebread et al., 2007). In particular, they may show greater ability to resist distractions, more persistence, and more efforts to encourage both themselves and others. These may often go hand in hand. One of us found that self-encouragement, for example, talking to oneself, often occurred as children struggled with something, persisting in completing a challenge (Robson, 2016b). Children may also be more likely to encourage one another when playing independently, both verbally and non-verbally, for example, with an encouraging smile, a 'thumbs up' gesture or a hug.

All of this point to the importance of thinking carefully about how and when to get involved in children's play. Adults can be present, and interactive, in young children's play in ways which do not inhibit children's activity. Key to this are adults' presence at a wide range of types of activity, not just those which might be perceived as having 'learning' outcomes, their use of open rather than closed questions, and opportunities for children to exercise choice and control (McInnes et al., 2011). In recent years, the idea of guided play or 'playful learning' has become more prevalent, with the idea that children take the lead, but adults support their exploration through props and by interacting in ways that scaffold the children's interest and learning. McInnes et al. (2010) suggest the value of adults being proximal. They found that an adult being nearby, rather than involved, resulted in better problem-solving and greater child involvement. In contrast, one of us specifically looked at children's self-regulation when the teacher was just present (but not involved in the activity) and found that this was linked to significantly fewer self-regulation behaviours compared to when the teacher was either absent or involved (Zachariou and Whitebread, 2021). It is, then, important to say that we have no conclusive evidence about the impact of teachers just being present.

Perry and Rahim (2011) advocate adults play a guiding and facilitating role, scaffolding children's understanding, talking about learning, self-regulation and metacognition, and supporting and modelling strategy use (Perry, 2013). O'Leary and Sloutsky (2017) found that providing instruction about strategy use improved the children's monitoring and control, and that feedback was valuable for improving children's ability to monitor what they were doing. They suggest that the experience of receiving feedback about their progress can help children to develop the ability to self-generate their own feedback and monitor progress for themselves.

From an affective perspective, an adult focus on nurturing a learning community (Perry, 2013), promoting an atmosphere of emotional warmth and security, and children's feelings of autonomy, self-awareness and control (Whitebread, 2012) can support the development of self-regulation. Frampton et al. (2009) found that practitioners with a positive interaction style used more metacognitive language with the 3–5-year-old children in their study. Interestingly, they also found that practitioners stimulated metacognitive thinking when they used a more punitive style of interaction, through their emphasis on perspective-taking, and seeing things from another child's point of view. There also seem to be benefits to children's emotional and social self-regulation when adult–child discussion supports the children in finding their own strategies and solutions in conflict situations (Bingham & Whitebread, 2009).

It is also useful to look back, too, at Chapters 4, 6 and 7, and ideas discussed there for adult involvement and engagement in children's talk and play, and the implications for self-regulation of children's peer relationships, and opportunities to play and work together.

The C.Ind.Le Project team identify a range of adult interactions to support young children's self-regulation:

- Explaining or introducing an activity;
- Making learning intentions explicit;
- Guiding/scaffolding children to help them complete a task;
- Monitoring progress and providing encouragement;
- Reviewing tasks/activities;
- Encouraging higher order/metacognitive thinking;
- Engaging in sustained shared thinking/genuine conversations;
- Discussing thinking and learning with children;
- Extending child-initiated interactions;
- Supporting children to resolve social conflicts.

(The C.Ind.Le Project, n.d.)

Look at an observation of an activity in which you were involved with a child or group of children:

1. Can you identify examples of some of these types of interaction? In your view, were they successful in supporting the children's self-regulation?

2. Can you identify a missed opportunity in your interactions? What might you do or say on another occasion?

3. Can you find evidence of the children's self-regulation, either in what they did or said?

4. Now identify one type of interaction which you would like to further develop and focus on this in your work with the children.

Some implications for practice: a summary

Table 8.1 brings together the ideas we have looked at about adult actions and adult–child interactions, with ideas for practice.

Adult actions and interactions	Thinking about practice
Promote an atmosphere of emotional warmth and security, nurturing a learning community	• Show you enjoy the children's company, and are interested in them. • Be playful. • Ensure there is sufficient predictability, familiarity and routine in the day to support a sense of security. • Display photographs that show daily routines, and talk about these. • Be sensitive to verbal and non-verbal signals of tiredness, hunger, boredom, sadness etc.
Support children's feelings of control, autonomy and self-awareness	• Design the environment to support children's independence, for example, resources are accessible, babies are in positions that they can get into and out of themselves. • Give children time to work through ideas. • Involve children in arranging the physical environment, and routines. • Use and model strategies that support children's agency, including ones children can later use for themselves.
Foreground child-initiated play, and ensure children have choices in terms of what they do, where and with whom, and see themselves as having choices	• Look at the balance between child- and adult-led activities. • Ensure the environment is accessible, offers choice and flexibility, and facilitates making connections between ideas and thinking. • Offer alternatives from which children can choose when providing more adult-structured activities.
Ensure children have opportunities to set their own learning goals, and to control challenge	• Give children time and opportunities to organise things for themselves, and avoid intervening too early. • This may be particularly important in adult-initiated activities: think about how to ensure that children see themselves as having some control in adult-led tasks, are clear about what they are doing, and can talk about it, for example deciding how much to write and with what level of support.
Ensure cognitive challenge, and opportunities for children to engage in complex, meaningful activities that extend over multiple sessions	• Ensure the environment supports independent and collaborative activity without distraction, for example, children do not have to walk through a space where children are building. • Ask open-ended questions that require higher-order thinking: 'what makes you say that?' why do you think…?' • Provide an accessible space for children to keep 'work in progress', such as models, so they can return to it, and ensure children understand that this should not be disturbed. • Revisit activities and build on them over multiple sessions.
Make learning intentions explicit in adult-led activities	• Talk about these with children before they begin, and also during an activity, restating them in conversation, as you work with children.
Play a guiding and facilitating role, scaffolding children's understanding	• See Chapter 6, supporting Sustained Shared Thinking list: observing, scaffolding, extending, discussing, modelling, playing. • Use gesture to accompany talk.
Get involved in children's self-initiated play, as appropriate, without taking it over	• Be sensitive in deciding if and when you should get involved. • Think about how: observe before entering, work and play alongside children, describe aloud what they are doing. • Enter pretend play in role.

Table 8.1 (Continued)

Adult actions and interactions	Thinking about practice
Look at how children's activity can be supported by being nearby rather than leading	• Think about where adults are positioned in the room. • Stay in one place for extended lengths of time, observe, and comment or add to children's conversation as appropriate.
Support and model strategy use	• Talk with children about strategies they are using, drawing attention to them. • Play alongside children and model self-commentary and actions, for example, how a block can be balanced on top of another, how to pour water into a cup without spilling it. • Describe what strategies you are trying, using self-talk.
Talk about thinking, learning and self-regulation with children, including providing feedback which focuses on aspects of self-regulation	• Use language that focuses on thinking and learning, with individuals, groups and the whole class: 'what do we have to remember?' 'think about your learning'. • Encourage children to talk (self-talk and to others) about what they are doing during an activity. • Focus on thinking and learning in feedback: 'good thinking', 'good remembering', 'that was a good plan'. • Use feedback which focuses on metacognitive knowledge – 'I can see you knew how to...', and regulation – 'I think your idea worked well because...' etc.
Encourage children to explain activities to one another, and to talk another child through an activity	• Encourage children to help one another, for example, when building, modelling etc, including talking about what they need, can do, etc. • Ensure collaborative activity. • Plan peer-tutoring activities. • Play barrier games (where players have an identical set of objects which are hidden from each other; one player makes an arrangement of objects and gives instructions to the other to try to make the same arrangement).
Think about how to maximise self-regulation opportunities in large group and whole class activities	• Encourage children to check ideas, and resolve roles, etc with other children in group and whole class activities, to avoid them seeing the adult as the person who helps or decides. • Look for opportunities for children to work cooperatively during large group or whole class activities. • Aim to ensure that adults are involved in all types of activity in all contexts, to ensure children do not think that smaller group activities are places for their control, and large group and whole class activities are times when they give responsibility to adults.
Ensure opportunities for children to cooperate and collaborate in pairs and small groups	• Arrange furniture so it supports pair and group activity. • Provide games, for example snakes and ladders, 'battleships', that require two or more children to play. • In a group task, talk through with the children what each will do. For example, one child collects resources, one is responsible for sharing things out, one for recording what they do – this can help children to develop skills of working in a group. • Resource areas in ways that support collaboration for them to be effective: drainpipes and pulleys in the sand, a two-person rocking boat, parachute games for larger groups.

(Continued)

Table 8.1 (Continued)

Adult actions and interactions	Thinking about practice
Ensure children are involved in setting evaluation criteria and reviewing and reflecting on their learning	• Encourage children to talk about what they are trying to do, and what, for them, counts as success in the activity. • When children say, for example, 'I'm done', 'I've finished' talk to them about how they know that. • Use photographs and video of children's activities as starting points for discussion, encouraging children to talk about what they were thinking and learning: 'what did you learn?', what they felt their best ideas were, and how they felt about the activity.
Stimulate metacognitive thinking in conflict situations, focusing on discussion that includes perspective-taking, and supporting children in finding their own strategies and solutions	• Talk about your own feelings, modelling how you manage them. • Use resources such as Persona Dolls, and books that feature a range of feelings to support discussion about managing feelings and dealing with conflicting views. • Ask children for their ideas on what to do if someone feels sad or angry. • Support children in recognising the consequences of their behaviour when they upset someone, and in developing strategies to deal with this. • This may be a particular challenge for children with Autism Spectrum Disorder: think about how dolls and puppets can be used to support talk.

Table 8.1 Adult actions and adult-child interactions that can support self-regulation

Thinking about the environment

Practitioners in Reggio Emilia talk of the environment as the 'third teacher' (Gandini, 1998), a constantly evolving space which can provoke children's thinking and help to make their learning meaningful. As we saw in Chapter 2, Roebers (2017) concludes that development of executive function is driven by the child's interaction with her environment.

In Chapters 1 and 2 we looked at the two key components of SRL: metacognitive knowledge and metacognitive regulation, and at how these are both affected by our metacognitive experiences. These experiences, by definition, occur within environments, both home and school. With that in mind, a useful starting question is:

> *How can the environment I create afford opportunities for experiences which can support the development of self-regulation?*

Answers to this question will differ, according to context, and also according to age and stage of development. Bronson (2000) looks in detail at this, and Table 8.2 includes highlights from her conclusions, differentiated by age.

It is worth looking at some aspects of the environment now in a little more detail:

An inclusive environment

The Early Years Coalition (2021: 35) emphasise that 'inclusive spaces are nurturing and supportive of all children'. This includes children having a sense of belonging, with things around them that support their senses of themselves and their families and communities. The environment needs to ensure access for all children. This includes the elimination of obstacles and furniture that could restrict mobility for all children, and provision of mobility aids, adapted equipment and clothing to ensure all areas, including outdoors, are fully accessible, especially for children with a physical disability.

Access alone, of course, is not enough. The environment needs to support engagement and achievement, and, in the context of self-regulation, opportunities for children to see themselves, and act as, thinkers and learners, with agency. This may mean, for example, careful attention to how the environment supports children's opportunities to develop concentration, attention and persistence. Children with dyslexia may experience difficulties in integrating visual and auditory data (Siegler et al., 2017), making it important to consider how the environment and adults' interactions support children in regulating aspects such as organisation of resources to support their thinking. Changes to routine, and alterations to the environment, need to be carefully considered for all children, but particularly for those with a special educational need, such as autism spectrum disorder.

Ages and areas of self-regulation (using Bronson's categories)	Role of the environment
Infants (0–12 months)	
Social/emotional	A consistent primary caregiver, and a reasonable amount of order and routine that an infant can recognise and come to anticipate; Alternating periods of stimulation and quiet that help children regulate arousal and sleep-wake cycles.
Prosocial	Others, including siblings, interact in gentle and appropriate ways.
Cognitive	Visual and auditory stimulation that an infant can distinguish, monitor and explore; Coherent and predictable patterns, routines and sequences.
Motivational	Safe for activity and exploration; Interesting, with appropriate levels of familiarity and novelty; Cause-effect opportunities that an infant can come to anticipate and manipulate.

(Continued)

Table 8.2 (Continued)

Ages and areas of self-regulation (using Bronson's categories)	Role of the environment
Toddlers (12–36 months)	
Social/emotional	A reasonable amount of order and routine that a toddler can recognise and predict; An appropriate level of freedom and constraint; Opportunities for observation, imitation, interaction and participation.
Prosocial	A climate of positive and caring social interactions.
Cognitive	Safe and interesting places for play and exploration; An appropriate range, and sufficient amount, of materials so toddlers can play with them as long as they are interested; Space and opportunity for action and investigation with protected spaces for uninterrupted play.
Motivational	Safe for activity and independent action; Opportunities for toddlers to practice self-regulation and choice; Appropriate levels of challenge, dependent on ability and interest.
Preschool and Kindergarten (3–5/6 years)	
Social/emotional	A trusted adult to support independence, self-control, and appropriate interactions with peers; Clear, age-appropriate guidelines for responsibilities, choices, expectations and consequences that are consistently implemented; Materials that support constructive peer interactions and pretend play.
Prosocial	Opportunities for positive and cooperative interactions; Includes materials and activities that encourage and support cooperative and prosocial behaviour and attitudes; Guidelines that encourage and support responsibility, respect and care for others, and sanction negative behaviour.
Cognitive	Coherent and predictable enough to support understanding and predictability; Flexible enough to ensure child can influence aspects of the environment; An appropriate range of materials; Provides choice and ensures time for choice; Space and opportunities for action and investigation, with protected spaces for uninterrupted, focused activities.

Table 8.2 (Continued)

Ages and areas of self-regulation (using Bronson's categories)	Role of the environment
Motivational	Enough coherence, predictability and flexibility to support children's understanding and engagement in self-regulated action;
	Appropriate level of challenge;
	Materials that children can structure independently;
	Opportunities to practice self-regulation and choice;
	Materials that children can access and use independently;
	Rules that support and protect independent action (individual and small group);
	Techniques for independent organisation (eg planning boards).

Table 8.2 Supporting self-regulation, the role of the environment (drawing on Bronson, 2000)

Provision for active play

In thinking about active play, we include children's mental as well as physical activity, but here we want to focus particularly on ways in which physical activity may be especially supportive of young children's self-regulation. At a neurological level, physical activity increases activation in the prefrontal cortex, which is linked to self-regulatory behaviour, including inhibitory control and working memory (Becker et al., 2014). Becker et al. found that higher levels of active play outdoors in young children predicted better self-regulation. As we saw in Chapter 6, gesture and body movement are supportive of memory, problem-solving and self-regulation in general. What does this mean for the environment? First, that it is important to incorporate movement and physical activity into children's lives both in and out of doors, at home and at school. Indoors, in particular, this means trying to ensure sufficient physical space for children to be appropriately active without hurting either themselves or others. This may be a particularly important consideration for children in wheelchairs, with limited mobility, or visual impairment. Second, that observing young children's active play can provide us with valuable insights into their self-regulation. For children in the school years this may be particularly important, given the pressure there is on aspects such as playtimes and opportunities for children in the primary years to engage in active play. A reduction in playtime has been related to difficulties in self-regulation and attention deficit, among other things (Pellegrini et al., 2007).

Play outdoors

Outdoors – in settings, local parks, forest school and elsewhere – offers opportunities that being inside just cannot match. Many of these opportunities are supportive of self-regulation. Outdoor space is often seen as more 'owned' by children (Davies et al., 2013), supporting their feelings of control and autonomy, and with more opportunities for child-initiated activity of all kinds. It is also often seen as more conducive to collaboration and collective activity (Davies et al., 2013). Canning (2013) links the potential that outdoor spaces have for (quite literally) seeing the world in new ways with pretend play, a key context for self-regulation.

Among other things, Tovey (2017) suggests that outdoors affords young children important opportunities for adventure, risk and challenge. As she says:

> *The willingness to take risks is an important characteristic of an effective learner. It can help develop a disposition to 'have a go', persist at something and see challenges as problems to enjoy rather than things to fear.*

(Tovey, 2017: 12)

In many instances, the challenges are ones that children have set for themselves – can I reach the top of the climbing frame? Can I balance on this plank? They embody important aspects of self-regulation such as knowledge of the task and of oneself as a learner, planning, monitoring and evaluating, motivation and persistence, in contexts which feature problem-solving, self-set goals, and opportunities for children to control challenge for themselves. Tovey (2017) identifies a range of features that are likely to be included in an outdoor space that provides challenge in play and exploration:

- Direct experience of nature in all the seasons;
- Child garden;
- Uneven ground;
- Wild areas;
- Diverse movement experiences;
- Open-ended materials;
- Provision for meaningful learning in all areas of the curriculum;
- Spaces to hide, make dens and to create their own secret worlds;
- Quiet spaces;
- Uninterrupted time.

OBSERVING RISK, CHALLENGE AND PROBLEM-POSING AND SOLVING IN OUTDOOR PLAY: BILL

Bill spent a long time one afternoon sliding repeatedly down the slide. He experimented with sliding on his back, his side, sitting up and lying down.

BILL: If you don't hold on with any hands then you slide down really fast.

(Continued)

He later went off to find a pillowcase, to put over his legs, saying this would help him to slide down faster.

Bill poses himself a challenge: What's the fastest way I can get down the slide? In attempting to solve his self-set problem he engages in a series of challenges, including the increased risk of sliding when not holding on. This necessitates a knowledge of what kinds of strategies are needed, as well as of himself. He persists and has sufficient uninterrupted time to see his problem through.

Time

Ensuring that children have sufficient, uninterrupted time to engage with and complete activities can be highly challenging, in an often-crowded curriculum. At the same time, there is evidence that if we can do so it can support deeper understandings and more complex knowledge in, for example, problem-solving (Lambert, 2000), and aid aspects such as possibility thinking (Craft et al., 2012; Davies et al., 2013), that is, the posing of 'what if?' questions, exploration, and finding and solving problems, all important aspects of self-regulation.

In addition, children will need to know, and be confident, that time is available for them. Gura (1992), looking at children's blockplay, for example, comments on the way in which a 'hit and run' attitude seemed to develop among children where lack of time prevented them from engaging in sustained play over a period of time. Giving children sufficient uninterrupted time can support them in persisting, and feeling in control, an important aspect of self-regulation. As the Early Years Coalition (2021) emphasise, too, sufficient time is important for children just to 'be' within the environment, to develop their sense of themselves, including themselves as thinkers and learners.

Making children's thinking visible: displays

In Chapter 5, we look at documentation and the value it has for supporting and developing young children's thinking. The documentation that children and adults develop together can be displayed, as work in progress, providing a context for discussion and continued development. Documentation like this can be valuable for metacognitive processes, helping to make visible the nature of the learning processes and strategies used by each child (Project Zero & Reggio Children, 2001), as children talk about what they think and know and have learned. Carr (2011) suggests the value of practitioners 'visiting' wall displays in the classroom with the children, revisiting and reviewing their learning with them, as a way of reflecting upon it and articulating their understanding.

Sustained Shared Thinking (SST), introduced in Chapter 6, is a term developed during the Researching Effective Pedagogy in the Early Years (REPEY) project (Siraj-Blatchford et al., 2002). It describes interactions in settings which contribute to the development of higher-order thinking, including self-regulation. Marion Dowling (2005) identifies a set of criteria for providing appropriate contexts for supporting SST:

Children should have:

- scope to become involved in activities and situations that interest and intrigue them

- access to a rich range of provision that is continuously available

- space inside and outside to move, make and do things without disturbing others

- time to practice and apply what they have learned, explore and experiment in depth, follow through their interests and decisions, even if they don't work, and make connections

- scope to link their home experiences with experiences in the setting

- opportunities to have their thinking made visible, through records of their ideas, in words and images

- opportunities to think which are embedded in their culture and language.

(Dowling, 2005: 7)

1. Using Dowling's list, take a tour of your environment(s) and look at it from the perspective of supporting the children's self-regulation.

2. Now take a tour and try to consider the environment from the children's perspective: do you see things differently, and do you notice different things?

3. Now do the same with a group of children. You might talk with them, or observe and record them; children could take photographs, draw pictures, or make models, etc. Are there particular places that children go to a lot? Are there spaces that are overlooked or under-used?

4. Using all of these different pieces of information, think about whether you want to make any changes, or develop aspects of the environment, to support the children's self-regulation.

The 'stuff' of self-regulation: materials and resources

The resources and materials in the environment act as 'things to think with' (Turkle, 2007) and as ways for children to represent and show their thinking. Gura (1992: 27), for example, believes that blockplay 'can be used to say certain kinds of things more powerfully than words or words alone can say'.

In the context of self-regulation and metacognition, opportunities to engage with open-ended props and resources may be particularly valuable. Why might this be?

- Open-ended resources support more self-initiated and sustained play themes (Broadhead, 2004, with children aged 3–5 years).

- The non-representational, open-ended nature of objects such as blocks and cardboard supports speculative talk and discussion about what they might become in the play, with the possibilities this has for developing both meta-cognition and theory of mind (Trawick-Smith, 1998, with children aged 2–6 years).

- Resourcing social and pretend play areas with items such as fabric and empty boxes can support increased highly social and collaborative activity (a key context for self-regulation). More structured themed role-play areas may be more closed in their potential for stimulating play themes and the social interactions required in negotiating roles, talking about the play and announcing symbolic transformations (Broadhead, 2004).

- Open-ended, non-representational, materials embody endless possibilities. Parker (2018), for example, cites the value of clay for giving children the opportunity to express their thoughts, feelings and experiences in both two and three dimensions.

- Including representational, replica play toys may even diminish the complexity of children's play, by limiting opportunities for representation. Including toy animals in the blockplay area, for example, can suggest the building of enclosures for the animals, and may limit the kinds of structures children choose to build, and prevent them thinking further (Trawick-Smith et al., 2017).

- In digital play, the presence of representational images in many software programs and apps can shape the types of narrative created during digital art-making, inspiring more 'as if' scenarios, rather than representations of personal experience and supporting less opportunity for children to think symbolically and develop their self-regulation and metacognition (Sakr et al., 2016).

As Gauntlett (2011: 176) asks: 'Does it (the material) want you to do your own thing, or does it want you to do its thing?'. At the same time, as Rogers (2015) suggests, when more 'closed-ended', thematic play areas are set up, children do often subvert them, transforming them into spaces and places that have more meaning for them. There may also be differences in relation to age. Umek and Musek (2001) found that younger children (aged 3–4 years) showed higher forms of symbolic play with structured materials rather than open-ended unstructured resources, while for the 5–6-year-old children in their study there was no difference.

The growth of digital technologies is an aspect of resourcing that has become particularly important in recent years, and which engenders much discussion, some of which is looked at in previous chapters. Here we want to emphasise the idea that 'technologies can be an effective part of a pedagogy that bridges digital and non-digital resources to create playful learning narratives for young children' (Arnott et al., 2018: 804). In effect, that digital technologies, like other kinds of resources, are valuable for the opportunities they afford for children's learning, and it is how we choose to use them which matters. At the same time, they also have unique properties, different to tools such as paper and pencils, and influence both how children make meaning and what meanings are made.

One advantage in the context of self-regulation is that digital technologies such as tablets and iPads offer opportunities for playfulness, for example, in the context of children's mark-making and art (Price et al., 2015). There is also evidence to suggest the value of digital devices, particularly touch-screen, for young children's problem-solving, planning and executive function (Herodotou, 2018; Huber et al., 2016), independent learning and peer assessment (Clarke & Abbott, 2016). Littleton and Mercer (2013) relate the ways in which children used an interactive whiteboard as a collaborative focus during peer discussion. It acted as a memory tool for them, and was also capable of repeated discussion, once saved and reloaded.

Working with parents

The starting point, as always, is to acknowledge and value parents' insights, experience and understanding of their own children and to seek to work with them in developing the children's self-regulation. In a study of children's well-being, Robson et al. (2019) found that both parents and practitioners placed high value on a number of aspects that contribute to children's self-regulation: time and space to play, feeling good about themselves and opportunities to express thoughts and feelings. Both also placed a lot of emphasis on the importance of the physical environment, citing opportunities to experience different spaces/places, a range of experiences, including first-hand, the affordance of the environment for exploration and opportunities to experiment. A study of parents in Moscow also showed them placing high importance on aspects of self-regulation in response to the question 'What are the most important features that a family must cultivate in children?' (Sobkin et al., 2018: 115). These features included persistence, tenacity and goal placement, and they came second only to 'kindness and empathy toward people'. So, it can be expected that parents will be receptive to and share practitioners' views about the importance of developing self-regulation. Larkin (2010) identifies parents' lack of familiarity with key terms as an issue, particularly ideas such as metacognition, and metacognitive knowledge and regulation. This suggests that an important task for practitioners in working with parents is to support their understanding of what these terms mean in practice, using analogies such as ideas of 'learning to learn' to help in this. Displays and parental workshops can be useful in giving examples that show what these ideas look like in the context of their own children. At the same time, practitioners can ensure that parents feel valued and included, by listening closely to their own ideas and theories about their children's thinking.

In this chapter, we have focused particularly on adult–child interactions and the provision of a physical environment which supports the development of self-regulation. Looking back at Vygotsky, parents have a similar role to practitioners, in being often a 'more experienced other', and supporting children's move from other- to self-regulation. So, much of what we have discussed here as valuable for practitioners holds true in thinking about parents and carers, including the principles we began with: emotional warmth and security – attachment, feelings of control, cognitive challenge and articulation of learning.

Throughout this book we have emphasised the importance of talk, and particularly talk about thinking and learning. This suggests that an important point in working with parents is to emphasise the value of this kind of metacognitive and mental state talk in their interactions with their children, drawing attention to it in their everyday conversations. This may be particularly important for children from lower socioeconomic status (SES) backgrounds, where the evidence is that they may be disadvantaged in relation to their peers from higher SES backgrounds, whose language skills may be more developed (Larkin, 2010). Not only does this mean that such children may be less experienced in articulating their thoughts, but, as a consequence, they may be more at risk of their knowledge and understanding being missed by practitioners.

We have already noted the links between physically active play and beneficial effects on brain structure in aspects such as attention, working memory and self-regulation. In addition to this, the importance of sleep is clear, with even minor reductions in sleep (one hour) potentially having a negative impact on brain processing in young children (Molfese et al., 2013).

Summarising a range of studies on parental interactions with their children in problem-solving tasks, Larkin (2010) concludes that sometimes parents actually supported their children too much and that what the children benefitted from was time and space to play independently, developing their persistence, and metacognitive knowledge and regulation, as a result of trying, failing, trying again and so on. Barker et al. (2014) found that the amount of less-structured time in 6–7-year-olds daily lives, including free play alone and with others, visits to places such as museums and social outings, was closely related to the children's self-regulation, and the OECD (2020) found that 'moderate' engagement in special activities was actually better for children's learning than very frequent, or even daily, special activities such as dance classes, extra sports, etc. Parents may often feel pressured to fill their children's lives with structured activities, and it may be that one thing practitioners can do is to reassure parents that the everyday activities they do with their children, including giving them time and space to play, and with everyday resources and toys, are supportive of the development of lifelong skills in self-regulation. Accessibility and opportunities for children to make their own choices of what to play with (within limits, particularly safety!) are important for practitioners to emphasise in their discussions with parents.

Conclusion

This chapter has had two purposes. First, it has been about the vital role of pedagogy in thinking about self-regulation. Second, it provides a summary for the book as a whole, bringing together ideas we have looked at throughout the book.

The most important message to emphasise here is that everyday life, at home and at school, provides constant opportunities for young children to develop self-regulation. As we have seen, all types of context, from child-led to adult-initiated, with adults involved and absent, are supportive. However, there is also clear evidence that child-initiated, independent activities often provide the richest contexts for young children to both develop and display their self-regulation. In addition, when adults are absent, children often exhibit more self-regulation, particularly in terms of meta-cognitive regulation, and emotional control.

While all sizes of grouping also potentially support self-regulation, the evidence is there to point to the value of small group and peer activity, particularly when this also supports co-operation and collaboration. The ways in which adults get involved, and the emphasis they place on helping children to become aware of their thinking, can make a clear difference to the development of the children's self-regulatory learning.

Complementing the ways in which activities are organised and managed is the physical environment in which they happen. Importantly, everyday spaces, places and resources, at home and in settings, are all that are needed to support young children's development of self-regulation. Crucial to this development are the ways in which the environment is organised to support young children's active play and feelings of control, autonomy and independence, in an atmosphere of emotional warmth and security. The environment needs to provide appropriate cognitive challenge and enough time and space for children to complete their self-set challenges.

Key further reading

Bronson, M. (2000). *Self-regulation in early childhood: Nature and nurture.* New York, NY: Guilford Press.

Early Years Coalition (2021). *Birth to 5 matters: Non-statutory guidance for the early years foundation stage.* Early Education. https://www.birthto5matters.org.ukp-content/uploads/2021/04/Birthto5Matters-download.pdf.

Perry, N., & Rahim, A. (2011). Studying self-regulated learning in classrooms. In **B. J. Zimmerman & D. H. Schunk** (Eds.), *Handbook of self-regulation of learning and performance* (pp. 122–136), London: Routledge.

Robson, S. (2016a). Self-regulation, metacognition and child- and adult-initiated activity: Does it matter who initiates the task? *Early Child Development and Care*, 186(5), 764–784.

Robson, S. (2016b). Self-regulation and metacognition in young children: Does it matter if adults are present or not? *British Educational Research Journal*, 42(2), 185–306.

Digital resources

Dowling, M. (2005) Supporting young children's sustained shared thinking: An exploration. *Training Materials*. Early Education. USB available from: https://www.early-education.org.uk/supporting-young-chil-drens-sustained-shared-thinking-usb.

The C.IndLe (Cambridge Independent Learning) Project (n.d.) *Supporting young children in becoming self-regulated learners. Double CD Training Pack for 5-day training course.* Available from: https://www.e-duc.cam.ac.uk/research/programmes/cindle/CDPack.html.

References

Adler, K., Salanterä, S., & Zumstein-Shaha, M. (2019). Focus group interviews in child, youth, and parent research: An integrative literature review. *International Journal of Qualitative Methods*, 18, 1–15.

Ahn, H. J. (2005). Child care teachers' strategies in children's socialization of emotion. *Early Child Development and Care*, 175(1), 49–61.

Alexander, J. M., Carr, M., & Schwanenflugel, P. J. (1995). Development of metacognition in gifted children: Directions for future research. *Developmental Review*, 15(1), 1–37.

Allan, N., Lonigan, C., Barkley, R., Becker, D., McClelland, M., Loprinzi, P., … Goswami, U. (2019). The development of self-regulation in young children. In D. Whitebread, V. Grau, K. Kumpulainen, M. M. McClelland, N. E. Perry, & D. Pino-Pasternak (Eds.), *SAGE handbook of developmental psychology and early childhood education* (pp. 471–486). London: Sage.

Annevirta, T., Laakkonen, E., & Kinnunen, R. (2007). Developmental dynamics of metacognitive knowledge and text comprehension skill in the first primary school years. *Metacognition and Learning*, 2, 21–39.

Aranda, G., & Tytler, R. (2017). Aligning neuroscience findings with socio-cultural perspectives on learning in science. In J. C. Horvath, J. M. Lodge, & J. Hattie (Eds.), *From the laboratory to the classroom: Translating science of learning for teachers* (pp. 139–154). Abingdon: Routledge.

Arnott, L., Palaiologou, I., & Gray, C. (2018). Editorial. Digital devices, internet-enabled toys and digital games: The changing nature of young children's learning ecologies, experiences and pedagogies. *British Journal of Educational Technology*, 49(5), 803–806.

Astington, J. (1994). *The child's discovery of the mind*. London: Fontana.

Australian Government Department of Education, Employment and Workplace Relations. (2009). *Belonging, being and becoming – The early years learning framework for Australia (EYLF)*. Retrieved from https://docs.education.gov.au/system/files/doc/other/belonging_being_and_becoming_the_early_years_learning_framework_for_australia_0.pdf

Azevedo, R. (2009). Theoretical, conceptual, methodological, and instructional issues in research on metacognition and self-regulated learning: A discussion. *Metacognition and Learning*, 4, 87–95.

Backer-Grøndahl, A., & Nærde, A. (2017). Self-regulation in early childhood: The role of siblings, center care and socioeconomic status. *Social Development*, 26(3), 530–544.

Barker, J. E., Semenov, A. D., Michaelson, L., Provan, L. S., Snyder, H. R., & Munakata, Y. (2014). Less-structured time in children's daily lives predicts self-directed executive functioning. *Frontiers in Psychology*, 5, 593.

Bartsch, K., & Wellman, H. M. (1995). *Children talk about the mind*. Oxford: Oxford University Press.

Basilio, M., & Rodriguez, C. (2017). How toddlers think with their hands: Social and private gestures as evidence of cognitive self-regulation in guided play with objects. *Early Child Development and Care*, 187(12), 1971–1986.

Becker, D. R., McClelland, M. C., Loprinzi, P., & Trost, S. G. (2014). Physical activity, self-regulation, and early academic achievement in preschool children. *Early Education and Development*, 25(1), 56–70.

Bergen, D., Schroer, J., & Woodin, M. (2018). *Brain research in education and the social sciences*. New York, NY; Abingdon: Routledge.

Berk, L. E., Mann, T. D., & Ogan, A. T. (2006). Make-believe play: Wellspring for development of self-regulation. In D. G. Singer, R. M. Golinkoff, & K. Hirsh-Pasek (Eds.), *Play = learning: How play motivates and enhances children's cognitive and social-emotional growth* (pp. 74–100). New York, NY: Oxford University Press.

Berkovits, L., Eisenhower, A., & Blacher, J. (2017). Emotion regulation in young children with autism spectrum disorders. *Journal of Autism and Developmental Disorders*, 47, 68–79.

Bernier, A., Carlson, S. M., & Whipple, N. (2010). From external regulation to self-regulation: Early parenting precursors of young children's executive functioning. *Child Development*, 81(1), 326–339.

Bialystok, E., & DePape, A.-M. (2009). Musical expertise, bilingualism, and executive functioning. *Journal of Experimental Psychology: Human Perception and Performance*, 35(2), 565.

Bingham, S., & Whitebread, D. (2009). Teachers supporting children's self-regulation in conflict situations within an early years setting. In T. Papatheodorou & J. Moyles (Eds.), *Learning together in the early years* (pp.90–97). London: Routledge.

Blair, C. (2002). School readiness: Integrating cognition and emotion in a neurobiological conceptualization of children's functioning at school entry. *American Psychologist*, 57(2), 111.

Blair, C., Calkins, S., & Kopp, L. (2010). Self-regulation as the interface of emotional and cognitive development: Implications for education and academic achievement. In R. H. Hoyle (Ed.), *Handbook of personality and self-regulation* (pp. 64–90). Malden, MA: Wiley-Blackwell.

Blair, C., & Diamond, A. (2008). Biological processes in prevention and intervention: The promotion of self-regulation as a means of preventing school failure. *Development and Psychopathology*, 20(3), 899–911.

Blair, C., & Raver, C. C. (2014). Closing the achievement gap through modification of neurocognitive and neuroendocrine function: Results from a cluster randomized controlled trial of an innovative approach to the education of children in kindergarten. *PloS One*, 9(11), e112393.

Blair, C., & Razza, R. P. (2007). Relating effortful control, executive function, and false belief understanding to emerging math and literacy ability in kindergarten. *Child Development*, 78(2), 647–663.

Blair, C., & Ursache, A. (2011). A bidirectional model of executive functions and self-regulation. In K. D. Vohs & R. F. Baumeister (Eds.), *Handbook of self-regulation: Research, theory and applications* (2nd ed., pp. 300–320). New York, NY; London: Guilford Press.

Bodrova, E. (2011). Promoting self-regulation in young children: Tools of the mind. In *BJEP psychological aspects of education current trends conference: Self-regulation and dialogue in primary classrooms*, University of Cambridge, 2nd and 3rd June 2011.

Bodrova, E., & Leong, D. J. (2006). *Tools of the mind: The Vygotskian approach to early childhood education*. Upper Saddle River, NJ: Pearson.

Bodrova, E., Leong, D. J., & Akhutina, T. V. (2011). When everything new is well-forgotten old: Vygotsky/Luria insights in the development of executive functions. *New Directions for Child and Adolescent Development*, 2011(133), 11–28.

Boekaerts, M. (2011). Emotions, emotion regulation, and self-regulation of learning. In B. J. Zimmerman & D. H. Schunk (Eds.), *Handbook of self-regulation of learning and performance* (pp. 408–425). New York, NY: Routledge.

Boekaerts, M., & Cascallar, E. (2006). How far have we moved toward the integration of theory and practice in self-regulation? *Educational Psychology Review*, 18, 199–210.

Boekaerts, M., & Niemivirta, M. (2000). Self-regulated learning: Finding a balance between learning goals and ego-protective goals. In M. Boekaerts, P. R. Pintrich, & M. Zeidner (Eds.), *Handbook of self-regulation* (pp. 417–450). San Diego, CA: Academic Press.

Bredikyte, M., & Hakkarainen, P. (2017). Self-regulation and narrative interventions in children's play. In T. Bruce, P. Hakkarainen, & M. Bredikyte (Eds.), *The Routledge international handbook of early childhood play* (pp. 246–257). Abingdon: Routledge.

Bretherton, I., & Beeghly, M. (1982). Talking about internal states: The acquisition of an explicit theory of mind. *Developmental Psychology*, 18(6), 906–921.

Bridges, L. J., & Grolnick, W. S. (1995). The development of emotional self-regulation in infancy and early childhood. *Social Development*, 15, 185–211.

Brinck, I., & Liljenfors, R. (2013). The developmental origin of metacognition. *Infant and Child Development*, 22(1), 85–101.

Broadhead, P. (2004). *Early years play and learning: Developing social skills and cooperation*. London: RoutledgeFalmer.

Bronson, M. (2000). *Self-regulation in early childhood: Nature and nurture*. New York, NY; London: Guilford Press.

Brown, A. L. (1987). Metacognition, executive control, self-regulation and other more mysterious mechanisms. In F. E. Weinert & R. H. Kluwe (Eds.), *Metacognition, motivation and understanding* (pp. 65–116). Hillsdale, NJ: Lawrence Erlbaum Associates.

Bruner, J. S. (1972). Nature and uses of immaturity. *American Psychologist*, 27(8), 687–708.

Bryce, D., & Whitebread, D. (2012). The development of metacognitive skills: Evidence from observational analysis of young children's behavior during problem-solving. *Metacognition and Learning*, 7(3), 197–217.

Bryce, D., Whitebread, D., & Szücs, D. (2015). The relationships among executive functions, metacognitive skills and educational achievement in 5 and 7 year-old children. *Metacognition and Learning*, 10, 181–198.

Burrage, M. S., Ponitz, C. C., McCready, E. A., Shah, P., Sims, B. C., Jewkes, A. M., & Morrison, F. J. (2008). Age-and schooling-related effects on executive functions in young children: A natural experiment. *Child Neuropsychology*, 14(6), 510–524.

Butler, D. L. (2011). Investigating self-regulated learning using in-depth case studies. In B. J. Zimmerman & D. H. Schunk (Eds.), *Handbook of self-regulation of learning and performance* (pp. 346–360). New York, NY: Routledge.

Cameron, C. E., Brock, L. L., Murrah, W. M., Bell, L. H., Worzalla, S. L., Grissmer, D., & Morrison, F. J. (2012). Fine motor skills and executive function both contribute to kindergarten achievement. *Child Development*, 83, 1229–1244.

Cameron, C. E., Cottone, E. A., Murrah, W. M., & Grissmer, D. W. (2016). How are motor skills linked to children's school performance and academic achievement? *Child Development Perspectives*, 10, 93–98.

Canning, N. (2013). 'Where's the bear? Over there!' – Creative thinking and imagination in den making. *Early Child Development and Care*, 183(8), 1042–1053.

Carlson, S. M., Moses, L. J., & Breton, C. (2002). How specific is the relation between executive function and theory of mind? Contributions of inhibitory control and working memory. *Infant and Child Development: An International Journal of Research and Practice*, 11(2), 73–92.

Carpendale, J., Lewis, C., & Müller, U. (2018). *The development of children's thinking*. London: Sage.

Carr, M. (2001). *Assessment in early childhood settings*. London: Paul Chapman.

Carr, M. (2011). Young children reflecting on their learning: Teachers' conversation strategies. *Early Years*, 31(3), 257–270.

Chaplin, T. M. (2015). Gender and emotion expression: A developmental contextual perspective. *Emotion Review*, 7(1), 14–21.

Clarke, C., & Abbott, L. (2016). Young pupils', their teacher's and classroom assistants' experiences of iPads in a Northern Ireland school: 'Four and five years old, who would have thought they could do that?' *British Journal of Educational Technology*, 47(6), 1051–1064.

Claxton, G. (2012). Turning thinking on its head: How bodies make up their minds. *Thinking Skills and Creativity*, 7, 78–84.

Coates, E., & Coates, A. (2015). Recognising 'the sacred spark of wonder': Scribbling and related talk as evidence of how young children's thinking may be identified. In S. Robson & S. Flannery Quinn (Eds.), *The Routledge international handbook of young children's thinking and understanding* (pp. 306–317). Abingdon: Routledge.

Council for the Curriculum Examinations and Assessment (CCEA), Northern Ireland. (2007). *The Northern Ireland curriculum: Primary*. Retrieved from https://ccea.org.uk/downloads/docs/ccea-asset/Curriculum/The%20Northern%20Ireland%20Curriculum%20-%20Primary.pdf

Council for the Curriculum Examinations and Assessment (CCEA), Northern Ireland. (2018). *Curricular guidance for pre-school education*. Retrieved from https://ccea.org.uk/downloads/docs/ccea-asset/Curriculum/Curricular%20Guidance%20for%20Pre-School%20Education.pdf

Craft, A., McConnon, L., & Paige-Smith, A. (2012). Child-initiated play and professional creativity: Enabling four-year-olds' possibility thinking. *Thinking Skills and Creativity*, 7(1), 48–61.

Curenton, S. M. & Gardner-Neblett, N. (2015). Narrative thinking: Implications for black children's social cognition. In S. Robson & S. Flannery Quinn (Eds.), *The Routledge international handbook of young children's thinking and understanding* (pp. 294–305). Abingdon: Routledge.

Damjanovic, V., Flannery Quinn, S., Branson, S., Caldas, E., & Ledford, E. (2017). The use of pedagogical documentation techniques to create focal points in a school-university partnership in early childhood education: Technologies that create a 'third space'. *School-University Partnerships*, 10(3), 30–50.

Danby, S., Evaldsson, A.-C., Melander, H., & Aarsand, P. (2018). Situated collaboration and problem solving in young children's digital gameplay. *British Journal of Educational Technology*, 49(5), 959–972.

Davies, D., Jindal-Snape, D., Collier, C., Digby, R., Hay, P., & Howe, A. (2013). Creative learning environments in education – A systematic literature review. *Thinking Skills and Creativity*, 8, 80–91.

Deans, J. (2016). Thinking, feeling and relating: Young children learning through dance. *Australasian Journal of Early Childhood*, 41(3), 46–57.

Deans, J., & Cohrssen, C. (2015). Young children dance mathematical thinking. *Australasian Journal of Early Childhood*, 40(3), 61–67.

Deci, E. L., Driver, R. E., Hotchkiss, L., Robbins, R. J., & Wilson, I. M. (1993). The relation of mothers' controlling vocalizations to children' s intrinsic motivation. *Journal of Experimental Child Psychology*, 55(2), 151–162.

Degé, F., Kubicek, C., & Schwarzer, G. (2011). Music lessons and intelligence: A relation mediated by executive functions. *Music Perception*, 29(2), 195–201.

Degotardi, S. (2015). Mind-mindedness: Forms, features and implications for infant-toddler pedagogy. In **S. Robson & S. Flannery Quinn** (Eds.), *The Routledge international handbook of young children's thinking and Understanding* (pp. 179–188). Abingdon: Routledge.

Degotardi, S. & Torr, J. (2008). A longitudinal investigation of mothers' mind-related talk to their 12- to 24-month-old-infants. In **R. Evans & D. Jones** (Eds.), *Metacognitive approaches to developing oracy* (pp. 199–212). London: Routledge.

DeLoache, J. S., & Brown, A. L. (1987). The early emergence of planning skills in children. In **J. Bruner & H. Haste** (Eds.), *Making sense* (pp. 108–130). London: Methuen.

Denham, S. A., Brown, C., & Domitrovich, C. E. (2010). 'Plays nice with others': Social-emotional learning and school success. *Early Education and Development*, 21(5), 652–680.

Department for Education (DfE), England. (2020a). *Early years foundation stage profile: 2021 handbook.* Retrieved from https://assets.publishing.service.gov.uk/government/uploads/system/uploads/attachment_data/file/919681/Early_adopter_schools_EYFS_profile_handbook.pdf

Department for Education (DfE), England. (2020b). https://assets.publishing.service.gov.uk/government/uploads/system/uploads/attachment_data/file/1007446/6.7534_DfE_Development_Matters_Report_and_illustrations_web__2_.pdf

Department for Education (DfE), England. (2021). *Statutory framework for the early years foundation stage: Setting the standards for learning, development and care for children from birth to five.* Retrieved from https://assets.publishing.service.gov.uk/government/uploads/system/uploads/attachment_data/file/974907/EYFS_framework_-_March_2021.pdf

Department of Education and Skills, Ireland. (2017). *Síolta user manual.* Retrieved from http://siolta.ie/media/pdfs/siolta-manual-2017.pdf

Desautel, D. (2009). Becoming a thinking thinker: Metacognition, self-regulation, and classroom practice. *Teachers College Record*, 111(8), 1997–2020. Retrieved from http://www.tcrecord.org. ID number 15504.

Diamond, A. (2002). Normal development of prefrontal cortex from birth to young adulthood: Cognitive functions, anatomy, and biochemistry. *Principles of frontal lobe function* (pp. 466–503). Oxford: Oxford University Press.

Diamond, A. (2006). The early development of executive functions. In **E. Bialystok & F. I. M. Craik** (Eds.), *Lifespan cognition: Mechanisms of change* (pp. 70–95). Oxford: Oxford University Press.

Dignath, C., Buettner, G., & Langfeldt, H. P. (2008). How can primary school students learn self-regulated learning strategies most effectively? A meta-analysis on self-regulation training programmes. *Educational Research Review*, 3(2), 101–129.

Dockett, S. (1998). Constructing understandings through play in the early years. *International Journal of Early Years Education*, 6(1), 105–116.

Dockett, S., Einarsdottir, J., & Perry, B. (2017). Photo elicitation: Reflecting on multiple sites of meaning. *International Journal of Early Years Education*, 25(3), 225–240.

Douglas, S., & Stirling, L. (2012). Metacommunication, social pretend play and children with autism. *Australasian Journal of Early Childhood*, 37(4), 34–43.

Drayton, S., Turley-Ames, K. J., & Guajardo, N. R. (2011). Counterfactual thinking and false belief: The role of executive function. *Journal of Experimental Child Psychology*, 108, 532–548.

Durlak, J. A., Weissberg, R. P., Dymnicki, A. B., Taylor, R. D., & Schellinger, K. B. (2011). The impact of enhancing students' social and emotional learning: A meta-analysis of school-based universal interventions. *Child Development*, 82(1), 405–432.

Early Education. (2019). *Early Education's response to the DfE consultation on the EYFS reforms: Draft as at 17.12.2019.* Retrieved from https://www.early-education.org.uk/sites/default/files/Draft%20EE%20response%20to%20EYFS%20consul-tation%202019%2017.12.19.pdf

Early Years Coalition. (2021). *Birth to 5 matters: Non-statutory guidance for the early years foundation stage, early education*. Retrieved from https://www.birthto5matters.org.uk/wp-content/uploads/2021/04/Birthto5Matters-download.pdf

Edossa, A. K., Schroeders, U., Weinert, S., & Artelt, C. (2018). The development of emotional and behavioral self-regulation and their effects on academic achievement in childhood. *International Journal of Behavioral Development, 42*(2), 192–202.

Education Endowment Foundation (EEF). (2019). *Metacognition and self-regulated learning*. Retrieved from https://educationendowmentfoundation.org.uk/public/files/Publications/Metacognition/EEF_Metacognition_and_self-regulated_learning.pdf

Education Scotland. (n.d.). *National improvement hub: Effective observation leading to effective assessment*. Retrieved from https://education.gov.scot/improvement/learning-resources/effective-observation-leading-to-effective-assessment/#

Edwards, C., Gandini, L., & Forman, G. (1998). *The hundred languages of children* (2nd ed.). Westport, CT: Ablex.

Efklides, A., & Misailidi, P. (2019). Emotional self-regulation in the early years: The role of cognition, metacognition and social interaction. In **D. Whitebread, V. Grau, K. Kumpulainen, M. M. McClelland, N. E. Perry, & D. Pino-Pasternak** (Eds.), *SAGE handbook of developmental psychology and early childhood education* (pp. 502–514). London: Sage.

Eisenberg, N., Spinrad, T. L., & Eggum, N. D. (2010a). Emotion-related self-regulation and its relation to children's maladjustment. *Annual Review of Clinical Psychology, 6*, 495–525.

Eisenberg, N., Valiente, C., & Eggum, N. D. (2010b). Self-regulation and school readiness. *Early Education and Development, 21*(5), 681–698.

Ekas, N. V., Lickenbrock, D. M., & Braungart-Rieker, J. M. (2013). Developmental trajectories of emotion regulation across infancy: Do age and the social partner influence temporal patterns. *Infancy, 18*(5), 729–754.

Elia, I., & Evangelou, K. (2014). Gesture in kindergarten mathematics classroom. *European Early Childhood Education Research Journal, 22*(1), 45–66.

Elias, C. L., & Berk, L. E. (2002). Self-regulation in young children: Is there a role for sociodramatic play? *Early Childhood Research Quarterly, 17*(2), 216–238.

Eme, E., Puustinen, M., & Coutelet, B. (2006). Individual and developmental differences in reading monitoring: When and how do children evaluate their comprehension? *European Journal of Psychology of Education, 21*(1), 91–115.

Fernyhough, C. (2008). *The baby in the mirror*. London: Granta.

Fitzsimons, G. M., & Finkel, E. J. (2011). The effects of self-regulation on social relationships. In **K. D. Vohs & R. F. Baumeister** (Eds.), *Handbook of self-regulation: Research, theory and applications* (2nd ed., pp. 407–421). New York, NY; London: Guilford Press.

Flavell, J. H. (1979). Metacognition and cognitive monitoring. *American Psychologist, 34*(10), 906–911.

Fleer, M. (2017). Digital role-play: The changing conditions of children's play in preschool settings. *Mind, Culture and Activity, 24*(1), 3–17.

Fleer, M., & Hammer, M. (2013). 'Perezhivanie' in group settings: A cultural-historical reading of emotion regulation. *Australasian Journal of Early Childhood, 38*(3), 127–134.

Fleer, M., Veresov, N., & Walker, S. (2020). Playworlds and executive functions in children: Theorising with the cultural-historical analytical lenses. *Integrative Psychological and Behavioral Science, 54*(1), 124–141.

Fletcher-Flinn, C. M., & Suddendorf, T. (1996). Do computers affect 'the mind'? *Journal of Educational Computing Research, 15*(2), 97–112.

Flewitt, R., & Cowan, H. (2019). *Valuing young children's signs of learning: Observation and digital documentation of play in early years classrooms*. Retrieved from https://www.froebel.org.uk/uploads/documents/Froebel-Trust-Final-Report-Cowan-and-Flewitt-Valuing-Young-Childrens-Signs-of-Learning.pdf

Forman, G. E. (1999). Instant video revisiting: The video camera as a 'tool of the mind' for young children. *Early Childhood Research and Practice, 1*(2). Retrieved from http://ecrp.uiuc.edu/v1n2/forman.html

Frampton, K. L., Perlman, M., & Jenkins, J. M. (2009). Caregivers' use of metacognitive language in child care centers: Prevalence and predictors. *Early Childhood Research Quarterly, 24*, 248–262.

Fuhs, M. W., Nesbitt, K. T., Farran, D. C., & Dong, N. (2014). Longitudinal associations between executive functioning and academic skills across content areas. *Developmental Psychology, 50*(6), 1698–1709.

Gabbard, C. (2015). Embodied cognition in children: Developing mental representations for action. In **S. Robson & S. Flannery Quinn** (Eds.), *The Routledge international handbook of young children's thinking and understanding* (pp. 229–237). Abingdon: Routledge.

Gagne, J. R., Liew, J., & Nwadinobi, O. K. (2021). How does the broader construct of self-regulation relate to emotion regulation in young children? *Developmental Review*, 60, 100965.

Galyer, K. T., & Evans, I. M. (2001). Pretend play and the development of emotion regulation in preschool children. *Early Child Development and Care*, 166(1), 93–108.

Gandini, L. (1998). Educational and caring spaces. In **C. Edwards, L. Gandini, & G. Forman** (Eds.), *The hundred languages of children* (2nd ed.: pp.161–178). Westport, CT: Ablex.

Gärtner, K. A., Vetter, V. C., Schäferling, M., Reuner, G., & Hertel, S. (2018). Inhibitory control in toddlerhood—The role of parental co-regulation and self-efficacy beliefs. *Metacognition and Learning*, 13(3), 241–264.

Garton, A. (2004). *Exploring cognitive development: The child as problem-solver.* Oxford: Blackwell.

Gascoine, L., Higgins, S., & Wall, K. (2017). The assessment of metacognition in children aged 4–16 years: A systematic review. *Review of Education*, 5(1), 3–57.

Gauntlett, D. (2011). *Making is connecting: The social meanings of creativity, from DIY and knitting to YouTube and Web 2.0.* Cambridge: Polity.

Gauvain, M., & Rogoff, B. (1989). Collaborative problem solving and children's planning skills. *Developmental Psychology*, 25(1), 139.

Georghiades, P. (2006). The role of metacognitive activities in the contextual use of primary pupils' conceptions of science. *Research in Science Education*, 36, 29–49.

Gianino, A., & Tronick, E. Z. (1988). The mutual regulation model: The infant's self and interactive regulation and coping and defensive capacities. In **T. M. Field, P. M. McCabe, & N. Schneiderman** (Eds.), *Stress and coping across development* (pp. 47–68). Hillsdale, NJ: Lawrence Erlbaum Associates.

Gioia, G., Guy, S., & Kenworthy, L. (2000). *Behaviour rating of executive function.* Lutz, FL: Psychological Assessment Resources.

Goldin-Meadow, S. (2015) Gesture as a window onto communicative abilities: Implications for diagnosis and intervention. *Perspectives on Language Learning and Education*, 22(2), 50–60.

Golinkoff, R., Hirsh-Pasek, K., & Singer, D. (2008). Why play = learning: A challenge for parents and educators. In **D. Singer, R. Golinkoff, & K. Hirsh-Pasek** (Eds.), *Play = Learning: How play motivates and enhances children's cognitive and social-emotional growth* (pp. 3–15). New York, NY: Oxford University Press.

Goswami, U. (2008). Cognitive development. In *The learning brain.* Hove: Psychology Press.

Graue, E., Clements, M. A. Reynolds, A. J., & Niles, M. J. (2004). More than teacher directed or child initiated: Preschool curriculum type, parent involvement, and children's outcomes in the child-parent centers. *Education Policy Analysis Archives*, 12(72), 1–36.

Grau, V., & Preiss, D. (2019). Supporting young children's self-regulation development. In **D. Whitebread, V. Grau, K. Kumpulainen, M. M. McClelland, N. E. Perry, & D. Pino-Pasternak** (Eds.), *SAGE handbook of developmental psychology and early childhood education* (pp. 535–553). London: Sage.

Grau, V., & Whitebread, D. (2012). Self and social regulation of learning during collaborative activities in the classroom: The interplay of individual and group cognition. *Learning and Instruction*, 22(6), 401–412.

Grazzani Gavazzi, I., & Ornaghi, V. (2011). Emotional state talk and emotion understanding: A training study with preschool children. *Journal of Child Language*, 38(5), 1124–1139.

Grolnick, W. S. (2009). The role of parents in facilitating autonomous self-regulation for education. *Theory and Research in Education*, 7(2), 164–173.

Grolnick, W., Frodi, A., & Bridges, L. (1984). Maternal control style and the mastery motivation of one-year-olds. *Infant Mental Health Journal*, 5(2), 72–82.

de Groot Kim, S. (2010). There's Elly, it must be Tuesday: Discontinuity on childcare programs and its impact on the development of peer relationships in young children. *Early Childhood Education Journal*, 38, 153–164.

Gura, P. (Ed.). (1992). *Exploring learning: Young children and blockplay.* London: Paul Chapman.

Hadwin, A. F., Järvelä, S., & Miller, M. (2011). Self-regulated, co-regulated, and socially shared regulation of learning. In B. J. Zimmerman & D. H. Schunk (Eds.), *Handbook of self-regulation of learning and performance* (pp. 65–86). New York, NY: Routledge.

Hadwin, A., & Oshige, M. (2011). Self-regulation, coregulation, and socially shared regulation: Exploring perspectives of social in self-regulated learning theory. *Teachers College Record*, 113(2), 240–264.

Hadwin, A. F., Winne, P. H., Stockley, D. B., Nesbit, J. C., & Woszczyna, C. (2001). Context moderates students' self-reports about how they study. *Journal of Educational Psychology*, 93(3), 477–487.

Hakkarainen, P., Bredikyte, M., Jakkula, K., & Munter, H. (2013). Adult play guidance and children's play development in a narrative play-world. *European Early Childhood Education Research Journal*, 21(2), 213–225.

Harwood, E. (1998). Music learning in context: A playground tale. *Research Studies in Music Education*, 11(1), 52–60.

Hattie, J., & Yates, G. (2014). *Visible learning and the science of how we learn*. Abingdon: Routledge.

Herodotou, C. (2018). Young children and tablets: A systematic review of effects on learning and development. *Journal of Computer Assisted Learning*, 34(1), 1–9.

Hill, M. (2006). Children's voices on ways of having a voice: Children's and young people's perspectives on methods used in research and consultation. *Childhood*, 13, 69–89.

Hill, M., Laybourn, A., & Borland, M. (1996). Engaging with primary-aged children about their emotions and well-being: Methodological considerations. *Children & Society*, 10(2), 129–144.

Hirsh-Pasek, K., Golinkoff, R., Berk, L. E., & Singer, D. (2008). *A mandate for playful learning in preschool: Presenting the evidence*. New York, NY: Oxford University Press.

Hoffmann, J. D., & Russ, S. W. (2016). Fostering pretend play skills and creativity in elementary school girls: A group play intervention. *Psychology of Aesthetics, Creativity, and the Arts*, 10(1), 114–125.

Holmes, C. J., Kim-Spoon, J., & Deater-Deckard, K. (2016). Linking executive function and peer problems from early childhood through middle adolescence. *Journal of Abnormal Child Psychology*, 44(1), 31–42.

Huber, B., Tarasuik, J., Antoniou, M. N., Garrett, C., Bowe, S. J., Kaufman, J., & Team, S. B. (2016). Young children's transfer of learning from a touchscreen device. *Computers in Human Behavior*, 56, 56–64.

Huber, B., Yeates, M., Meyer, D., Fleckhammer, L., & Kaufman, J. (2018). The effects of screen media content on young children's executive functioning. *Journal of Experimental Child Psychology*, 170, 72–85.

Hurme, T. R., & Järvelä, S. (2005). Students' activity in computer-supported collaborative problem solving in mathematics. *International Journal of Computers for Mathematical Learning*, 10(1), 49–73.

Hutt, J., Tyler, S., Hutt, C., & Christopherson, H. (1989). *Play, exploration and learning: A natural history of the preschool*. London: Routledge.

Hyson, M., Copple, C., & Jones, J. (2007). Early childhood development and education. In K. A.Renninger, I. E.Sigel, W.Damon, & R. M.Lerner (Eds.), *Handbook of child psychology: Child psychology in practice* (pp. 3–47). New York: John Wiley & Sons Inc.

Iiskala, T., Vauras, M., & Lehtinen, E. (2004). Socially shared metacognition in peer-learning? *Hellenic Journal of Psychology*, 1, 147–178.

Jenvey, V. B., & Newton, E. (2015). The development of theory of mind and its role in social development in early childhood. In S. Robson & S. Flannery Quinn (Eds.), *The Routledge international handbook of young children's thinking and understanding* (pp. 163–178). Abingdon: Routledge.

Jokić, C. S., & Whitebread, D. (2011). The role of self-regulatory and metacognitive competence in the motor performance difficulties of children with developmental coordination disorder: A theoretical and empirical review. *Educational Psychology Review*, 23(1), 75–98.

Kaler, S. R., & Kopp, C. B. (1990). Compliance and comprehension in very young toddlers. *Child Development*, 61(6), 1997–2003.

Kallia, E., & Dermitzaki, I. (2017). Assessing maternal behaviours that support children's selfregulated learning. *Hellenic Journal of Psychology*, 14(2), 83–112.

Karmiloff-Smith, B. A. (1994). Beyond modularity: A developmental perspective on cognitive science. *European Journal of Disorders of Communication*, 29(1), 95–105.

Karpov, Y. V. (2005) *A neo-Vygotskian approach to child development.* New York, NY; Cambridge: Cambridge University Press.

Kettlewell, K., Sharp, C., Lucas, M., Gambhir, G., Classick, R., Hope, C., ... **National Foundation for Educational Research.** (2020). *International early learning and well-being study (IELS): National report for England.* London: Department for Education. Retrieved from https://assets.publishing.service.gov.uk/government/uploads/system/uploads/attachment_data/file/939718/IELS_national_report_Dec_2020.pdf

Knauf, H. (2017). Documentation as a tool for participation in German early childhood education and care. *European Early Childhood Education Research Journal*, 25(1), 19–35.

Kochanska, G., Coy, K. C., & Murray, K. T. (2001). The development of self-regulation in the first four years of life. *Child Development*, 72(4), 1091–1111.

Kochanska, G., Murray, K. T., & Harlan, E. T. (2000). Effortful control in early childhood: Continuity and change, antecedents, and implications for social development. *Developmental Psychology*, 36(2), 220.

Kopp, C. B. (1982). Antecedents of self-regulation: A developmental perspective. *Developmental Psychology*, 18(2), 199–214.

Kopp, C. B. (1989). Regulation of distress and negative emotions: A developmental view. *Developmental Psychology*, 25(3), 343.

Krafft, K. C., & Berk, L. E. (1998). Private speech in two preschools: Significance of open-ended activities and make-believe play for verbal self-regulation. *Early Childhood Research Quarterly*, 13(4), 637–658.

Krumm, G., Filippetti, V. A., & Gutierrez, M. (2018). The contribution of executive functions to creativity in children: What is the role of crystallized and fluid intelligence? *Thinking Skills and Creativity*, 29, 185–195.

Kuhn, D. (2005). Metacognitive development. In L. Balter & C. C. Tamis-LeMonda (Eds.), *Child psychology: A handbook of contemporary issues* (pp. 259–286). New York, NY; Hove: Psychology Press.

Kuhn, L. J., Willoughby, M. T., Wilbourn, M. P., Vernon-Feagans, L., Blair, C. B., & **The Family Life Project Key Investigators.** (2014). Early communicative gestures prospectively predict language development and executive function in early childhood. *Child Development*, 85(5), 1898–1914.

Lagattuta, K. H., Wellman, H. M., & Flavell, J. H. (1997). Preschoolers' understanding of the link between thinking and feeling: Cognitive cuing and emotional change. *Child Development*, 68(6), 1081–1104.

Lambert, B. (2000). Problem-solving in the first years of school. *Australian Journal of Early Childhood*, 25(3), 32–38.

Lambert, B. (2005). Children's drawing and painting from a cognitive perspective: A longitudinal study. *Early Years*, 25(3), 249–269.

Lamm, B., Keller, H., Teiser, J., Gudi, H., Yovsi, R., Freitag, C., ... Lohaus, A. (2018) Waiting for the second treat: Developing culture-specific modes of self-regulation. *Child Development*, 89(3), e261–e277.

Larkin, S. (2007). A phenomenological analysis of the metamemory of five six-year-old children. *Qualitative Research in Psychology*, 4(4), 281–293.

Larkin, S. (2010). *Metacognition in young children.* London: Routledge.

Larkin, S. (2015). Metacognitive experiences: Taking account of feelings in early years education. In S. Robson & S. Flannery Quinn (Eds.), *The Routledge international handbook of young children's thinking and Understanding* (pp. 189–198). Abingdon: Routledge.

Lecce, S., Caputi, M., & Pagnin, A. (2014). Long-term effect of theory of mind on school achievement: The role of sensitivity to criticism. *European Journal of Developmental Psychology*, 11, 305–318.

Lever, R., & Sénéchal, M. (2011). Discussing stories: On how a dialogic reading intervention improves kindergartners' oral narrative construction. *Journal of Experimental Child Psychology*, 108(1), 1–24.

Lew, J. C. T., & Campbell, P. S. (2005). Children's natural and necessary musical play: Global contexts, local applications. *Music Educators Journal*, 91(5), 57–62.

Lewis, H. (2019). Supporting the development of young children's metacognition through the use of video-stimulated reflective dialogue. *Early Child Development and Care*, 189(11), 1842–1858.

Liew, J., Eisenberg, N., Spinrad, T. L., Eggum, N. D., Haugen, R. G., Kupfer, A., & Baham, M. E. (2011). Physiological regulation and fearfulness as predictors of young children's empathy-related reactions. *Social Development*, 20(1), 111–134.

Lillard, A. S., Lerner, M. D., Hopkins, E. J., Dore, R. A., Smith, E. D., & Palmquist, C. M. (2013). The impact of pretend play on children's development: A review of the evidence. *Psychological Bulletin*, 139(1), 1–34.

Littleton, K., & Mercer, N. (2013). *Interthinking. Putting talk to work.* Abingdon: Routledge.

Ljung-Djärf, A. (2008). The owner, the participant and the spectator: Positions and positioning in peer activity around the computer in pre-school. *Early Years*, 28(1), 61–72.

Lloyd, B., & Howe, N. (2003). Solitary play and convergent and divergent thinking skills in preschool children. *Early Childhood Research Quarterly*, 18(1), 22–41.

Lobo, F. M., & Lunkenheimer, E. (2020). Understanding the parent-child coregulation patterns shaping child self-regulation. *Developmental Psychology*, 56(6), 1121.

Löfdahl, A. (2005). 'The funeral': A study of children's shared meaning-making and its developmental significance. *Early Years*, 25(1), 5–16.

Luna, B., Doll, S. K., Hegedus, S. J., Minshew, N. J., & Sweeney, J. A. (2007). Maturation of executive function in autism. *Biological Psychiatry*, 61(4), 474–481.

Marsh, K., & Young, S. (2007). Musical play. In G. McPherson (Ed.), *The child as musician: A handbook of musical development* (pp. 289–310). Oxford: Oxford University Press.

Marulis, L. M., & Nelson, L. J. (2021). Metacognitive processes and associations to executive function and motivation during a problem-solving task in 3–5 year olds. *Metacognition and Learning*, 16(1), 207–231.

Marulis, L. M., Palincsar, A. S., Berhenke, A. L., & Whitebread, D. (2016). Assessing metacognitive knowledge in 3–5 year olds: The development of a metacognitive knowledge interview (McKI). *Metacognition and Learning*, 11(3), 339–368.

Mattanah, J. F. (2001). Parental psychological autonomy and children's academic competence and behavioral adjustment in late childhood: More than just limit-setting and warmth. *Merrill-Palmer Quarterly*, 47(3), 355–376.

Mazefsky, C. A., Herrington, J., Siegel, M., Scarpa, A., Maddox, B. B., Scahill, L., & Whoite, S. W. (2013). The role of emotion regulation in autism spectrum disorder RH: Emotion regulation in ASD. *Journal of the American Academy of Child and Adolescent Psychiatry*, 52(7), 679–688.

McClelland, M. M., Acock, A. C., & Morrison, F. J. (2006). The impact of kindergarten learning-related skills on academic trajectories at the end of elementary school. *Early Childhood Research Quarterly*, 21(4), 471–490.

McClelland, M. M., & Cameron, C. E. (2012). Self-regulation in early childhood: Improving conceptual clarity and developing ecologically valid measures. *Child Development Perspectives*, 6(2), 136–142.

McClelland, M. M., John Geldhof, G., Cameron, C. E., & Wanless, S. B. (2015). Development and self-regulation. In *Handbook of child psychology and developmental science* (pp. 1–43). Hoboken, NJ: Wiley.

McClelland, M. M., & Tominey, S. L. (2011). Introduction to the special issue on self-regulation in early childhood. *Early Education and Development*, 22(3), 355–359.

McGuinness, C. (1999). *From thinking skills to thinking classrooms (research report 115).* London: DfEE.

McInnes, K., Howard, J., Miles, G., & Crowley, K. (2010). Differences in adult-child interactions during playful and formal practice conditions: An initial investigation. *The Psychology of Education Review*, 34(1), 14–20.

McInnes, K., Howard, J., Miles, G., & Crowley, K. (2011). Differences in practitioners' understanding of play and how this influences pedagogy and children's perceptions of play. *Early Years*, 31(2), 121–133.

Mead, D., & Winsler, A. (2015). Children's private speech. In S. Robson & S. Flannery Quinn (Eds.), *The Routledge international handbook of young children's thinking and understanding* (pp. 150–162). Abingdon: Routledge.

Meins, E. (1999). Sensitivity, security and internal working models: Bridging the transmission gap. *Attachment and Human Development*, 1, 325–342.

Mercer, N. (2000). *Words and minds: How we use language to think together.* London: Routledge.

Miller, L. (1999). Babyhood: Becoming a person in the family. In D. Hindle & M. V. Smith (Eds.), *Personality development: A psychoanalytic perspective* (pp. 33–47). London: Routledge.

Miller, P. H., & Aloise-Young, P. A. (2018). Revisiting young children's understanding of the psychological causes of behavior. *Child Development*, 89(5), 1441–1461.

Ministry of Education Republic of Singapore. (2013a). *Nurturing early learners: A curriculum for kindergartens in Singapore: Educators' guide: Overview*. Retrieved from https://www.nel.moe.edu.sg/qql/slot/u143/Resources/Download-able/pdf/nel-guide/nel-edu-guide-overview.pdf

Ministry of Education Republic of Singapore. (2013b). *Nurturing early learners: A curriculum for kindergartens in Singapore: Social and emotional development*. Retrieved from https://www.nel.moe.edu.sg/qql/slot/u143/Resources/Downloadable/pdf/nel-guide/nel-edu-guide-social-emotional-development.pdf

Ministry of Education Republic of Singapore. (n.d.). *Singapore kindergarten impact project: Fine and gross motor skills are important for self-regulation and early academic skills*. Retrieved from https://www.nel.moe.edu.sg/qql/slot/u143/Resources/Research/Motor%20Skills%20Self-Regulation%20and%20Early%20Academic%20Skills.pdf

Ministry of Education, New Zealand. (2017). *Te Whāriki: Early childhood curriculum*. Retrieved from https://www.education.govt.nz/assets/Documents/Early-Childhood/Te-Whariki-Early-Childhood-Curriculum-ENG-Web.pdf

Mischel, W., Ayduk, O., Berman, M. G., Casey, B. J., Gotlib, I. H., Jonides, J., … Shoda, Y. (2011). 'Willpower' over the life span: Decomposing self-regulation. *Social Cognitive and Affective Neuroscience*, 6(1), 252–256.

Moffitt, T. E., Arseneault, L., Belsky, D., Dickson, N., Hancox, R. J., Harrington, H., & Caspi, A. (2011). A gradient of childhood self-control predicts health, wealth, and public safety. *Proceedings of the National Academy of Sciences*, 108(7), 2693–2698.

Molfese, D. L., Ivanenko, A., Key, A. F., Roman, A., Molfese, V. J., O'Brien, L. M., … Hudac, C. M. (2013). A one-hour sleep restriction impacts brain processing in young children across tasks: Evidence from event-related potentials. *Developmental Neuropsychology*, 38(5), 317–336.

Monette, S., Bigras, M., & Guay, M.-C. (2011). The role of the executive functions in school achievement at the end of grade 1. *Journal of Experimental Child Psychology*, 109, 158–173.

Montroy, J. J., Bowles, R. P., & Skibbe, L. E. (2016a). The effect of peers' self-regulation on preschooler's self-regulation and literacy growth. *Journal of Applied Developmental Psychology*, 46, 73–83.

Montroy, J. J., Bowles, R. P., Skibbe, L. E., McClelland, M. M., & Morrison, F. J. (2016b). The development of self-regulation across early childhood. *Developmental Psychology*, 52(11), 1744.

Moreno, S., Friesen, D., & Bialystok, E. (2011). Effect of music training on promoting preliteracy skills: Preliminary causal evidence. *Music Perception*, 29(2), 165–172.

Morgan, A. (2007). Using video-stimulated recall to understand young children's perceptions of learning in classroom settings. *European Early Childhood Education Research Journal*, 15(2), 213–226.

Moss, E., & Strayer, F. F. (1990). Interactive problem-solving of gifted and non-gifted preschoolers with their mothers. *International Journal of Behavioral Development*, 13(2), 177–197.

Moss, P., Dahlberg, G., Grieshaber, S. et al. (2016). The organisation for economic co-operation and development's international early learning study: Opening for debate and contestation. *Contemporary Issues in Early Childhood*, 17(3), 343–351.

Murray, D. W., Rosanbalm, K., Christopoulos, C., & Hamoudi, A. (2015). *Self-regulation and toxic stress: Foundations for understanding self-regulation from an applied developmental perspective*. OPRE Report #2015-21. Washington, DC: Office of Planning, Research and Evaluation, Administration for Children and Families, U.S. Department of Health and Human Services. Retrieved from https://www.acf.hhs.gov/sites/default/files/documents/report_1_foundations_paper_final_012715_submitted_508_0.pdf

National Association for the Education of Young Children (NAEYC). (2009). *Developmentally appropriate practice in early childhood programs serving children from birth through age 8: Position statement*. Retrieved from https://www.naeyc.org/sites/default/files/globally-shared/downloads/PDFs/resources/position-statements/PSDAP.pdf

National Association for the Education of Young Children (NAEYC). (2019). *NAEYC early learning program accreditation standards and assessment items*. Retrieved from https://www.naeyc.org/sites/default/files/globally-shared/downloads/PDFs/accreditation/early-learning/standards_and_assessment_2019.pdf

National Council for Curriculum and Assessment (NCCA), Ireland. (2009). *Aistear: The early childhood curriculum framework: Principles and themes*. Retrieved from http://www.ncca.biz/Aistear/pdfs/PrinciplesThemes_ENG/PrinciplesThemes_ENG.pdf

Neal, J. W., Durbin, C. E., Gornik, A. E., & Lo, S. L. (2017). Codevelopment of preschoolers' temperament traits and social play networks over an entire school year. *Journal of Personality and Social Psychology*, 113(4), 627.

Neale, D., & Whitebread, D. (2019). Maternal scaffolding during play with 12- to 24-month-old infants: Stability over time and relations with emerging effortful control. *Metacognition and Learning*, 14(3), 265–289.

Novack, M., & Goldin-Meadow, S. (2015). Learning from gesture: How our hands change our minds. *Educational Psychology Review*, 27(3), 405–412.

O'Leary, A. P., & Sloutsky, V. (2017). Carving metacognition at its joints: Protracted development of component processes. *Child Development*, 88(3), 1015–1032.

O'Neill, G., & Miller, P. H. (2013). A show of hands: Relations between young children's gesturing and executive function. *Developmental Psychology*, 49(8), 1517–1528.

Organisation for Economic Co-operation and Development (OECD). (2018). *Early learning matters: Findings from the international early learning and child well-being 2017 field trial, November 2018. In Focus 1.* Retrieved from http://www.oecd.org/education/school/publicationsdocuments/brochure/IELS-Field-Trial-Report.pdf

Organisation for Economic Co-operation and Development (OECD). (2020). *Early learning and child well-being: A study of five-year-olds in England, Estonia and the United States.* Retrieved from https://www.oecd-ilibrary.org/education/early-learning-and-child-well-being_debef904-en

Organisation for Economic Co-operation and Development (OECD). (n.d.). *The international early learning and child well-being study: The study.* Retrieved from http://www.oecd.org/education/school/the-international-early-learning-and-child-well-being-study-the-study.htm

Özbaran, B., Kalyoncu, T., & Köse, S. (2018). Theory of mind and emotion regulation difficulties in children with ADHD. *Psychiatry Research*, 270, 117–122.

Pagani, L. S. & Messier, S. (2012). Links between motor skills and indicators of school readiness at kindergarten entry in urban disadvantaged children. *Journal of Educational and Developmental Psychology*, 2, 95–107.

Pahigiannis, K., & Glos, M. (2020). Peer influences in self-regulation development and interventions in early childhood. *Early Child Development and Care*, 190(7), 1053–1064.

Palaiologou, I. (2019). *Child observation.* London: Sage.

Paley, V. G. (1981). *Wally's stories.* Cambridge, MA: Harvard University Press.

Paley, V. G. (1986). On listening to what the children say. *Harvard Educational Review*, 56(2), 122–131.

Palincsar, A. S., & Brown, A. L. (1984). Reciprocal teaching of comprehension-fostering and comprehension-monitoring activities. *Cognition and Instruction*, 1, 117–175.

Panksepp, J. (1998). Attention deficit hyperactivity disorders, psychostimulants, and intolerance of childhood playfulness: A tragedy in the making? *Current Directions in Psychological Science*, 7(3), 91–98.

Papaeliou, C. F., & Trevarthen, C. (2006). Prelinguistic pitch patterns expressing communication and apprehension. *Journal of Child Language*, 33(1), 163.

Papaleontiou-Louca, E. (2008). *Metacognition and theory of mind.* Newcastle: Cambridge Scholars Publishing.

Parker, L. (2018). *Exploring clay.* London: Froebel Trust. Retrieved from https://www.froebel.org.uk/resources/pamphlets/

Patrick, H., & Middleton, M. J. (2002). Turning the kaleidoscope: What we see when self-regulated learning is viewed with a qualitative lens. *Educational Psychologist*, 37(1), 27–39.

Paulus, M., Licata, M., Kristen, S., Thoermer, C., Woodward, A., & Sodian, B. (2015). Social understanding and self-regulation predict pre-schoolers' sharing with friends and disliked peers: A longitudinal study. *International Journal of Behavioral Development*, 39(1), 53–64.

Pellegrini, A., Dupuis, D., & Smith, P. K. (2007). Play in evolution and development. *Developmental Review*, 27, 261–276.

Pellicano, E. (2010). The development of core cognitive skills in autism: A 3-year prospective study. *Child Development*, 81(5), 1400–1416.

Perels, F., Merget-Kullmann, M., Wende, M., Schmitz, B., & Buchbinder, C. (2009). Improving self-regulated learning of preschool children: Evaluation of training for kindergarten teachers. *British Journal of Educational Psychology*, 79, 311–327.

Perry, N. E. (1998). Young children's self-regulated learning and contexts that support it. *Journal of Educational Psychology, 90*(4), 715–729.

Perry, N. E. (2002). Introduction: Using qualitative methods to enrich understandings of self-regulated learning. *Educational Psychologist, 37*(1), 1–3.

Perry, N. E. (2013). Understanding classroom processes that support children's self-regulation of learning. In D. Whitebread, N. Mercer, C. Howe, & A. Tolmie (Eds.), *Self-regulation and dialogue in primary classrooms. British. The British Journal of educational psychology, monograph series II: Psychological aspects of education - Current trends no. 10* (pp. 45–68). Leicester: British Psychological Society.

Perry, N. E., Phillips, L., & Hutchinson, L. (2006). Mentoring student teachers to support self-regulated learning. *The Elementary School Journal, 106*(3), 237–254.

Perry, N. E., & Rahim, A. (2011). Studying self-regulated learning in classrooms. In B. J. Zimmerman & D. H. Schunk (Eds.), *Handbook of self-regulation of learning and performance* (pp. 122–136). New York, NY: Taylor & Francis.

Perry, N. E., & VandeKamp, K. J. (2000). Creating classroom contexts that support young children's development of self-regulated learning. *International Journal of Educational Research, 33*(7), 821–843.

Perry, N. E., VandeKamp, K. O., Mercer, L. K., & Nordby, C. J. (2002). Investigating teacher-student interactions that foster self-regulated learning. *Educational Psychologist, 37*(1), 5–15.

Perry, N. E., & Winne, P. H. (2013). Tracing students' regulation of learning in complex collaborative tasks. In S. Volet & M. Vauras (Eds.), *Interpersonal regulation of learning and motivation. New perspectives on learning and instruction* (pp. 45–66). London: Routledge.

Piaget, J. (1950). *The psychology of intelligence.* London: Routledge & Kegan Paul.

Piaget, J. (1953). *The origins of intelligence in children.* London: Routledge and Kegan Paul.

Piaget, J. (1959). *The language and thought of the child.* London: Routledge & Kegan Paul.

Picchio, M., Di Giandomenico, I., & Musatti, T. (2014). The use of documentation in a participatory system of evaluation. *Early Years, 34*(2), 133–145.

Piotrowski, J. T., Lapierre, M. A., & Linebarger, D. L. (2013). Investigating correlates of self-regulation in early childhood with a representative sample of English-speaking American families. *Journal of Child and Family Studies, 22*(3), 423–436.

Pino-Pasternak, D., Basilio, M., & Whitebread, D. (2014). Interventions and classroom contexts that promote self-regulated learning: Two intervention studies in United Kingdom primary classrooms. *Psykhe, 23*(2), 1–13. doi:10.7764/psykhe.23.2.739

Pino-Pasternak, D., & Whitebread, D. (2010). The role of parenting in children's self-regulated learning. *Educational Research Review, 5*(3), 220–242.

Pino-Pasternak, D., Whitebread, D., & Tolmie, A. (2010). A multidimensional analysis of parent–child interactions during academic tasks and their relationships with children's self-regulated learning. *Cognition and Instruction, 28*(3), 219–272.

Pintrich, P. R. (2000). The role of goal orientation in self-regulated learning. In M. Boekaerts, P. Pintrich, & M. Zeidner (Eds.), *Handbook of self-regulation* (pp. 451–502). San Diego, CA: Academic.

Pintrich, P. R., & Zusho, A. (2002). The development of academic self-regulation: The role of cognitive and motivational factors. In A. Wigfield & J. Eccles (Eds.), *Development of achievement motivation* (pp. 249–284). San Diego, CA: Academic Press.

Piotrowski, J. T., Lapierre, M. A., & Linebarger, D. L. (2013). Investigating correlates of self-regulation in early childhood with a representative sample of English-speaking American families. *Journal of Child and Family Studies, 22*(3), 423–436.

Planalp, E. M., & Braungart-Rieker, J. M. (2015). Trajectories of regulatory behaviors in early infancy: Determinants of infant self-distraction and self-comforting. *Infancy, 20*(2), 129–159.

Ponitz, C. E. C., McClelland, M. M., Jewkes, A. M., Connor, C. M., Farris, C. L., & Morrison, F. J. (2008). Touch your toes! Developing a direct measure of behavioral regulation in early childhood. *Early Childhood Research Quarterly, 23*(2), 141–158.

Ponizovsky-Bergelson, Y., Dayan, Y., Wahle, N., & Roer-Strier, D. (2019). A qualitative interview with young children: What encourages or inhibits young children's participation? *International Journal of Qualitative Methods, 18*, 1–9.

Portugal, A. M., Bedford, R., Cheung, C. H. M., Mason, L., & Smith, T. J. (2021). Longitudinal touchscreen use across early development is associated with faster exogenous and reduced endogenous attention control. *Scientific Reports*, 11, 2205. doi:10.1038/s41598-021-81775-7

Pramling, I. (1988). Developing children's thinking about their own thinking. *British Journal of Educational Psychology*, 58: 266–278.

Price, S., Jewitt, C., & Crescenzi, L. (2015). The role of iPads in pre-school children's mark making development. *Computers & Education*, 87, 131–141.

Project Zero and Reggio Children. (2001). *Making learning visible: Children as individual and group learners.* Reggio Emilia: Reggio Children.

Puustinen, M. (1998). Help-seeking behaviour in a problem-solving situation: Development of self-regulation. *European Journal of Psychology of Education*, 13(2), 271–282.

Pyle, A. (2013). Engaging young children in research through photo elicitation. *Early Child Development and Care*, 183(11), 1544–1558.

Qu, L. (2011). Two is better than one, but mine is better than ours: Pre-schoolers' executive function during co-play. *Journal of Experimental Child Psychology*, 108, 549–566.

Rabaglietti, E., Vacirca, M. F., & Pakalniskiene, W. (2013). Social-emotional competence and friendships: Prosocial behaviour and lack of behavioural self-regulation as predictors of quantity and quality of friendships in middle childhood. *European Journal of Child Development, Education and Psychopathology*, 1(1), 5–20.

Rademacher, A., & Koglin, U. (2019). The concept of self-regulation and preschoolers' social-emotional development: A systematic review. *Early Child Development and Care*, 189(14), 2299–2317.

Radziszewska, B., & Rogoff, B. (1988). Influence of adult and peer collaborators on children's planning skills. *Developmental Psychology*, 24(6), 840.

Ramani, G. B. (2012). Influence of a playful, child-directed context on preschool children's peer cooperation. *Merrill-Palmer Quarterly*, 58(2), 159–190.

Raver, C. C. (2012). Low-income children's self-regulation in the classroom: Scientific inquiry for social change. *American Psychologist*, 67(8), 681–689.

Razza, R. A., Bergen-Cico, D., & Raymond, K. (2015). Enhancing preschoolers' self-regulation via mindful yoga. *Journal of Child and Family Studies*, 24(2), 372–385.

Razza, R. A., & Blair, C. (2009). Associations among false-belief understanding, executive function, and social competence: A longitudinal analysis. *Journal of Applied Developmental Psychology*, 30, 332–343.

Razza, R., & Raymond, K. (2015). Executive functions and school readiness: Identifying multiple pathways for success. In S. Robson & S. Flannery Quinn (Eds.), *The Routledge international handbook of young children's thinking and under-standing* (pp. 133–149). Abingdon: Routledge.

Robson, S. (2010). Self-regulation and metacognition in young children's self-initiated play and reflective dialogue. *International Journal of Early Years Education*, 18(3), 227–241.

Robson, S. (2012). Children's experiences of creative thinking. In H. Fumoto, S. Robson, S. Greenfield, & D. J. Hargreaves (Eds.), *Young children's creative thinking* (pp. 93–106). London: Sage.

Robson, S. (2015). Whose activity is it? The role of child- and adult-initiated activity in young children's creative thinking. In S. Robson & S. Flannery-Quinn (Eds.), *The international handbook of young children's thinking and understanding* (pp. 433–447). Abingdon: Routledge.

Robson, S. (2016a). Self-regulation, metacognition and child- and adult-initiated activity: Does it matter who initiates the task? *Early Child Development and Care*, 186(5), 764–784.

Robson, S. (2016b). Self-regulation and metacognition in young children: Does it matter if adults are present or not? *British Educational Research Journal*, 42(2), 185–306.

Robson, S. (2016c). Are there differences between children's display of self-regulation and metacognition when engaged in an activity and when later reflecting on it?: The complementary roles of observation and reflective dialogue. *Early Years*, 36(2), 179–194.

Robson, S. (2017). Play, creativity and creative thinking. In T. Bruce, P. Hakkarainen, & M. Bredikyte (Eds.), *Routledge international handbook of play* (pp. 328–339). Abingdon: Routledge.

Robson, S. (2019). *Developing thinking and understanding in young children: An introduction for students.* Abingdon: Routledge.

Robson, S. (2020). Self-regulation in early childhood policy and practice in england. In **W. Pink** (Ed.), *Oxford encyclopedia of school reform.* New York, NY: Oxford University Press. https://doi.org/10.1093/acrefore/9780190264093.013.1599

Robson, S., Brogaard Clausen, S. & Hargreaves, D. J. (2019). Loved or listened to?: Parent and practitioner perspectives on young children's well-being. *Early Child Development and Care*, 189(7), 1147–1161.

Robson, S., & Rowe, V. (2012). Observing young children's creative thinking: Engagement, involvement and persistence. *International Journal of Early Years Education*, 20(4), 349–364.

Rodríguez, C., & Palacios, P. (2007). Do private gestures have a self-regulatory function?: A case study. *Infant Behaviour and Development*, 30(2), 180–194.

Roebers, C. M. (2017). Executive function and metacognition: Towards a unifying framework of cognitive self-regulation. *Developmental Review*, 45, 31–51.

Roebers, C. M., Schmid, C., & Roderer, T. (2009). Metacognitive monitoring and control processes involved in primary school children's test performance. *British Journal of Educational Psychology*, 79(4), 749–767.

Rogat, T. K., & Adams-Wiggins, K. R. (2014). Other-regulation in collaborative groups: Implications for regulation quality. *Instructional Science*, 42(6), 879–904.

Rogat, T. K., & Linnenbrink-Garcia, L. (2011). Socially shared regulation in collaborative groups: An analysis of the interplay between quality of social regulation and group processes. *Cognition and Instruction*, 29(4), 375–415.

Rogers, S. (2015). Pretend play and its integrative role in young children's development. In **S. Robson & S. Flannery Quinn** (Eds.), *The Routledge international handbook of young children's thinking and understanding* (pp. 282–293). Abingdon: Routledge.

Rothbart, M. K., & Bates, J. E. (2006). Temperament. In **N. Eisenberg** (Ed.), *Handbook of child psychology* (pp. 3–166). Hoboken, NJ: Wiley.

Rothbart, M. K., Ellis, L. K., & Posner, M. I. (2004). Temperament and self-regulation. In **R. F. Baumeister & K. D. Vohs** (Eds.), *Handbook of self-regulation: Research, theory, and applications* (pp. 357–379). New York, NY: Guilford Press.

Rothbart, M. K., Posner, M. I., & Kieras, J. (2006). Temperament, attention, and the development of self-regulation. In **K. McCartney & D. Phillips** (Eds.), *Blackwell handbooks of developmental psychology. Blackwell handbook of early childhood development* (pp. 338–357). Malden, MA: Blackwell.

Rueda, M. R., Fan, J., McCandliss, B. D., Halparin, J. D., Gruber, D. B., Lercari, L. P., & Posner, M. I. (2004). Development of attentional networks in childhood. *Neuropsychologia*, 42(8), 1029–1040.

Sakr, M., Connelly, V., & Wild, M. (2016). Narrative in young children's digital art-making. *Journal of Early Childhood Literacy*, 16(3), 289–310.

Särkämö, T., Tervaniemi, M., & Huotilainen, M. (2013). Music perception and cognition: Development, neural basis, and rehabilitative use of music. *Wiley Interdisciplinary Reviews: Cognitive Science*, 4(4), 441–451.

Savina, E. (2014). Does play promote self-regulation in children? *Early Child Development and Care*, 184(11), 1692–1705.

Schellenberg, E. G. (2011). Examining the association between music lessons and intelligence. *British Journal of Psychology*, 102(3), 283–302.

Scottish Government. (2009). *Curriculum for excellence (CfE).* Retrieved from https://education.gov.scot/Documents/All-experiencesoutcomes18.pdf

Scottish Government. (2011). *Curriculum for excellence: Building the curriculum 5: A framework for assessment (btc5).* Retrieved from https://www.education.gov.scot/Documents/btc5-framework.pdf

Shiakalli, M. A., & Zacharos, K. (2012). The contribution of external representations in pre-school mathematical problem solving. *International Journal of Early Years Education*, 20(4), 315–331.

Shuey, E., & Kankaraš, M. (2018). *The power and promise of early learning: OECD education working paper no. 186.* doi: 10.1787/f9b2e53f-en

Siegler, R. S., & Lin, X. (2010). Self-explanations promote children's learning. In **H. S. Waters & W. Schneider** (Eds.), *Metacognition, strategy use, and instruction* (pp. 85–112). New York, NY: Guilford Press.

Siegler, R. S., Saffran, J. R., Eisenberg, N., DeLoache, J., & Gershoff, E. (2017). *How children develop* (5th ed.). New York, NY: Worth Publishers.

Sigel, I. E. (2002). The psychological distancing model: A study of the socialization of cognition. *Culture & Psychology*, 8(2), 189–214.

Silkenbeumer, J. R., Schiller, E. M., & Kärtner, J. (2018). Co-and self-regulation of emotions in the preschool setting. *Early Childhood Research Quarterly*, 44, 72–81.

Silva, K. M., Spinrad, T. L., Eisenberg, N., Sulik, M. J., Valiente, C., Huerta, S., … School Readiness Consortium. (2011). Relations of children's effortful control and teacher–child relationship quality to school attitudes in a low-income sample. *Early Education and Development*, 22(3), 434–460.

Siraj-Blatchford, I., Sylva, K., Muttock, S., Gilden, R., & Bell, D. (2002). *Researching effective Pedagogy in the early years (research report 356)*. London: DfES.

Siraj, I., Kingston, D., & Melhuish, E. (2015). *Assessing quality in early childhood education and care. Sustained shared thinking and emotional well-being (SSTEW) scale for 2-5-year-olds provision.* London: IOE Press.

Skolverket, S. (2019). *Curriculum for the preschool, Lpfö 18*. Retrieved from https://www.skolverket.se/portletresource/4.6bfaca41169863e6a65d9f5/12.6bfaca41169863e6a65d9fe?file=4049

Slaughter, V., Peterson, C. C., & Moore, C. (2013). I can talk you into it: Theory of mind and persuasion behavior in young children. *Developmental Psychology*, 49(2), 227–231.

Slot, P. L., Mulder, H., Verhagen, J., & Leseman, P. P. M. (2017) Preschoolers' cognitive and emotional self-regulation in pretend play: Relations with executive functions and quality of play. *Infant and Child Development*, 26(6), e2038.

Smith-Donald, R., Raver, C. C., Hayes, T., & Richardson, B. (2007). Preliminary construct and concurrent validity of the Preschool Self-regulation Assessment (PSRA) for field-based research. *Early Childhood Research Quarterly*, 22, 173–187.

Sobkin, V. S., Skobeltsina, K. N., & van Oudenhoven, N. (2018). The interactions between parents with their preschool children during leisure time: Key features. In N. Veraksa & S. Sheridan (Eds.), *Vygotsky's theory in early childhood education and research* (pp. 113–128). Abingdon: Routledge.

So, W. C., Chen-Hui, C. S., & Wei-Shan, J. L. (2012). Mnemonic effect of iconic gesture and beat gesture in adults and children: Is meaning in gesture important for memory recall? *Language and Cognitive Processes*, 27(5), 665–681.

Sperling, R. A., Walls, R. T., & Hill, L. A. (2000). Early relationships among self-regulatory constructs: Theory of mind and pre-school children's problem solving. *Child Study Journal*, 30(4), 233–253.

Stefanou, C. R., Perencevich, K. C., DiCintio, M., & Turner, J. C. (2004). Supporting autonomy in the classroom: Ways teachers encourage student decision making and ownership. *Educational Psychologist*, 39(2), 97–110.

Stenseng, F., Belsky, J., Skalicka, V., & Wichstrøm, L. (2015). Social exclusion predicts impaired self-regulation: A 2-year longitudinal panel study including the transition from preschool to school. *Journal of Personality*, 83(2), 212–220.

Sun, J., & Tang, Y. (2019). Maternal scaffolding strategies and early development of self-regulation in Chinese pre-schoolers. *Early Child Development and Care*, 189, 1525–1537.

Sylva, K., Bruner, J. S., & Genova, P. (1976). The role of play in the problem-solving of children 3 to 5-years old. In J. S. Bruner & K. Sylva (Eds.), *Play: It's role in development and evolution* (pp. 55–67). Harmondsworth: Penguin.

Sylva, K., Melhuish, E., Sammons, P., Siraj-Blatchford, I., & Taggart, B. (2010). *Early childhood matters*. London: Routledge.

Taggart, G., Ridley, K., Rudd, P., & Benefield, P. (2005). *Thinking skills in the early years: A literature review*. Slough: NFER.

Tarnowski, S. M. (1999). Musical play and young children: A music teacher can enhance a child's learning and development by encouraging musical play activities. *Music Educators Journal*, 86(1), 26–29.

Tarricone, P. (2011). *The taxonomy of metacognition*. Hove: Psychology Press.

Thorpe, K. J., & Satterly, D. J. H. (1990). The development and inter-relationship of metacognitive components among primary school children. *Educational Psychology*, 10(1), 5–21.

Timmons, K., Pelletier, J., & Corter, C. (2016). Understanding children's self-regulation within different classroom contexts. *Early Child Development and Care*, 186(2), 249–267.

Tominey, S. L., & McClelland, M. M. (2011). Red light, purple light: Findings from a randomized trial using circle time games to improve behavioral self-regulation in preschool. *Early Education and Development*, 22(3), 489–519.

Tovey, H. (2017). *Outdoor play and exploration*. London: Froebel Trust. Retrieved from https://www.froebel.org.uk/uploads/documents/FT-Outdoor-Play-Pamphlet.pdf

Trawick-Smith, J. (1998). A qualitative analysis of metaplay in the preschool years. *Early Childhood Research Quarterly*, 13(3), 433–452.

Trawick-Smith, J., Swaminathan, S., Baton, B., Danieluk, C., Marsh, S., & Szarwacki, M. (2017). Block play and mathematics learning in preschool: The effects of building complexity, peer and teacher interactions in the block area, and replica play materials. *Journal of Early Childhood Research*, 15(4), 433–448.

Trentacosta, C. J., & Shaw, D. S. (2009). Emotional self-regulation, peer rejection, and antisocial behavior: Developmental associations from early childhood to early adolescence. *Journal of Applied Developmental Psychology*, 30(3), 356–365.

Trevarthen, C. (1995). The child's need to learn a culture. *Children and Society*, 9(1), 5–19.

Turkle, S. (2007). *Evocative objects: Things we think with.* Cambridge, MA: MIT Press.

Umek, L. M., & Musek, P. L. (2001). Symbolic play: Opportunities for cognitive and language development in preschool settings. *Early Years*, 21(1), 55–64.

United Nations. (1989) *Convention on the rights of the child.* Retrieved from http://www.unicef.org/crc

Urban, M., & Swadener, B. B. (2016). Democratic accountability and contextualised systemic evaluation. *International Critical Childhood Policy Studies*, 5(1), 6–18.

Vallotton, C., & Ayoub, C. (2011). Use your words: The role of language in the development of toddlers' self-regulation. *Early Childhood Research Quarterly*, 26, 169–181.

Van der Stel, M., & Veenman, M. V. (2010). Development of metacognitive skilfulness: A longitudinal study. *Learning and Individual Differences*, 20(3), 220–224.

Van der Stel, M., & Veenman, M. V. (2014). Metacognitive skills and intellectual ability of young adolescents: A longitudinal study from a developmental perspective. *European Journal of Psychology of Education*, 29(1), 117–137.

Vauras, M., & Volet, S. (2013). The study of interpersonal regulation in learning and its challenge to the research methodology. In S. Volet & M. Vauras (Eds.), *New perspectives on learning and instruction. Interpersonal regulation of learning and motivation* (pp. 1–13). New York, NY: Routledge.

Veenman, M. V., & Spaans, M. A. (2005). Relation between intellectual and metacognitive skills: Age and task differences. *Learning and Individual Differences*, 15(2), 159–176.

Veenman, M. V., Van Hout-Wolters, B. H., & Afflerbach, P. (2006). Metacognition and learning: Conceptual and methodological considerations. *Metacognition and Learning*, 1(1), 3–14.

Veenman, M. V., Wilhelm, P., & Beishuizen, J. J. (2004). The relation between intellectual and metacognitive skills from a developmental perspective. *Learning and Instruction*, 14(1), 89–109.

Vieillevoye, S., & Nader-Grosbois, N. (2008). Self-regulation during pretend play in children with intellectual disability and in normally developing children. *Research in Developmental Disabilities*, 29(3), 256–272.

Vitiello, V. E., Greenfield, D. B., Munis, P., & George, J, (2011). Cognitive flexibility, approaches to learning, and academic school readiness in head start preschool children. *Early Education and Development*, 22(3), 388–410.

Vitiello, V. E., Booren, L. M., Downer, J. T., & Williford, A. P. (2012). Variations in children's classroom engagement throughout a day in preschool: Relations to classroom and child factors. *Early Childhood Research Quarterly*, 27: 210–220.

Vygotsky, L. S. (1962). *Thought and language.* Cambridge, MA: MIT Press.

Vygotsky, L. S. (1978). *Mind in society: The development of higher mental processes.* Cambridge, MA: Harvard University Press.

Vygotsky, L. S. (2016). Play and its role in the mental development of the child. *International Research in Early Childhood Education*, 7(2), 3–25.

Walker, R. A., Pressick-Kilborn, K., Arnold, L. S., & Sainsbury, E. J. (2004). Investigating motivation in context: Developing sociocultural perspectives. *European Psychologist*, 9(4), 245–256.

Wall, K., & Higgins, S. (2006). Facilitating metacognitive talk: A research and learning tool. *International Journal of Research and Method in Education*, 29(1), 39–53.

Wanless, S. B., McClelland, M. M., Tominey, S. L., & Acock, A. C. (2011). The influence of demographic risk factors on children's behavioral regulation in prekindergarten and kindergarten. *Early Education and Development*, 22(3), 461–488.

Watts, T. W., Duncan, G. J., & Quan, H. (2018). Revisiting the marshmallow test: A conceptual replication investigating links between early delay of gratification and later outcomes. *Psychological Science*, 29(7), 1159–1177.

Webb, N., Franke, M., Turrou, A., & Ing, M. (2013). Self-regulation and learning in peer-directed small groups. In *Self-regulation and dialogue in primary classrooms. The British Journal of Educational Psychology, Monograph Series II: Psychological Aspects of Education – Current Trends, No. 10* (pp. 69–92). Leicester: British Psychological Society.

Welsh Government. (2015). *Curriculum for wales: Foundation phase framework.* Retrieved from https://hwb.gov.wales/storage/d5d8e39c-b534-40cb-a3f5-7e2e126d8077/foundation-phase-framework.pdf

Whitebread, D. (2012). *Developmental psychology and early childhood education,* London: Sage.

Whitebread, D. (2013). Self-regulation in young children: Its characteristics and the role of communication and language in its early development. In *Self-regulation and dialogue in primary classrooms. British Journal of Educational Psychology Monograph Series II: Psychological Aspects of Education – Current Trends, No. 10* (pp. 25–44). Leicester: British Psychological Society.

Whitebread, D. (2016). Self-regulation in early childhood education. *Early Education Journal,* 80, 3–5.

Whitebread, D., Anderson, H., Coltman, P., Page, C., Pasternak, D. P., & Mehta, S. (2005). Developing independent learning in the early years. *Education 3-13,* 33(1), 40–50.

Whitebread, D., Basilio, M., Kuvalja, M., & Verma, M. (2012). The importance of play. *Toy Industries of Europe,* 1–55.

Whitebread, D., Basilio, M., O'Sullivan, L., & Zachariou, A. (2019). The importance of play, oral language and self-regulation in children's development and learning; implications for quality in early childhood education. In D. Whitebread, V. Grau, K. Kumpulainen, M. M. McClelland, N. E. Perry, & D. Pino-Pasternak (Eds.), *SAGE handbook of developmental psychology and early childhood education* (pp. 554–569). Los Angeles, CA: Sage Publications.

Whitebread, D., Basilio, M., Torres, P., & Kim, M. K. (2015). *Characteristics of playful collaborative groups that support metacognitive abilities, creativity and narrative skills.* Unpublished paper presented at 16th Biennial EARLI Conference, Limassol, Cyprus.

Whitebread, D., Bingham, S., Grau, V., Pasternak, D. P., & Sangster, C. (2007). The development of metacognition and self-regulated learning in young children: The role of collaborative and peer-assisted learning. *Journal of Cognitive Education and Psychology,* 6(3), 433–455.

Whitebread, D., & Cárdenas, V. G. (2012). Self-regulated learning and conceptual development in young children: The development of biological understanding. In A. Zohar & Y. J. Dori (Eds.), *Metacognition in science education: Trends in current research* (pp. 101–132). Dordrecht: Springer.

Whitebread, D., Coltman, P., Jameson, H., & Lander, R. (2009a). Play, cognition and self-regulation: What exactly are children learning when they learn through play? *Educational and Child Psychology,* 26(2), 40.

Whitebread, D., Coltman, P., Pasternak, D. P., Sangster, C., Grau, V., Bingham, S., ... Demetriou, D. (2009b). The development of two observational tools for assessing metacognition and self-regulated learning in young children. *Metacognition and Learning,* 4, 63–85.

Whitebread, D., & O'Sullivan, L. (2012). Preschool children's social pretend play: Supporting the development of metacommunication, metacognition and self-regulation. *International Journal of Play,* 1(2), 197–213.

Whitebread, D., Pino-Pasternak, D., & Coltman, P. (2015). Making learning visible: The role of language in the development of metacognition and self-regulation in young children. In S. Robson & S. Flannery Quinn (Eds.), *The Routledge international handbook of young children's thinking and understanding* (pp. 199–214). Abingdon: Routledge.

Williams, K. E. (2018). Moving to the beat: Using music, rhythm, and movement to enhance self-regulation in early childhood classrooms. *International Journal of Early Childhood,* 50(1), 85–100.

Williams, K. E., & Berthelsen, D. (2019). Implementation of a rhythm and movement intervention to support self-regulation skills of preschool-aged children in disadvantaged communities. *Psychology of Music,* 47(6), 800–820.

Wilson, R. V., & Foglia, L. (2015). *Embodied cognition.* Stanford Encyclopedia of Philosophy. Retrieved from https://plato.stanford.edu/entries/embodied-cognition/?utm_medium=website&utm_source=archdaily.com

Winne, P. H. (2010). Improving measurements of self-regulated learning. *Educational Psychologist,* 45(4), 267–276.

Winne, P. H., Hadwin, A. F., & Perry, N. E. (2013). Metacognition and computer-supported collaborative learning. In C. Hmelo-Silver, C. Chinn, C. K. Chan, & A. O'Donnell (Eds.), *The international handbook of collaborative learning* (pp. 462–479). New York, NY: Taylor & Francis.

Winne, P. H., & Perry, N. E. (2000). Measuring self-regulated learning. In M. Boekaerts, P. R. Pintrich, & M. Zeidner (Eds.), *Handbook of self-regulation* (pp. 531–566). San Diego, CA: Academic Press.

Winsler, A., & Diaz, R. M. (1995). Private speech in the classroom: The effects of activity type, presence of others, classroom context, and mixed-age grouping. *International Journal of Behavioral Development*, 18, 463–488.

Winsler, A., Ducenne, L., & Koury, A. (2011). Singing one's way to self-regulation: The role of early music and movement curricula and private speech. *Early Education and Development*, 22(2), 274–304.

Wood, D. J., Bruner, J. S., & Ross, G. (1976). The role of tutoring in problem-solving. *Journal of Child Psychology and Psychiatry*, 17(2), 89–100.

Wood, E. (2013). *Play, learning and the early childhood curriculum*. London: Sage.

Yelland, N. J. (2018). A pedagogy of multiliteracies: Young children and multimodal learning with tablets. *British Journal of Educational Technology*, 49(5), 847–858.

Young, S. (2003). *Music with the under-fours*. London: Routledge.

Young, S. (2004). The interpersonal dimension: A potential source of musical creativity for young children? *Musicae Scientiae*, 7(1 suppl), 175–191.

Young, S. (2005). Changing tune: Reconceptualizing music with under three year olds. *International Journal of Early Years Education*, 13(3), 289–303.

Zachariou, A., & Bonneville-Roussy, A. (under review). The role of autonomy support from teachers in young learners' self-regulation in dyadic contexts. *Learning and Instruction*.

Zachariou, A., & Whitebread, D. (2015). Musical play and self-regulation: Does musical play allow for the emergence of self-regulatory behaviours? *International Journal of Play*, 4(2), 116–135.

Zachariou, A., & Whitebread, D. (2017). A new context affording for regulation: The case of musical play. *International Journal of Educational Psychology*, 6(3), 212–249.

Zachariou, A., & Whitebread, D. (2019). Developmental differences in young children's self-regulation. *Journal of Applied Developmental Psychology*, 62, 282–293.

Zachariou, A., & Whitebread, D. (2021). The relation between early self-regulation and classroom context: The role of adult presence, the task's source of initiation, and social context. *British Journal of Educational Psychology*, e12476.

Zeidner, M., Boekaerts, M., & Pintrich, P. (2000). Self-regulation. Directions and challenges for future research. In M. Boekaerts, P. Pintrich, & M. Zeidner (Eds.), *Handbook of self-regulation* (pp. 749–768). San Diego, CA: Academic Press.

Zelazo, P. D., Müller, U., Frye, D., Marcovitch, S., Argitis, G., Boseovski, J., & Carlson, S. M. (2003). The development of executive function in early childhood. *Monographs of the Society for Research in Child Development*, 68(3), i–151.

Zhang, H., & Whitebread, D. (2017). Linking parental scaffolding with self-regulated learning in Chinese kindergarten children. *Learning and Instruction*, 49, 121–130.

Zimmer-Gembeck, M. J., & Skinner, E. A. (2011). The development of coping across childhood and adolescence: An integrative review and critique of research. *International Journal of Behavioral Development*, 35(1), 1–17.

Zimmerman, B. J. (1989). A social cognitive view of self-regulated academic learning. *Journal of Educational Psychology*, 81(3), 329–339.

Zimmerman, B. J. (1994). Dimensions of academic self-regulation: A conceptual framework for education. In D. H. Schunk & B. J. Zimmerman (Eds.), *Self-regulation of learning and performance* (pp. 3–21). Hillsdale, NJ: Lawrence Erlbaum Associates.

Zimmerman, B. J. (2011). Self-regulated learning and performance: An introduction and an overview. In B. J. Zimmerman & D. H. Schunk (Eds.), *Handbook of self-regulation of learning and performance* (pp. 1–12). London: Routledge.

Digital resources

Dowling, M. (2005). *Supporting young children's sustained shared thinking: An exploration*. Training Materials. Early Education. USB available from: https://www.early-education.org.uk/supporting-young-childrens-sustained-shared-thinking-usb

The C.Ind.Le (Cambridge Independent Learning) Project (n.d.) *Supporting young children in becoming self-regulated learners. Double CD Training Pack for 5-day training course*. Retrieved from: https://www.educ.cam.ac.uk/research/pro-grammes/cindle/CDPack.html.

Websites

Early Years Coalition, https://www.birthto5matters.org.uk.

Ministry of Education, New Zealand *Te Whāriki online: Self management and regulation.* https://tewhariki.tki.org.nz/en/teaching-strategies-and-resources/self-management-and-regulation/.

Organisation for Economic Co-operation and Development, https://www.oecd.org/education/school/early-learning-and-child-well-being-study/.

TABLET (Toddler Attentional Behaviours and Learning with Touchscreens) project, https://www.cinelabresearch.com/tablet-project.

Index